# THE MARSHALL CAVENDISH
☆ ☆ ☆ ILLUSTRATED ☆ ☆ ☆
# ENCYCLOPEDIA OF
# WORLD WAR II

**VOLUME 24**

# THE MARSHALL CAVENDISH ☆ ☆ ☆ ILLUSTRATED ☆ ☆ ☆ ENCYCLOPEDIA OF

# WORLD WAR II

*Based on the original text by*
Lieutenant Colonel Eddy Bauer

## CONSULTANT EDITOR

Brigadier General James L. Collins, Jr., U.S.A.
CHIEF OF MILITARY HISTORY,
DEPARTMENT OF THE ARMY

MARSHALL CAVENDISH CORPORATION/NEW YORK

# CONTENTS

Editorial Director: Brian Innes
Editor-in-chief; Brigadier Peter Young, D.S.O., M.C., M.A.
Managing Editor: Richard Humble
Editor: Christopher Chant
Art Editor: Jim Bridge

# CHAPTER 185

# The American Fighting man

Previous page: *The end of 4½ years' fighting as Corporal C. Dunn, U.S.M.C., runs up the U.S. flag over Yokosuka Naval Base in Japan.*
▷ *Marines in training on Santa Lucia, British West Indies. They are, from left to right, Pfc Joe Racer of Manassas, Virginia; Corporal Max Akin of Bernice, Louisiana; Sergeant Skinner of McCrachen, Kansas; 1st Sergeant Champ Faircloth of Homerville, Georgia; Corporal Earnest Todd and Corporal Fred Durant, both of Laurenberg, North Carolina.*
▽▷ *Converging fire exercise by three machine guns of the Puerto Rican 65th Regiment at Punta Salinas, near San Juan.*
▽▽▷ *Battery E, 91st Coast Artillery, drills in the Philippines.*
▽ *Machine gun training.*

The mass production and big business skills which were employed in the production and distribution of weapons, ammunition, and equipment were also used in training, posting, and employment of the American soldier in World War II.

Aware of his status in a military chain of production and consumption, the U.S. soldier gave himself the nickname "G.I.", taken from the initials stamped on his equipment. He was "Government Issue".

As America moved steadily towards war in 1940 and 1941, she began to increase her war production and expand her forces. On August 27, 1940, Congress authorised the President to call up the National Guard and other reserves for active duty for a year. On September 16, the Burke-Wadsworth Bill provided for selective

service for a year. These men, howe could only be employed in the wes hemisphere and the possessions of United States.

There were optimistic plans for trai conscripts in special recruit cadres, the limited facilities meant that they straight into Regular Army divisions had both to train them and also enga; advanced exercises themselves.

When Major-General Lesley Mc] came away from one unit in Septer 1940, he said he had the impression o "blind leading the blind, and offi generally elsewhere". Despite this, ground was being prepared for gre expansion and the system could alr claim some success: the quality of young officers produced by the Res Officers' Training Corps. At the en

1 General Marshall called them "prob-
y our greatest asset during this present
ansion".

ut what of the draftees, the men who
been called up, and had come "to get
job done".

y about April 1941, recruits were no
ger being sent from reception centres
ctly into tactical units, but to Re-
ement Training Centers for 13 weeks'
ic training. G.H.Q. added three ad-
onal phases of training to follow
ematically: small unit training, com-
ed training with the various weapons
he regiment, and division and large-
t manoeuvres.

here were proficiency tests at every
e and an emphasis on elementary
ning and general proficiency. Exer-
s were free and not rigorously con-

trolled but could include live firing to simulate battle conditions. De-briefs and meticulous umpiring reinforced lessons learned in the field.

Road runs, physical training, and the assault course hardened up the young men who now began to be inducted into the forces in greater numbers. The Army too began to lose its surplus fat.

## The infantry division revamped

Under General McNair, Chief of Army Ground Forces, the infantry division, which had a full strength of 15,500 men in 1942, lost 1,250 men in the reforms. The chief savings were in defensive weapons and specialists. Infantrymen were expect-

ed to take on a variety of tasks which h been the reserve of specialists: they came radio operators, truck drivers, simple mine-clearing, and took on ene tanks with their rocket launchers.

Major tank attacks or complex eng eering operations could be handled by t specialists who had been pooled in n divisional units. The task of the infant division was to advance, and so it w equipped with weapons which were mob or man-portable.

A division had 27 rifle companies tot ling 5,184 men. Each company had thr rifle platoons and a weapons platoon. T rifle platoon contained three squads of men armed with ten M1 Garand rifles, o automatic rifle, and one Model 19 Springfield rifle. The weapons plato contained two .30-inch light machi guns, three 60-mm mortars, three an tank rocket launchers, and one .50-in machine gun which was intended for an aircraft defence, but could fire armo piercing ammunition.

Three rifle companies were group with a heavy weapons company to for an infantry battalion. The heavy weapo company contained 162 officers and m with six 81-mm mortars, eight .30-in medium machine guns, seven anti-ta rocket launchers, and three .50-inch hea machine guns.

The battalion headquarters compa had had an anti-tank platoon armed wi three 37-mm anti-tank guns (later replac by 57-mm guns), three .30-inch machi guns, one .50-inch machine gun, and eig rocket launchers.

Three infantry battalions with a hea quarters company (supported by six 10 mm howitzers, a service company, and anti-tank company with 12 guns, one . inch and four .30-inch machine gun made up the infantry regiment.

Three infantry regiments were su ported by three artillery battalions make up the combat elements of a divisio The artillery battalions contained o 155-mm howitzer battery with 12 gun two 105-mm howitzer batteries with guns, and a headquarters and a servi battery.

## Support elements

The division was supported by engine signal, ordnance, quartermaster, medic and military police units, with a hea

▷ *The crew of a 40-mm light anti-aircraft gun drills during an exercise near Barstow, California. It is hard to see how the crew's eyes could have become adjusted to the dark, however, with the cameraman's lights pointing in their eyes!*

▽ *Working his way up from the bottom: Private Francis Warren Pershing, son of General of the Armies John Pershing, learns the tricks of the machine gunner's trade with Private Jacob Kruithop (right) at Fort Belvoir, Virginia.*

quarters company and a mechanised reconnaissance troop. In practice the infantry division operated in the field with a tank battalion and other supporting elements semi-permanently attached.

The division remained a standardised unit throughout the war, and was kept up to strength by a steady stream of replacements, or "reppl's" in Army slang. In three months of heavy fighting, an infan-try regiment could suffer 100 per c casualties. By early 1945, 47 infan regiments in 19 divisions had suffered 1 and in some cases over 200, per c casualties.

Men, like equipment, made their v through a series of depots and stag posts between the United States a arriving at the front. In McNair's wo there was always "the invisible horde ople going here and there but seemingly ever arriving".

Whatever the flair and skill of generals, without these nameless men, the G.I.s, the war could never have been brought a successful conclusion. Many already ossessed skills they had learned in the ty or on the farm. Trucks and cars, and eir engines and maintenance, were no ovelty. These men came from a gadget-minded nation, and many had used rifles and shotguns from an early age.

General George S. Patton asserted "The soldier is the Army. No army is better than its soldiers. The soldier is also a citizen. In fact, the highest obligation and privilege of citizenship is that of bearing arms for one's country. Hence it is a proud privilege to be a soldier – a good soldier."

The U.S. Army also held some of the

▽ *American infantry exercise in Northern Ireland (note the early pattern British-style steel helmets). Although the first U.S. troops arrived in Great Britain in 1942, most of them had to wait until Operation "Overlord" in 1944 before getting their first taste of action.*

CE GUESTS

*The spoils of war?
...cans relax on the shores of
...e Lake in Berlin with local
...fter the war.
...erican soldiers entertain
...elves with the help of
...ment supplied by the Young
... Christian Association in
...oking area of Surrey,
...nd.*

*...merican troops in Great
...in at an alfresco
...ainment show.
...me-from-home: American
...rs enjoy themselves at a
... given by Mrs. Rees Evans
... Finchley Road in London.
... hospitality by their hosts
...d an important part in
...g American troops feel at
... on "alien" shores.*

world's most educated and best informed soldiers, and General Bradley explained that in Sicily they had their own opinions about Patton.

"George irritated them by flaunting the pageantry of his command. He travelled in an entourage of command cars followed by a string of nattily uniformed staff officers. His own vehicle was gaily decked with oversize stars and the insignia of his command. These exhibitions did not awe the troops as perhaps Patton believed. Instead, they offended the men as they trudged through the clouds of dust left in the wake of that procession."

## Army newspapers

The soldiers had their own newspapers, *Yank* and *The Stars and Stripes*, and most divisions and higher commands produced their own duplicated news sheets, using the journalistic talent that had been drafted into the Army. In addition there was the Armed Forces Radio, which provided news and music.

The American public demanded a ceived news coverage of their f abroad which emphasised a human est angle. Men were named in photog and stories and their home town and included. For as Bradley learned, fo 80,000 men in his corps there were " than a quarter-million fathers, mot wives, and what-have-you in the U States, all of them worrying about men. A good many of them are pro asking themselves: What sort of a g this Omar Bradley? Is he good enou take care of my man?"

Surprisingly, this literate, democ and well-informed army made war fectively as many more autocratic fo One of the chief reasons for this wa feeling that they were fighting a just Japan had made a treacherous atta Pearl Harbor and, after swallowin Europe, Germany had declared war o United States. Both countries wer gressors, and the war was being wag beat them and bring peace to Europe Asia.

The Army was well paid; by Br standards the men seemed very wel

△ *Lt.-Col. James A. Clark (with map), deputy commander of the 4th Fighter Group, briefs his pilots at Debden before a sweep over France on April 10, 1944. Two of the "aces" in the photograph are Captain Don S. Gentile (extreme right) and Major James A. Goodson (on Clark's right). During the sweep, 28 German aircraft were downed.*
△▷ *Corporal W. H. Porter, U.S.M.C., is eased onto a stretcher-blanket after being wounded in the battle for Iwo Jima.*
▷ *Mail-call for Marines of the 2nd Marine Division on Tinian island in the Marianas.*

for a staff sergeant could take home as much as a British Army captain. Serving overseas, a private made $60 a month, roughly three times as much as his British counterpart. In a country that had been denuded of its men, the invasion by large numbers of comparatively wealthy young men was welcomed by many British girls. The "G.I. brides" who were carried off to the United States at the end of the war bore witness to the charms of these friendly invaders.

However, before he landed in Britain, the U.S. serviceman was given a 32-page booklet, *A Short Guide to Great Britain*. It warned him against such social blun-

ders as stealing a British soldier's girl spending his money too freely, and ad the following admonition: "The Bri don't know how to make a good cu coffee. You don't know how to mak good cup of tea. It is an even swap."

But these domestic and social subtle were only light relief for soldiers continued their training in Britain preparation for D-Day.

Infantry assault tactics had evol from the covering-fire tactics of Wo War I. Each 12-man rifle squad had a t man scout section, a four-man fire secti and a five-man manoeuvre and ass section. In theory the squad leader

t section would locate the enemy, and
le one section with Browning Auto-
ic Rifles pinned down the enemy, the
d section would advance.

his theory, however, only used a small
t of the squad's fire-power, and often
squad leader was pinned down with
scout section. In practice the infantry
n worked with tanks – between three
seven tanks were assigned to an in-
try company. Sometimes the armour
t at point, sometimes with the infantry
extended line), and when there was
le resistance expected, the infantry
e on them.

he tanks would take on the centres of
istance, the infantry would attack the
i-tank guns.

As an alternative to this system there
s the "marching fire offensive" em-
yed by Patton. It was costly, but could
ld dramatic results. The infantry ad-
nced in a skirmish line with close tank
pport. With them went all the portable
apons, including the B.A.R.s and .30-
h machine guns. All available fire
uld be directed at centres of resistance;
s had a favourable effect on the assault
ops, and looked and sounded terrifying
the defenders. Artillery and mortars
uld be brought forward behind this line
give supporting fire if necessary.

## ood rations for the
## ghting man

the field the G.I. usually received at
ast one hot meal a day, but sometimes
had to fall back on the three varieties
emergency rations. The K-ration came
a small cardboard box which held a can
cheese, ham and egg mixture, or beef
ash, a fruit bar or hard candy, four cigar-
tes, hard crackers, a few sheets of lava-
ry paper, and coffee or fruit juice
oncentrate.

The C-ration included a can of meat
ew, hamburger, or spaghetti with sauce.
he "10-in-1" ration held dehydrated or
anned food in a large carton which fed
n men for a day. A less popular item was
he D-ration, which was a protein enrich-
d bar of bitter hard chocolate.

While air force units had satisfactory
ashing facilities, front line soldiers had
o make do with their helmets as wash
asins until they visited the shower tent.
ere they could leave their soiled clothes

at one entrance and at the exit colle
clean uniform.

Medical care was excellent, for m
doctors, nurses, and dentists had
drafted. Each company or equivalent
had a medical aid man, or corpsr
trained in first aid. If a man was hi
trod on a mine, the corpsman would
emergency treatment and attach a ta
him, giving details of the wound.
casualty would be sent back to the
talion aid station, where a doctor
equipped to do limited emergency surg
A motor ambulance would then move
casualty to a division collecting comp
where more sophisticated emergency
gery would be performed, then to a "fi
or "evacuation" hospital. More ser
cases passed on further to the rear
"station" hospital and in some case
air or ship to the United States.

In some theatres, specialised med

△ ◁ A Browning .50-inch
machine gun crew in Italy. On
the left is Pfc James E. Rhodes of
Hayesville, South Carolina, and
on the right Private Casimer W.
Bielic of Niagara Falls, New
York. The two men have coffee
and doughnuts provided by the
U.S. front line services.
◁ ◁ A bazooka team lurks in
wait for a German tank in the
Forêt d'Andaine in France.
△ Men of Company K of the
398th Infantry Regiment (100th
Division) ready themselves for
action in the Rosteic area in
France.
◁ A Negro patrol probes into a
French village.

△ *American infantry move up through Caiazzo, north of the Volturno river, in Italy. This was yet another theatre where the huge American presence was felt.*

units were moved close to the front. At Cassino, where many men were wounded in the head by flying stones and mortar fragments, eye specialists and neurosurgeons were moved up to the front line. The prompt use of their skills could save the life or sight of a soldier who would not have survived if he had been sent back through the normal medical chain.

Out of all the U.S. Army and Army Air Force casualties who received medical treatment at battalion level or above, the mortality rate was 4.5 per cent. In World War I this rate had stood at 8.1 per cent. Most of the wounded men were returned to their units after treatment, some even after their second and third wounds.

## Proper burial

For those men who were killed in action there was the assurance that their body would receive a proper burial. Each man's identity tags, "dog tags", worn round his neck listed his name, service serial number, religion, and next of kin. In the event of death he could be identified, and one tag left with the body. After his personal effects had been checked for damage or blood stains, they were sent with the identity tag to the next of kin. With a mattress cover as a shroud, the body was buried in a temporary cemetery, and after

the war it could be sent home to a pe nent cemetery if the relatives so wis

The combat infantryman was with the grim prospect of death or wo as the only permanent break from fig at the front. Though he might be ro back to a rest camp, he did not have t missions and the opportunity to r home which was the prerogative o crew in the Army Air Forces.

In the end a scheme was introduce it was the exception rather than the that men could return to the U States, for they had to fulfill a numl strict requirements before they were sidered.

In the Pacific a whole unit cou pulled out for a spell in a rest camp, Europe only small groups would be back to enjoy the simple but very wel luxuries of beds with sheets, baths, and hot food served on plates. The would be located beyond the ran enemy artillery fire, but the soldier' was only about 48 hours. Some men, ever, did get brief passes to the cit Australia, to London, Paris, and Ro

An efficient mail service made up a for the enforced separation of the Officers and men enjoyed a free servi their outgoing letters. Those of th listed men were subject to censorshi officers were relied on to observe se restrictions—though their letters given a random spot-check withi

tal service. The quickest way to send
receive letters was by the V-mail, a
cial form which was microfilmed and
onstituted at the receiving end. There
one letter however which was not
come. "Dear John", which was the
e of a popular song, became the name
he letter from the G.I.'s girl friend in
United States writing to say that she
found a new boy.

## creased age and
aturity

World War I America had raised a
ce of 5,000,000 men, composed very
gely of young men. They tripled that
re in World War II and took men aged
to 45, thus raising the average age of
Army to 26.

One service policy which remained un-
nged in both wars was the segregation
of Negroes. Although they were employed
largely in service units, there were also
tank and tank destroyer battalions, chem-
ical mortar and artillery battalions, a
fighter-bomber group, and two infantry
divisions, one of which fought in Italy and
the other in the Pacific.

The training of these units in the
United States caused some racial tension
and outbursts, particularly when the
camps were situated near small provincial
towns in the southern states. An added
complication was that Negro Military
Police were usually unarmed. Dramatic
and often biased accounts in the local
press served to inflame further the Negro
soldiers and white community.

With the exception of the fighter-
bomber group and some individual battalions, the record of these combat units
has become a matter of controversy.

However, if their performance was un-
satisfactory, an experiment forced on the
U.S. Army in Europe in the winter of
1944–45 proved that integrated fighting

▽ *The end of the long road in the
European theatre: American
soldiers greet their Russian
counterparts on a shattered
bridge over the Elbe on April 28,
1945.*

As others saw him:
△ Eduard Thöny's comment in the Munich edition of Simplicissimus *on the "gentlemen of North Italy"– "And now, Billy, let's find an altar-cloth to put on the mantelpiece."*
△ ▷ *From the* Sveglia *of the Salo Fascist régime in northern Italy– "Well, Italian, what did you do before the Liberation?" "I was a university professor."*
▷ *One of the greatest American fighter aces, Francis Gabreski.*

units were just as efficient as many all-white ones. Some 4,500 Negro volunteers, many taking reductions from ranks as high as master sergeant to private soldier, fought in the 6th Army Group as provisional companies attached to infantry regiments and in the 12th Army Group as extra platoons attached to companies. The service of these units, particularly the platoons, led to the post-war policy of integrated units.

## Distinct national units

There were other racially separate units in the U.S. Army. One infantry battalion contained Norwegian-Americans who spoke little or no English. Japanese-Americans, after some confusion in the early years of the war, formed an effective combat team which fought in Italy, France, and Germany. The Philippine Scouts and other units of the Philippine Army fought under American command in both the regular and irregular war against the Japanese. At the beginning of the war, some National Guard divisions reflected their regional background, but

reinforcements and replacements s[o] blurred any distinction between Regu[lar] National Guard, and selective service draftee, divisions.

## The United States Army Air Forces

In the first War Powers Act of 1941, United States Army Air Forces beca[me] autonomous in all but name. Betwe[en] 1939 and 1945 they expanded enormous[ly] in July 1939 there were only 3,991 [Air] Corps personnel abroad, at the end of [the] war the total strength of the U.S.A.A[.F] stood at 2,253,000 men and women.

Though effectively a separate orga[niz]ation, this did not prevent the G.I. fr[om] envying his brother in the air. There w[ere] simple things, like the way they were p[er]mitted to shape and batter their issue ca[ps] and the more profound suspicion that [the] air force had an easier war. Their [pay] was good, the food and living quarters [at] their bases seemed luxurious to the fr[ont] line soldier and the promotion policy w[as] more liberal.

Undoubtedly the Army Air Forces enjoyed all these privileges, but theirs was no easy war. The bomber and fighter crews needed a special sort of courage to take their aircraft deep into enemy territory. In early operations over Germany, before the advent of long range escort fighters, B-17 Flying Fortresses suffered heavily from German *Flak* and fighter attacks. In the Schweinfurt raid, 60 bombers out of a force of 291 failed to return, but the next day the remaining aircraft were readied, the formations adjusted, and the crews briefed in preparation for their next mission. In May 1944 one bomber would be lost for every 13 damaged by *Flak* in operations by the 8th Army Air Force.

## Non-combat deaths

Sometimes the violent death caused by *Flak* or fighters was preferable to ditching at sea. In the later months of the war German civilians attacked crewmen who had parachuted from their burning aircraft. Of the eight men captured by the Japanese in the Doolittle Raid on April 18, 1942, three were executed and one died

▽ *Cheerful faces around one of the most dangerous positions in the Boeing B-17 Flying Fortress— the ventral ball turret. In the turret is Technical Sergeant Robert Myllyskoski of Painsville, Chicago, and on the right is Staff Sergeant H. Jessup of Union City, Indiana.*

malnutrition, and others were to die daring to trespass in "Imperial air-ace".

The ground crews too were sometimes the wrong end of air raids. In Europe severely-stretched Luftwaffe still man-ed to mount attacks on advanced air ips. At Pearl Harbor, sailors, soldiers, d airmen were all victims of the Japan-e air assault.

In the fighting in the Bataan Peninsula January 1942, a handful of obsolescent rtiss P-40's fought an unequal battle th faster Japanese Zeros and Betties. ough the aircraft had fuel, the pilots d ground crews were suffering from ense fatigue and malnutrition, but despite this they kept the P-40's flying. In the end, the Japanese overran the extemporised landing grounds, and the remaining personnel were caught in savage close-quarter fighting.

Enemy action was not the only cause of casualties. Aircrew died when their oxygen failed, or suffered frost-bite in the grim high altitude raids over Germany. Crash-landings by damaged aircraft could be as dangerous to the crash crew as they fought the fire as to the escaping air crew or pilot. More dangerous still was the crash on take-off by a loaded bomber.

Though it was the man on the ground who guaranteed the ultimate victory, the Army Air Forces were responsible for

△ *Loading the rear turret of a B-26 Marauder. From left to right the men are Technical Sergeant Robert P. Morris of Wheeling, West Virginia, Staff Sergeant Francis C. Barabe of Detroit, Michigan, and Staff Sergeant John T. McQueeney of Washington, D.C.*

▷ *Ground crew prepare a B-26 for a sortie from England. On the left, Lieutenant Glenn Abbot of Akron, Ohio, checks the bomb-load, with the help of Staff Sergeant Gustav J. Sylvan of Columbia, South Carolina.*

▽ *Thunderbolt pilots pose on the wing of one of their aircraft. These were the men, with the Mustang pilots, who defended the American daylight bomber fleets.*

◀ *Before a 9th Air Force sortie: from left to right the men are Major Robert Keller of Lititz, Pennsylvania, Captain Samuel Monk of Memphis, Tennessee, Lieutenant Thomas James of Ashville, North Carolina, Lieutenant George Hines of Knoxville, Tennessee, and Captain George Kunde of Milwaukee, Wisconsin.*

some war-winning blows. The most obvious examples are the two atomic bomb attacks on Hiroshima and Nagasaki. However, post-war evaluation of the B-29 Blitz shows that the atomic bombs were the final blow in a campaign that was already forcing Japan towards annihilation or surrender. Even the vanguard of the massive Tokyo fire raids, the comparatively modest Doolittle Raid, prompted the Japanese fleet to sail to their defeat at Midway.

In Europe the U.S.A.A.F. made two major raids on the Rumanian oil fields at Ploieşti, and their later attacks on the German synthetic oil plants led to the slow immobilisation of the enemy mechanised forces.

Fighters and fighter-bombers perfected ground attack operations which made enemy movement in daylight almost impossible. And Lockheed P-38 Lightnings were responsible for death of Admiral were responsible for the death of Admiral who had planned the Pearl Harbor attack.

It was a plodding, unglamorous, but no less courageous job that fell to the transport pilots who flew "over the Hump" to China. Their comrades in Europe ear lasting respect and admiration fr ground forces for their delivery of a and supplies, notably at Bastogne.

Throughout the war, in many lands, G.I. remained unmistakable. Like army, his contained a few men who c mitted grave crimes. They looted, tur away from the enemy, raped, or murde But in Europe these men represented o one half of one per cent of all the U forces employed in that theatre. No ar is guiltless in any war, but the U.S. Ar had one of the best records in World V II.

In this war the G.I. was typified less the impetuous "Lafayette here we com attitude than his father's generation World War I. Major-General Carl Spa spoke for most U.S. servicemen on Ju 18, 1942, when at Bushy Park in Engla he said: "We won't do much talking u we've done more fighting. We hope t when we leave you'll be glad we ca Thank you."

In the light of subsequent ever Western Europe and the countries of Far East have much to thank America 1

*▽ Apparently unruffled, members of the crew of a heavily-damaged Marauder pose in their aircraft. From left to right they are Lieutenant Tom Trainer (navigator) of Haverill, Massachusetts, Lieutenant Jim Davis (pilot) of Elligay, Georgia, Staff Sergeant Ritcher King (gunner) of Dallas, Texas, Staff Sergeant Joseph G. White (radio operator) of Eureka, and Staff Sergeant George Lemberger (gunner) of Ashkos.*

# CHAPTER 186
# The Cold War

by Professor D. C. Watt

The cold war was a war that never was. There was no declaration of war, no employment of troops in vast and bloody attacks on defended trenches, no Blitzkrieg, and no armistice or formal surrender. Equally there was no treaty of peace. The term was invented by the American politician, Bernard Baruch, to describe the very great deterioration of relations between the Soviet Union and the United States and their allies and associates after the grand alliance of the Soviet Union, the United States, and Great Britain in the war against Nazi Germany. Since it had no formal beginning and no formal end, historians are likely to argue about when it began, what it was about and when or whether it ended, for as long as relations between the Soviet Union and the non-Soviet world are based on the ideological differences that divide them.

There is one very powerful group of writers who argue that the cold war began with the Russian revolution of November 1917 and the intervention of Britain, France, the United States, Canada, and Japan in the Russian civil war that followed. This group is in turn divided. One section argues that the cold war began with the intervention by these five

powers into the Russian civil war, that without this, the cold war w never have happened. The other re that the leaders of the November re tion in Russia expected it to sp immediately through Europe, and this expectation itself amounted declaration of "cold war". They cont to say that the failure of the revolutic spread created a situation which, acc ing to Soviet doctrine, could not be than warlike, since, between the s that practised capitalism and the S Union, relations could not be other hostile, it being the declared aim of S political philosophy to destroy the talist system. In Soviet doctrine capitalist world was certain to perish its own internal contradictions. It always possible, however, that capit political leaders might seek to avoi internecine conflict in which their sy was bound to end by seeking unity i attack on the one state which embo the socialist ideal. If that happe socialism could destroy capitalism; in the more pessimistic of doctr derived by the Bolshevik leader, Le from Karl Marx's writings, it was possible that both systems might pe in mutual destruction. In the view of group of writers, the Soviet leader thought war to be the normal abi state of relations between the S Union and capitalist states. Thin this, they conducted relations with capitalist states on a basis of host which negated any attempts by indivi capitalist states to put their relations the Soviet Union on any other basis.

The difficulty which has led n historians to avoid applying the "cold war" to the whole of the histo Soviet relations with the principal talist states is that a historical term w is so all-embracing becomes virtu meaningless. The majority of histor in the countries of Europe and the Ur States uses the term to cover relat between the Soviet Union and the st bordering on the North Atlantic from end of the fighting in Europe in 194 some date in the 1950-1972 period. S see its ending in the process of Ameri Soviet détente which began after Cuban missile crisis of 1962. Some se ending in the series of treaties concl by the West German Government Russia, Poland, and East German 1971-72, and in the Soviet-Amer understanding which accompanied

erican military withdrawal from Viet-
m. Others put its ending earlier.

The real point to decide is what issue
s at stake in the cold war. It was
sically concerned with the question of
e control of central Europe, and that
s issue was settled to all intents and
rposes by the meeting of President
senhower, Sir Anthony Eden, and the
viet leaders at the Geneva Summit
nference in 1955, at which both sides
me to accept the partition of Germany
o two states, one in alliance with the
tes of western Europe and of North
erica, and one in alliance with the
viet Union and its associates. Soviet
licy thereafter, with its attempt to
ploit the Middle Eastern situation in
5-56 and its opening of the question of
st Berlin in November 1958, entered a
ite different phase. If one is to use the
m "cold war" to describe this one must
tinguish between the first and the
ond "cold war".

If Germany was the main battlefield of
e "cold war" it was not of course the
ly one. The civil wars in Greece in
4-45 and 1946-48 were clearly part of
e same process. The wars which began
1946 in Indo-China and in 1950 in Korea,

though not lacking in effect on the cold
war, were coincidental in time to it and
not part of the same process any more
than were the fighting in Palestine in the
years 1947-49, in Malaya from 1949-59, the
Hungarian rising of 1956, or the covert
American intervention in Guatemala in
1954. The Indo-Chinese war lay between
a Communist-dominated nationalist movement and its French colonial overlords
and is different from the fighting in 1947-
49 in Indonesia between the Indonesian
nationalists and their Dutch overlords
only in that the Indonesian nationalists
defeated the attempts by the Indonesian
Communist party to take over and domi-
nate the Indonesian nationalist movement, while the Indo-Chinese Communist
party had largely taken command of the
Indo-Chinese nationalist movement before the Japanese surrender made the
return of the French possible. The con-
sequent difference, that the United States
played a large part in forcing the Dutch
withdrawal from Indonesia, while agree-
ing after 1950 to finance and support the
French, is thus understandable.

As for Korea, it seems now much more
likely that the sudden attack launched by
North Korean troops across the 38th

*One aspect of the cold war was
the formation of two military
"camps" in Europe–the Warsaw
Pact countries in the East and
the N.A.T.O. alliance in the
West, dominated by the Soviet
Union and the U.S.A.
respectively.*
△ *Foreign ministers of some of
the N.A.T.O. countries take a
break during a meeting in late
1952. From left to right:
Secretary of State Dean
Acheson, French Foreign
Minister Robert Schuman, Bjorn
Ole Kraft of Denmark, and the
British Foreign Secretary,
Anthony Eden.*

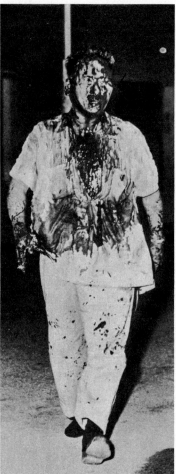

parallel against the South Korean state was not inspired by the Russians but was done to force their hand. The subsequent involvement of the Communist Chinese was a direct consequence of the decision by the American commander-in-chief of the United Nations forces not to stop after he had destroyed the bulk of the North Korean armies and driven them back across the 38th parallel, but to continue, to occupy North Korea and to unify the north and south of the country by force. If successful this would have established a state, in alliance with and dependent upon the United States, with a common frontier with China on the Yalu river. The Chinese Communist leadership, only having established their victory over the American-aided Chinese Nationalist government and forces the previous year, when the remains of the Nationalist forces withdrew to Formosa from the mainland, chose to regard this as a direct threat to the security of their new state. Their intervention prolonged the fighting for nearly four years, restored the north Korean state to its previous boundaries, and eventually resulted in the Panmunjon armistice. But it was not a direct part of the cold war between the Soviet Union,

the United States, and their allies associates. The cold war was a Europ war. Korea was an American-Chin conflict. It belongs to a quite separate of developments which date back to opening of Japan, the scramble of European powers for spheres of influe in the decaying Chinese empire and American proclamation of the Open D which if accepted by the other pow would have put the United States on equal if not superior footing in scramble.

The cold war then was about the con of central Europe in general and Germa in particular. It developed quite logica out of the German attack on the Sov Union in July 1941 and the British a American decision to treat the Sov Union as an ally against Hitler. T decision doomed Hitler and made defeat merely a question of time. It possible that the Soviet Union could h defeated Nazi Germany and her all even without British and American a possible but not certain. What that gave the Soviet Union was the food, fuel, the raw materials, and the transp tation which enabled that part of Sov heavy industry which survived the t

t German offensives of 1941-42 to
centrate on the provision of the tanks,
, aircraft, and munitions which made
Soviet defeat of these offensives and
great counter-offensive of 1943-45
ible. Without that aid it is con-
able, no more, that a Soviet-German
istice and compromise peace might
e been arranged. There certainly were
destine Soviet-German conversations
he early part of 1943 in Stockholm,
igh we know very little about them
ind the fact of their occurrence.
ie decision to aid Soviet Russia made
Nazi defeat inevitable. That in turn
id the question of the future of central
ipe. Hitler's attack on Russia had
id a period in which Russia had
inced her frontiers westwards by
ixing, with German agreement, the
le eastern section of the pre-war
ish state. In 1940 Russia had similarly
ipied and annexed from Rumania the
ince of Bessarabia. When Hitler's
es invaded Russia, the Rumanian and
garian armies fought alongside them.
sia could be expected therefore to be
erned about the nature of the post-
régimes in these countries. She was
lly concerned to secure from Britain

recognition of her annexation in 1939-40
of the eastern section of the pre-1939
Polish state, of the three little Baltic
republics of Estonia, Latvia, and Lithua-
nia, and of Bessarabia.

The matter was greatly complicated by
two circumstances. Britain had declared
war on Germany in consequence of the
German attack on Poland with whom
Britain had, on August 26, 1939, signed
an alliance. Although Hitler had defeated
the Polish forces and overrun and occupied
the territory of the Polish state, there
were sizable Free Polish forces fighting
on the British side, and there was a Polish
government-in-exile, living in London
and recognised by the British and, for that
matter, the Americans, as the legitimate
interim government of Poland.

The German attack on the Soviet Union,
the British decision to support the Soviets
and, still more, the signature of the Anglo-
Soviet alliance in 1942, raised the question
of relations between the free Polish
government-in-exile and the Soviet Union.
It was an awkward question in itself. So
far as the free Poles were concerned the
Soviet Union had illegally occupied the
eastern part of their country, had carried
off into imprisonment a very sizable part

*The cold war was confined to
Europe, while unrest in the Far
East could be attributed to a
variety of factors – the success of
the Communists in China, the
crumbling of colonial empires,
the desire for self-determination.
The Japanese had proved to the
people of Asia that the ruling
Europeans could be defeated.
Was it possible to emulate them?
The Malayan peninsula, scene of
one of the British Army's
greatest débâcles, was a case
in point. The nationalist
movement was well-grounded by
1945, when the British returned,
and the move to self-government
and independence was delayed
only by the police action against
Communist guerrillas operating
in the interior.
◁ and ◁▽ Scenes of violent
rioting in Singapore.
▽ R.A.F. and R.A.A.F. Avro
Lincoln bombers head out for a
raid on terrorists hidden in the
Malayan swamps.*

△ *The result of a raid by Lincoln bombers of the R.A.F. and R.A.A.F. – a terrorist jungle camp bombed out of existence.*
▷ *A young Malay watches two patrols prepare to leave their base on a sweep through the jungle.*

of the Polish armed forces and had stage-managed a plebiscite by which the inhabitants of these eastern areas appeared to have voted in overwhelming numbers for incorporation into the Soviet Union. The free Poles did not for a moment accept that procedure or its results as legitimate. Moreover in their view they were only an interim caretaker government. Until elections, held in a Poland free from foreign occupation, had produced a new representative government they felt, or said they felt, unable to make any far-reaching decisions about the future of any part of pre-war Poland.

There were, in the meantime, a nu[m] of practical issues on which Polish-S[o] talks could be held. Principally these [con]cerned the whereabouts in Russia o[f] prisoners taken in 1939 and of thei[r] organisation into Polish fighting fo[rce] Discussions were held, some though b[y no] means all of the prisoners located, [and] progress made with the formatio[n of] Polish units on Russian soil. There [was] however far too little trust betwee[n the] Polish ex-prisoners and their former So[viet] captors for these units to be effectiv[e. It] was decided therefore to evacuate all [who] wanted to go to non-Soviet terri[tory]

*△ The end of the line: a Tamil terrorist surrenders during an all-out police drive against insurgents in northern Malaya.*

through Persia. Several thousands of former Polish citizens were evacuated and the able-bodied among them formed the Polish Corps which under General Anders played an important part in the fighting in Italy. There were, however, about 10,000 men, mainly officers, unaccounted for.

In April 1943 the German propaganda agencies announced the discovery of the bodies of over 2,000 of these officers in a series of mass graves in Belorussia near a place called Katyn. The victims had been tied together and shot. The Germans ascribed these deaths to Russian actions and produced a medical commission of the most distinguished forensic experts they could find in Europe, whose report on the corpses ascribed the date of the victims' deaths to a time when the area was under Soviet control. The Polish government-in-exile in London regarded this as confirmation of their worst fears and called for an investigation by the International Red Cross. The Soviet leadership, who had stigmatised the whole thing as a German propaganda trick, accused the London Poles of lending themselves to the purposes of Dr. Goebbels and promptly broke off relations with

them. They produced in their stea⬩ group of Polish Communists, the plia survivors of those who had sought ref in Russia in the inter-war years from dictatorship of Marshal Piłsudski, whom the Stalinist purges of the ye 1935-39 had fallen with particular sever This group of stooges and nobodies ⬩ originally established in the Polish to of Lublin and was known as the Lub Committee. The Soviet authorities m it clear that, so far as they were c cerned, the Lublin Committee was only acceptable representative Pol body with whom they were prepared deal.

This was the position then when Big Three, President Roosevelt for United States, Prime Minister Wins Churchill for Britain, and Stalin for Soviet Union met in late 1943 in Teher Their formal agenda was mainly milit⬩ as the state of the British records sho The political discussions that took pl were only preliminary. But when meeting took place it was clear that ⬩ tory was merely a matter of time. It had already surrendered and British ⬩ American troops were already establis⬩ on the European mainland, though a l⬩

lay ahead up the long and mount
ous Italian peninsula. The Red Army
met and defeated the last major
man offensive in the East at Kursk in
, and had begun its steady and relent-
westward drive. It was still a time for
peration; but the seeds of conflict
e already there.

hey were to lie mainly in the overriding
iet concern for security on her western
tier which led the Russians to insist,
hey had in Poland, on a take-over by
munist-dominated régimes in the coun-
s of eastern Europe as the Red Army
erated" them. At the same time the
sians made no effort to help or
ally suppress the military and politi-
organisations that had existed on an
derground" basis. Thus no effort was
le to help the risings of the Polish
ne Army in Warsaw or the Slovak
ng in 1944, and British and American
mpts to aid them were thwarted.
ders of the Polish underground in the
iet-occupied areas were arrested and
of them flown to Moscow for a "show-
l" of the 1930's kind, obviously in-
ded to discredit them entirely. In
imes such as that which switched
s in Rumania, the Russians insisted

on the control of the ministry of justice
and the ministry responsible for the police
being in the hands of the local Communist
party.

The Communist parties of eastern
Europe had never been very strong in the
inter-war years. They had borne the
brunt of police repression during the
1920's and of local Fascism in the 1930's.
Many of their bravest and ablest men had
taken part in the Communist emigration
and ended up fighting in Spain or in exile
in Russia. There only the most pliant had
survived. The only countries where a
large-scale local party with an armed
resistance movement existed were those
that had fought against the Nazis in 1941,
Greece and Yugoslavia. In each of these,
Communist partisan forces had co-existed
side by side with non-Communist guerrillas. Only the most tenuous contacts with
Moscow had been possible, and the parties
had followed their own course of action.
In each country the main source of arms
and aid was the British Special Operations Executive.

The lack of contact with Moscow can
be seen in the very different course followed by the Communist resistance movements in Yugoslavia and Greece. In

*The Communist resistance
movement in Greece, though
increasingly well-armed, had
done little in the way of
harassing the Germans. Instead,
it concentrated its efforts on
eliminating the non-Communist
resistance groups and–after the
arrival of British troops in late
1944–guerrilla action against
these latter.*
▽ *During demonstrations in
Athens, a member of E.L.A.S.,
the armed wing of the
Communist movement, is
arrested by a British soldier.*

YOU ARE LEAVING
THE AMERICAN SECTOR
ВЫ ВЫЕЗЖАЕТЕ ИЗ
АМЕРИКАНСКОЙ ЗОНЫ
VOUS SORTEZ
DU SECTEUR AMERICAIN

*Following complete disagreement between the Soviet Union and the Western Powers over the administration of Berlin, the Soviet Union enforced a total blockage of road, rail, and water traffic between Berlin and the West. The Western Powers replied by organising the Berlin air lift, and for almost a year flew into the beleaguered western part of the city everything required to keep its residents alive, if not in luxury.*

*△ With the road blocks due to be dismantled, banners are hoisted over the Russian-American sector boundary. This one reads "The Sector of Freedom Welcomes the Fighters for Freedom and Right of the Western Sectors".*

*△▷ The first buses leave Berlin for the Western Zone after the lifting of the Soviet blockade, on May 14, 1949.*

*▷ On the same day, the first road convoy of supplies from the Western Zone to reach Berlin receives an enthusiastic welcome.*

Yugoslavia the non-Communist underground, the Četniks, did little active fighting against the German occupying authorities, for fear of provoking reprisals against the civilian population. In the Italian-occupied areas some local commanders co-existed quite peaceably with the Italians or even co-operated with them against the Communists. The Communist underground, the Partisans, by contrast, fought actively against the Germans, pinning down considerable German forces by their efforts. In Greece the opposite was the case. The Greek Communist movement, E.A.M and its armed wing, E.L.A.S., did very little active fighting against the Germans, save when the longest and most patient of British efforts succeeded in getting them to co-operate with non-Communist forces. The rest of the time they concentrated on eliminating the non-Communist guerrillas, until the only surviving organisation of any strength was in the Peloponnese, where E.A.M. never really succeeded in establishing itself. In October 1944 when British troops landed in Greece to take over from the retreating Germans, the E.A.M. forces rose against the British and attempted to seize power.

Much of this could be explained terms of local initiative. But it did look that way at the time, when tal with the Soviet behaviour over Pola A pattern of ruthless suppression of genuine democratic forces seemed to emerging. Both in Britain and in Ameri a section of the governments' advis began to warn against what seemed them to be a Soviet imperialism a expansionism differing little in kind fr that of Hitler. Their misgivings w overruled or passed unheeded at the ti since, in the minds of Roosevelt and of British Cabinet, no post-war secur system stood a chance without Sov participation. On the Polish issue t concentrated on trying to persuade Russians of the need to widen the Lub Committee to take in leading non-Co munist figures both from Poland itself a from the Polish emigration. At the Ya Conference of February 1945, they s ceeded. A similar agreement was negot ted with the Russians over the Partis régime in Yugoslavia. Stalin made protest against the suppression of Greek Communist revolt. His main an eties, often brutally and roughly voic were that the western powers would si

▽ Before the blockade was lifted: a new runway being built at Gatow airfield, in the British sector.

◁ ◁ ◁ The millionth bag of coal to be delivered by air is lowered by Sergeant Clyde Peterson of Fairfield, California, and Group Captain B. C. Yarde, the Gatow station commander.

◁ ◁ One of the first cars to arrive in Berlin after the lifting of the blockade.

◁ Unloading supplies from an R.A.F. Sunderland on the Havel river near Berlin. The skill of pilots landing and taking off in heavily built-up areas or—as in this case—using inland waterways, was a vital factor in keeping Berlin supplied during the blockade.

*For two years the bitter fighting in Korea swept back and forth across the country as first one side, then the other, gained the upper hand.*
△ *American-equipped South Korean troops march* en route *to the battle zone.*

a separate armistice with the German forces in the west, which would enable a Nazi or nationalist government to survive in Germany and turn its forces exclusively against Russia.

The main issue at Yalta was, however, territorial. Since Russia insisted on retaining the territories she had taken from Poland in 1939, Poland would have to be compensated in the west. At Teheran it had more or less been agreed that this should be at Germany's expense. Now this was settled and it was agreed that eastern Germany up to the rivers Oder and Neisse should be taken over by Poland. Königsberg was to become Russian, Danzig Polish. But this in turn had consequences. If post-war Germany was not to become inspired by the idea of recovering these territories, then she would have to have a government that the Soviet Union could rely on. For Russia this meant a Communist or fellow-travelling government. The issue of the control of Germany was raised inevitably.

Up to that point, although the Russians, alone among the belligerents, had fostered a free German movement, the Russian representatives had been committed to the idea of splitting Germany into a num-

ber of small, weak states. Only Britain ha resisted this, convinced that this wou not only sow the seeds of a new war, b that it would saddle Britain with the co of supporting the economy of whateve part of Germany she occupied and mak her own post-war economic recovery a well as that of Europe itself virtual impossible. After Yalta the Soviet Unio sharply reversed its position. At the sam time it began preparing small teams o German Communists to enter German behind the Red Army and set up 'ant Fascist' committees which would serve a the centres of new German politic activities under Soviet control.

It was at this point that Roosevelt die and was succeeded by Harry Truman Roosevelt had been prepared to make ver far reaching concessions to get the Sovie Union to join the United Nations and t provide a secure basis for post-war peace Truman, as it turned out, was less in clined to make this his overriding priorit; and more concerned that the Unitec States should receive their due share o respect and attention and that the post war settlement should be based on justice and a true balance of power. Soviet action in forcing a Communist puppet govern

on Rumania in February 1945, and
aking it virtually impossible for any
ern representation to move freely in
gary or Bulgaria, struck him as being
red by unfriendly sentiments towards
rica. He felt, as he said, that American
eements with the Soviet Union so far
been a one-way street". He was "fed
he said, "with babying the Soviets".
ractice, however, there was little he
d do: and as seen from London, the
se American pressure for demobili-
n and an end to all wartime aid to
pe, Lend-Lease, etc., seemed to be
ng the Soviets an entirely free hand
urope. On the ground Soviet obstruc-
was holding up western occupation
e zones agreed on at Yalta, in Berlin,
in Vienna. And at Potsdam the
ricans in essence accepted the divi-
of Germany into two by accepting
trade between the Soviet and non-
et zones should be regulated by
ement rather than be free, and accep-
that the Soviets should have an
ely free hand in their own occupation
American conciliation of the Soviet
n was to continue until early in 1946.
Soviet satellite governments in
ania and Hungary and Bulgaria were

recognised: and the level of economic
activity in Germany was fixed at a level
so low that British money continued to be
necessary to keep the population of north-
west Germany alive.

The turning point came in America over
the winter of 1945-46. Congressional
opinion was outraged by Soviet pressure
on Turkey, for joint control of the Dardanelles, by the attempt to set up pro-
Communist separatist states in the Soviet
occupied zone in northern Persia, and by
the Soviet sponsorship of a new Greek
Communist rising in March 1946. Moreover, the Republican party saw a chance of
making heavy inroads in the urban areas
of the American midwest, with their
Polish and other east European minority
groups, if they attacked the American
government for making concessions to
the Soviets over these countries. They
succeeded in causing the Truman administration to issue a number of severe
moral condemnations of Russian actions.
But American unwillingness to do anything more was shown conclusively in
March 1946 when Winston Churchill,
speaking at Fulton, Missouri, declared
that the Soviet Union had divided Europe
by an "iron curtain", created police states

▽ *Primitive but practical, given
the terrain: a South Korean
cavalry unit on the road.*

suppressed liberty behind it, and was
king to spread her system wherever
could. He called for a "fraternal
ociation" of the "English-speaking
ples", in close military relationship
h each other, to stand up to Russia.
rchill was disowned by the American
ernment, jeered at on a drive through
v York, and accused of trying to com-
the United States "to the task of pre-
ing the far flung British empire". To
ease American opinion the American
ernment adopted a much firmer, more
alistic stand. This secured some con-
sions from the Russians at the con-
nce which met in Paris from April to
e 1946 to draft treaties of peace with
y, Rumania, Hungary, and Bulgaria.
American forces were still being run
n in Europe. In Germany, however,
Americans ended reparation deliveries
he Soviet Union from their zone. The
tish followed suit and negotiations
an for a fusion of the American and
tish zones into a single economic unit.
he change in the American position
much too slow for the realities of the
er relationships in Europe. In the
mer of 1946 the British had been
ed to introduce bread rationing in

Britain to provide any margin of food for
their zone. The harvest failed in France.
The winter of 1946-47 was one of the worst
in recent history; the British economy
came to a virtual halt. That of the Bizone
broke down almost entirely. There was
widespread starvation and malnutrition.
The British were forced to finance the
Bizone entirely. The cost of maintaining
aid to Greece and Turkey, and occupation
troops in Greece and northern Italy, in
addition to military responsibilities the
globe over, was bankrupting Britain. The
British government had been driven to
the reluctant conclusion in the summer
of 1946 that the Soviet Union was deliberately trying to wreck the economy of
Britain and western Europe so as to
create conditions for the growth of Com-
munism. In February 1947 therefore, determined to force America's hand, they
informed the American government that
Britain could no longer undertake the
economic support of Greece and Turkey
and would have to resign herself to see
them go Communist unless America would
intervene.

The message arrived at an auspicious
moment. President Truman's relations
with his Secretary of State, James Byrnes,

had deteriorated throughout 1946 and
toward the end of the year he had replaced
him by General Marshall, the war-time
chief of the American Joint Chiefs-
of-Staff, whose judgement and integrity
were respected by everyone. The State
Department's Russian experts had been
combining to warn the President against
either assuming that Russia was planning
an all-out war or that the Soviet judgement of the fundamental differences between the Soviet system and that of the
west could be reconciled. What was
needed was a policy of quiet containment,
not one of self-proclaimed "toughness".
At the same time a joint State-War-Navy
Committee had been concerned for the
better part of the past year with the possibilities of bolstering the European
economy.

Between February and July 1947, five
significant developments marked the
change in American foreign policy. The
first was the enunciation of the so-called
"Truman doctrine" in President Truman's
message to Congress on March 12, 1947,
which declared it to be "the policy of the
United States to support free peoples who
are resisting attempted subjugation by
armed minorities or by outside pressures"

and appropriated $400 million for eco
mic and military aid to Greece and Turk
two specific commitments disguised
hind an open-ended undertaking to eng
on an ideological crusade. The second
the establishment of the State Departm
Policy Planning Staff in April 1947. T
third was a speech by Marshall's assist
under-secretary, Dean Acheson, at Cle
land, Mississippi, promising "top prior
for American reconstruction aid"
"free peoples who are seeking to prese
their independence and democr
institutions and human freedoms agai
totalitarian pressures, either internal
external".

The fourth was the presentation
George Kennan's thesis on "containme
which gave the Truman administratio
philosphical defence for the policy
was embarking upon. (It was publis
under the pseudonym "X" in the Americ
journal *Foreign Affairs* in July 1947.) T
fifth was Mr. Secretary Marshall's fam
speech at the Harvard University Grad
tion Day ceremonies on June 5, 1947,
origin of the Marshall Plan.

In this speech General Marshall offe
American aid to all nations which wo
co-operate in the programme. The init

in determining their needs and co-
ordinating them would have to be taken
by the European nations. The speech was
aimed at starting a process the nature of
which, even the scale of which, had not
been worked out in Washington. It was
not couched in terms which would exclude
the Soviet Union or its satellites. But it
was not expected they would go along
with it.

The British Government equally had
spent much of 1946 wondering how the
American government could be persuaded
to unlock its funds to aid Europe's economic recovery. In the autumn of 1945 the
British had negotiated a seemingly im-
mense loan from the United States: the
criticism the Labour Government had had
to face while Congress was ratifying this
loan determined its members never to
repeat the experience. Much of the loan
had had to be spent buying food and raw
materials for the British and American
zones in Germany. But the British had
found it difficult to establish friendly
relations with Byrnes or his underlings.
The message abandoning Greece and
Turkey was a desperate attempt to shock
the Americans into awareness.

The British Foreign Secretary, Ernest

Bevin, therefore had devoted much of his
energies to cultivating the French. For
the first 18 months of the occupation of
Germany, French obsession with the
dangers of a German revival of power and
President de Gaulle's anti-American fixa-
tions had made France and the Soviet
Union natural allies in preventing any
recovery of the German economy or the
establishment of any central German
administration. In January 1947, however,
after President de Gaulle's resignation
in January 1946 had removed the doctrinal
obstacles to a reorientation of French
foreign policy, Britain's patient cultivation of France throughout the previous
year paid off in the shape of an Anglo-
French alliance, the Treaty of Dunkirk.
At the Moscow Foreign Ministers' Conference in March 1947, the French were
finally convinced that the Soviet Union
was not to be counted upon as an ally to
keep Germany weak, and came to abandon
their independent position and lean towards Britain.

The way was open for Bevin to seize on
the Marshall speech, and, in conjunction
with Bidault, the French Foreign Minister,
to summon a conference of the European
states in Paris. Molotov, the Soviet

*In the mid-1950's Marshal Bulganin, as Chairman of the Council of Ministers, and Nikita Khrushchev, as First Secretary of the Communist Party's Central Committee, travelled extensively boosting Russia's image—and trade—in many countries.*

△ *A new era of good relations with Yugoslavia is opened as they are greeted at the airport in Belgrade by President Tito.*

foreign minister, attended the conference with 80 advisers, a sign that at first the Russians took the idea of participation seriously. During the meeting, however, he was instructed by Stalin to break off all participation. The British and French went ahead with a second conference a month later in Paris. Very heavy Soviet pressure had to be exerted on Czechoslovakia and Poland not to accept the invitation. As by September those nations which did attend agreed on a joint statement of their needs and the machinery to handle it, the effects of the Marshall speech were to confirm and institutionalise the division of Europe. France's agreement to merge her occupation zone in Germany with those of Britain and America translated that division into German terms.

In the winter of 1946 Soviet policy in Germany had received a serious set-back. Up to that point the Soviets had hoped to secure power by the formation of a "front organisation", the Socialist Unity Party (S.E.D.), which in their zone was composed of a fusion of the Communist party and sections of the Social Democratic, Christian Democratic, and German Liberal parties which had been allowed to restart operations in Germany in the winter of

1945-46. In October 1946, however, l[ocal?] government elections were held thro[ugh]out the Soviet zone in Germany an[d] Berlin. Despite the most far-reach[ing] assistance from the Russian occupa[tion] authorities, the S.E.D. was resoundi[ngly] defeated in Berlin, where the Social De[mo]cratic party had repudiated any links [with] the S.E.D. The experience made it clea[r to] the Russians that there was no hope of [the] S.E.D. winning power in Germany by [free] elections.

Instead they determined to make [an] increased bid for the support of Ger[man] nationalist sentiment. In March 194[7 at] the Moscow conference of Foreign M[ini]sters, and again in London in Novem[ber] Molotov called for an independent Ger[man] government to be set up by agreem[ent] between the German political parties [and] alleged that west Germany was be[ing] reduced by Britain and America to [the] status of a colony. A People's Cong[ress] was assembled in eastern Berlin in Dec[em]ber and prominent representatives f[rom] west Germany of the idea of a new Ger[man] Soviet agreement as the price of reunif[ica]tion were given their heed. The So[viet] appeal for a revival of German nationa[lism] was, however, rather marred by a dem[and] for £10,000 million in reparations.

At the same time the Soviet leader[s] began to tighten its hold on the satel[lite] countries. In Poland, Rumania, and H[un]gary, police persecution and all kind[s of] other pressures were turned on the [sur]viving non-Communist parties to fo[rce] them to merge with the Communist[s in] "united front" parties controlled by [the] Communists. Individual political lead[ers] who proved recalcitrant were arrested [on] trumped-up charges. From Hung[ary] which at least had a common border w[ith] Austria, refugees flooded across into [the] British-occupied zone of Austria by t[ens] of thousands throughout the summe[r of] 1947. The Rumanians were less hap[pily] placed. And from Poland only a few of th[ose] whom the Russians had been forced [to] accept in 1945, including the Peas[ant] Party leader, Mikolaczyk, managed [to] escape. In February 1948, the Russi[ans] staged a *coup d'état* in Czechoslovakia, [the] one country that they had had most trou[ble] with over the Marshall plan. Presid[ent] Benes was forced, under threat of civil w[ar] to accept a government dominated [by] Russian nominees. The Foreign Minis[ter] Jan Masaryk, was found dead in suspici[ous] circumstances. And a number of Cze[chs] were added to those from Hungary in [the]

△ Leaving the Geneva Summit Conference in July 1955; Khrushchev, Bulganin, and Marshal Zhukov, the Defence Minister.

P. camps in the British and American ...es in Austria and Western Germany.

The Prague coup seemed so exactly like ...tler's annexation of Austria or his ...cupation of Prague in March 1939 that ...stern Europe was galvanised with ...tivity. Mr. Bevin had been turning over ...ns for creating some kind of institu-...nalised community of western Europe ...ce the previous summer at the very ...st. On January 22, 1948, speaking in the ...use of Commons, he had described ...viet policy as attempting to unsettle ...nd intimidate west Europe by political ...sets, economic chaos and even revolu-...nary methods". In March 1948 he ...rsuaded France and the three Benelux ...untries to sign a treaty establishing ...vestern European Union, a permanent ...litary alliance with a standing council ...Foreign Ministers. The first item on the ...uncil's agenda was the setting in motion ...western Germany of discussions on the ...fting of a Federal constitution and the ...ntual establishment of a west German ...vernment.

This challenge to Soviet plans for Ger-...ny was a turning of Soviet methods ...ainst their originators. A logical corol-...y to this was a drastic reform of the German currency, since without this the economy in west Germany would remain dominated by barter and the black market. The admission of the "trizone" (the three western zones of occupation now shared a common administration in economic affairs) to the Marshall plan in February 1948 made this even more essential. The Soviet Union was confronted with the possibility of a west German state, strong economically and welded into western Europe, in a way which would not only put the establishment of Soviet control over it beyond all possibility but was certain to exercise a strong emotional pull on the Soviet-occupied zone.

The Soviet reply was a series of graduated measures of pressure on the western powers' occupation of Berlin. On March 20, 1948, the Soviet members walked out of the Control Commission. Road, rail, and air links with Berlin were harassed. On June 16 the Soviet representatives walked out of the Allied *Kommandatura* in Berlin. Between June 19 and July 10, 1948, they suspended all road, rail, and water communications between Berlin and western Germany.

Thus began the blockade of Berlin, a thoroughly alarming period for all con-

cerned. The Soviet Union had an almost overwhelming military superiority on land in Europe. Soviet troops only had to move westward to sweep away almost overnight the small and pathetically unprepared western occupation forces in Germany and Austria. Only one military restraint on them existed – the American possession of the atomic bomb.

The blockade was to last until May 1949. It was broken by the air lift, a massive use of air transport, heavily subsidised, to bring food, coal, raw materials, etc., into Berlin, and to bring Berlin's exports out again. Its effect was to turn the western European Union from a purely European security organisation, designed to control the new west German State and to allay the fears of those western Europeans who had only four years earlier been liberated

from German occupation, into an an Soviet security system under Americ leadership. In September 1948 the Britis postponed demobilisation of those co scripts whose term of service was up ar secured the stationing in Britain American aircraft, armed with atom bombs, to be used against any Sovi aggression in Europe. In December 194 the American government eventual committed itself to the idea of a Nort Atlantic alliance. The Treaty establis ing N.A.T.O. was signed in April 1949.

In the meantime the Soviet Union ha suffered three other serious defeats. A the beginning of October 1947 as the Ma shall Plan was being organised by the we: European governments, a Russian-orgar ised conference, meeting in Warsaw, atter ded by delegates not only from Sovie

open. Yugoslavia was formally expelled from the Cominform, and the "Tito clique", which had isolated and arrested the Soviet cats'-paws in its midst, denounced as imperialist agents. The Yugoslav defection was followed by the collapse of the Greek Communist guerrillas, deprived of their bases in the Yugoslav mountains. The experience led Stalin to carry out a series of purges of the Communist leadership of eastern Europe, Rajk in Hungary, Gomulka in Poland, Kostov in Bulgaria, Xoxe in Albania and, lastly and most extensively, Slansky and his allies in Czechoslovakia. Only those Communist leaders, whose presence in Russia during the war years and survival of the Great Purges of the 1930's guaranteed their loyalty, were immune.

## East Germany

The formation of N.A.T.O. and the setting up of the West German Federal Republic in 1949 was answered by the establishment of an East German state, for which the Soviets had already, in 1948, begun recruiting a paramilitary armed and regimented police of 50,000 men with armoured cars and light artillery. At that point the most stringent prohibition on the establishment of any West German armed forces had been accepted by the West German Government despite the advice of the N.A.T.O. military staffs that without a sizable German military contribution western Europe could hardly be defended. In the summer of 1950 when the new Federal Chancellor, Dr. Adenauer, approached the Allied High Commissioners for permission to raise a Federal West German police force to match the armed *Volkspolizei* of the east, despite British support neither the French nor the American Governments would hear of the matter, even after the outbreak of the Korean War in July 1950.

By September, however, the American government had changed its mind. Its decision to press its N.A.T.O. allies to allow the raising of a 12-division West German army was unveiled at a special N.A.T.O. meeting in New York. The French replied by proposing that this new German army should only be allowed within the framework of a European army, the German forces being integrated at a unit level so small that no separate German army could ever come into existence. This pro-

△ *"K & B", as they became known to the Western press, arrive at Victoria Station at the start of an official visit to Britain in 1956. They are being greeted by Sir Anthony Eden, the Prime Minister.*

nmunist parties and those of the ssian satellites, but also from the French Italian Communist parties, had set up Communist Information Bureau, .ch had immediately called for the eat of the Marshall Plan, "a European nch of the general world plan of expan- being realised by the United States", claration of political warfare against west. An all-out campaign of general kes and demonstrations was launched France and Italy. It failed. A major rt was made to win the 1948 elections taly. Again the effort failed.

he third, and worst, failure came in the mer of 1948 when long-standing difnces between the Soviet Union and goslavia, stemming from Soviet efforts stablish full control over the Yugoslav nmunist leadership, broke into the

posal was so novel, so controversial, and so antipathetic to the British that it took from 1950 to 1952 to negotiate, the European Defence Community treaty being signed in Paris only in May of that year.

During the long debate on the setting up of the E.D.C., the Soviet Union had remained comparatively inactive on the European front. Her main attention was taken up with monitoring the Korean War and her main propaganda effort put into organising the Stockholm peace petition, a massive and fortunately quite unsuccessful attempt to arouse what was coming to be called "neutralist" opinion in Europe against the United States, where the initial stage of the Korean War had been followed in January 1951 by an enormous rearmament programme, the distribution of American strategic air command bases all round the Soviet borders and the establishment of a sizable military force and an integrated military command under General Eisenhower within N.A.T.O. The American hydrogen bomb programme had already been launched. The first test bomb was to be exploded in November 1952.

It was the prospect of West German rearmament and the E.D.C. actually

going through which stirred the Sov Union into new diplomatic action central Europe. In March 1952, the Sov leadership called for a Four Power C ference to negotiate a German pe treaty and a German unification. T Soviet position was a weak one. In Septe ber 1951 the United Nations had be persuaded into appointing an intern tional commission of neutral states investigate the possibility of holding fr elections in both parts of Germany. It h been denied entry into the Soviet occupi zone. Soviet chances of a successful appe to German nationalism had been grea weakened by the conclusion of a trea between East Germany and Poland cognising the Oder-Neisse line as t frontier, something it was to take years to get West German opinion to acce

The reply of the three western occupyi powers opened a period of shadow boxir The rules of the game were that it w about the rules by which Germany was be reunified. Was it to be by free electio to an all-German parliament that all-German government would emerg as the western powers demanded? C was it to be by the prior establishment an all-German government drawn fro

a policy of diplomacy by bombastic rhetoric; phrases such as "the liberation of the captive nations", "rolling back the enemy", "massive retaliation", and "not being scared to go to the brink" concealed a gradual realisation that the limits on American action observed by the Democratic administration were objective restraints, not subjective inhibitions.

The second was the death of Stalin and the absorption of the successors in a struggle for the leadership which was to last for the next four to five years. The new leadership was originally headed by Georgi Malenkov and Molotov, the Soviet Foreign Minister, but gradually they were ousted from power by Nikolai Bulganin and his successor, Nikita Khruschev. In the struggle for power the unconscious longing for a relaxation of the tensions of Stalin's police state, at least for the Soviet élite, was Khruschev's most potent weapon.

The third event was the development of a Soviet thermo-nuclear bomb in the first year of the Eisenhower régime. The fourth was the East German rising of June 1953 which revealed both the thinness of Soviet control over its satellites and the willingness to use force, armed force, to suppress dissidence. It showed also the total inability of the west, despite all Dulles's rhodomontades, to do anything to assist popular movements within the Soviet bloc. A "balance of terror" had been established which was to prove the most stabilising factor in the new situation. It was under these circumstances that the British Government under Winston Churchill began its great drive for an armistice if not a settlement in the "cold war", to be settled "at the summit", that is by a meeting of heads of government. France duly failed to ratify E.D.C. despite Dulles's threats of an "agonising reappraisal" of American policy leading to a withdrawal from Europe. The British drive began in May 1953. Its dominant idea was a central European security pact based on mutual guarantees.

The first stage, the four-power foreign ministers' conference which met in Berlin in February 1954, was largely devoted to reiterating past proposals. It was followed by the failure of the French Assembly to ratify the E.D.C. agreements. In its place the British revived the 1948 establishment of western European Union to include West Germany. Britain broke the practice of centuries and committed a large part of her armed forces to the continent as a guarantee against France finding herself

governments of the two German states, the Soviets insisted? The first would ...p away the S.E.D. and the East ...man Government. The second would ...ide chances for all kinds of shenani-... The aim of the western allies was to ...eve a position of reasonable military ...ngth and then, and only then, nego-... This aim was very much that of the ...ral German chancellor, Dr. Adenauer. ...e shadow-boxing lasted for two years, ...Soviets concentrating on delaying the ...fication of the E.D.C. treaties by the ...ch parliament, and on attempting to ...upt support for them in Germany. The ...ets had a good deal of success with ...these ploys.

## e players changed

...r major events, however, changed the ...le thrust and scale of the game. The ...was Eisenhower's election to the U.S. ...idency in November 1952 and his ...ointment of John Foster Dulles as ...etary of State, whose crusading anti-...munism and hostility to containment ...cringing to the Soviets" led him into

▽ *Matyas Rakosi, 1st Secretary of the Hungarian Workers Party just before the 1956 uprising.*

△ *Russian tanks roll through the streets of Budapest, crushing the last flickers of revolt.*
△▷ *A 15-year-old freedom fighter; her fate is unknown.*
△▷▷ *The huge head from Stalin's statue lies in the street, decorated with a traffic sign. The vast statue symbolised the oppressive presence of the hated Russians and was toppled by cheering crowds in the early days of the Rising.*
▷ *Hacking the statue to pieces – parts of it were taken away as souvenirs.*

alone against Germany. This the French Assembly accepted, the Germans following suit in March 1955. West Germany joined N.A.T.O. The Soviets replied in May 1955 by setting up the Warsaw Pact.

In February 1955 Bulganin replaced Malenkov as Soviet premier and Khruschev, the Party secretary, became more and more prominent. At Geneva in April 1954, Britain and Russia had collaborated in negotiating an ending to the French war in Indo-China and a prevention of its escalation into a Sino-American confrontation. The experience heartened the British foreign minister, Anthony Eden, sufficiently to play on Eisenhower's desire, the year before he was due to retire or run again for re-election, to do something serious about peace. Bulganin and Khruschev co-operated, most noticeably by proclaiming their belief in co-existence and suddenly abandoning their ten-year-old opposition to a peace treaty with Austria. At the same time, the Soviet feud with Yugoslavia was brought to an end.

The Geneva summit conference duly met in July 1955. The Soviet position was by no means a flexible one. The British hope had been that some kind of alternative security could be found to that provided

for the Soviets by the presence of of their divisions in East Germany. Soviets made it clear that only the w drawal of American forces from Eur and the dismantling of N.A.T.O. wo lead them to accept the unification Germany. Superficially these disag ments were patched over. But when Foreign Ministers met in Geneva October 1955, the same problems emer again. Nothing was achieved save acceptance of the existence of the German states, each integrated into military, economic, and political syste of the two blocs. This was to be confirm a year later with West German partic tion in the setting up of the Comn Market. The Soviet acceptance of this symbolised in the Soviet recognition of Federal German Government and invitation to Dr. Adenauer to v Moscow.

## The cold war ends

With this tacit acceptance by each s of the division of Germany, the cold properly considered had ended. The li

△ *Before the establishing of its permanent home in New York, the U.N. General Assembly met in several different countries. Here the 1948 session gets under way in the Palais de Chaillot, Paris.*

drawn in central Europe by the tripartite agreements reached at Yalta and afterwards on the zonal boundaries between the areas of Germany and Austria to be occupied by each of the four occupying powers had hardened into a division of Europe into two power blocs. No serious possibility existed of intervention across those dividing lines, extended as they were up to the north cape by the addition of Denmark and Norway to N.A.T.O. in the north, and to the Dardanelles by the entry of Greece and Turkey into N.A.T.O. in the south. Even here the line followed that agreed between Churchill and Stalin in October 1944 as dividing British and Soviet spheres of influence with Yugoslavia, divided 50:50 between the two countries in 1944, occupying since 1948 a half-way position of neutrality between the two blocs.

In this the Geneva summit and the Foreign Ministers' conference of 1955

marked a recognition of the balanc power which had existed since 194 balance between Soviet contentic forces and the American nuclear deterr The addition of N.A.T.O.'s minimal fo and the Soviet deterrent to that bala did nothing really to disturb a situatio which for once only a madman could any profit in a new war. The near mis culation of the 1962 Cuban missile cri and Khruschev's long but in the end successful attempt to exploit weaknesses and ambiguities of the west position in Berlin only underlined stability of the balance. Its concomit was the western acceptance of episo such as the bloody suppression by Soviets of the Hungarian rising in and the Czechoslovak "liberalisi régime of Mr. Dubcek in 1968. The war had become a cold stalemate, armistice which no one was really in ested in breaking.

# rganisationsbuch der N.S.D.A.P.
## The Nazi Party Handbook

k the compilers of the Nazi Handbook 550 pages to ex- l the intricacies of Party isation. From this, much of is too technical to be of al interest, only the most icant passages have been ated. It is hoped that they provide readers with an r to the puzzle of how the persuaded the German e that the way to a Golden f Teutonic glory lay in the bracing folds of National lism.

answer emerges only too y from the Handbook: there d, from 1934, an incredibly ex Party organisation, one ose aims was the inclusion ery Aryan German within ds. This was achieved effi- y by means of a comprehen- Party hierarchy, at the m of which was the Block r, in charge of 40 to 60 holds. He knew, or soon out, all that went on in

s, however, is only one t; plausibility is another. often the long-winded sen- s of ideological claptrap are tively, insidiously persua- there was to be a fellowship

of the people, and in this ability, rather than standing, was to be the criterion. In this system, therefore, the Block Leader was not a snooper but a confidant and aide. Anyone who took the Block Leader into his confidence did so at his own peril, however, for the information was passed through the hierarchy and could be used to ensure the loyalty of the original informant. The whole etiquette of precedence and pre- rogative implicit in the system of subordinates and superordinates effectively cancelled out any sup- posed feeling of fellowship even in the first years of the Nazi era.

There is in the Handbook all that a German could desire: a para-military organisation, uni- forms, ranks, ceremonies, rallies, and parades—the trappings of power without its responsibilities.

It is hoped that the passages chosen will illustrate the frightening completeness with which every German was caught up in the Nazi net. In translating the text, every effort has been made to preserve the crude and often clumsy sentence construc- tion of the German original. The translation and notes are by **Suzanne Flatauer.**

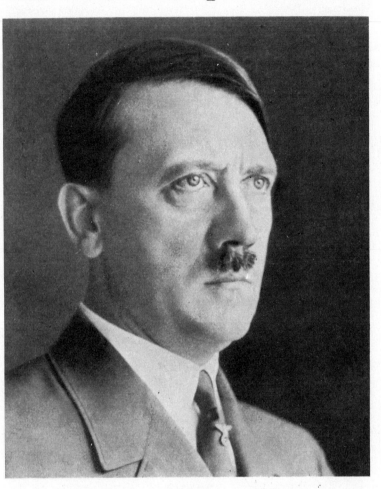

1936

*Commemorative badges:*
△ △ △ *The S.A. Rally of 1931 in Brunswick.*
△ △ *The Coburg Decoration.*
△ *The Party Day of 1929 in Nuremberg.*

# 1. The National Socialist's General Conduct

Every Party member must think of himself as a servant of the Movement and of his people, and act accordingly. That applies particularly to Political Leaders, to Leaders of all Sections of the Party, to Administrators and Wardens.

It is the most important task of every National Socialist to keep alive and continually strengthen the idea of national unity within Party and State.

It is incompatible with this task to keep oneself aloof from one's fellow Party members and citizens, to imagine oneself to be superior, and thus to open up a gulf, to bridge which has caused deep-felt anguish to the best of German men. When he accepts higher office, a National Socialist accepts higher duties. He holds absolute power only to enable him to carry out his higher duties. It does not entitle him to become overbearing, arrogant, and conceited. He will never win the confidence and the ready obedience of his Junior Leaders and men by threats, tyranny, and parade-ground language.

On duty he should be a leader and supporter, off duty he should act as good companion and helper to his Junior Leaders, fellow Party members, and fellow citizens. The more his deeds are in keeping with his words, the more readily his fellow Party members as well as his fellow citizens will follow him with a will.

In his behaviour, every National Socialist must remain as simple and as modest as was customary among National Socialists during the times of struggle. He should not want to appear to be greater than he really is, and just as he will reject any obsequiousness towards those above him, he should not allow obsequiousness towards himself. A leading Party member must not be vain and sensitive at any time; he is bound to prefer a well-tried fighter's true and candid speech to the honeyed words of creatures who fawn on him.

Always he is to keep in touch with the most humble of his fellow citizens, lending a willing ear to their troubles. They will be pleased to come to him if he has remained the same as ever, and if he still moves in the same society and circles as in the times of struggle.

Political Leaders, Administrators, and Wardens should not take part in banquets; they should not go after presents and after becoming freemen of cities; they should not patronise the most expensive restaurants; and they should always behave, on duty and off duty, in the manner expected of them as representatives of the German Freedom Movement and as collaborators in the unutterably hard task of building a better Germany.

Above all they should avoid excessive consumption of alcohol at a time when there are still many German families who lack the barest necessities of life and who are bound to lose their painfully regained faith while men belonging to the Movement – possibly by breaking licensing laws – are holding drinking parties, damaging by their behaviour in a state of intoxication the reputation of the Movement.

A true National Socialist does not boast of his actions and does not demand thanks. He finds his greatest reward in the knowledge of having performed his duty, in the success of his work, and in the confidence in him of his following.

A National Socialist is bound to act correctly if he examines himself daily, asking himself if he could justify his behaviour before his Führer.

# 2. The Party Member

## (1) Admission

Every member of the German nation, of unblemished character and of German stock, not belonging to any Masonic Lodge (or any of its subsidiary organisations), and having completed his 18th year, may become a member of the N.S.D.A.P. (*National Sozialistische Deutsche Arbeiterpartei* = National Socialist German Workers' Party) on completion of the application form of the N.S.D.A.P. and on payment of the fixed admission fee. The Party management may, at any time, impose a bar on the admission of new members, or restrict admission to certain persons. Announcements in this connection will be issued by the National Treasurer of the N.S.D.A.P. only.

Rejection of an application for admission will be made, no reasons being stated, either by the respective Leader of the local branch or by the Base Leader, as the case may be, in agreement with the competent Party Tri-

bunal. There is no legal re[course] against rejection.

Admission has officially [taken] place upon issue of a memb[ership] card or a membership book. [Who]ever becomes a National So[cialist] is not merely joining an org[anis]ation, but is turning into a s[oldier] of the German Freedom [Move]ment, and that implies far [more] than simply paying one's [dues] and attending Party mee[tings.] In making this step, he take[s] on himself the obligation of s[etting] aside the self and of vent[uring] everything he possesses, hi[mself] and his property, for his pe[ople.] Only he who knows how [to do] this should become a Nat[ional] Socialist: the selection has [to be] made with this aim in mind.

**Fighting spirit**
**A spirit of Sacrifice**
**Strength of Char[acter]**

those are the qualifications [of a] true National Socialist. M[inor] blemishes (e.g. if someone s[hould] have committed a youthf[ul of]fence) may be overlooked. [Per]formance in the struggl[e for] Germany is all-decisive. [A] healthy organism will [spon]taneously expel what is dise[ased] as long as the will to be he[althy] has been proved through su[itable] leadership and achieve[ment.] Thus the criteria for admissi[on to] the Party should be not bour[geois] but soldierly standpoints, an[d the] decisive factor for judgi[ng a] man's character should b[e his] bearing when he is face to [face] with the enemy. The Party [must] always remain the élite o[f the] people. Therefore care has [to be] taken as to who is admitted [as a] Party member, and all philis[tines] and "big shots" who are s[elfish] and lacking in character a[re to] be kept out or expelled.

In order to prevent unsui[table] elements from slipping thro[ugh,] a fellow citizen may only [be] admitted into and carried o[n the] register of the Party at his [place] of residence. Every applica[tion] form has to pass through [the] hands of the local Block Le[ader.] Should the prospective me[mber] apply to the Cell, the Base [or] Local Branch, the District B[oard] or any other place rather [than] directly to his Block Leader[, the] application form must be [re]turned as quickly as possib[le to] the local Block Leader for ev[alu]ation. It is the duty of the B[lock] Leader, who knows every pe[rson] in his block, to initial this a[ppli]cation form and to forward [it to] the Local Branch without d[elay.] This procedure is applicable [also] to people proposed for admis[sion]

1923

1925

... and △ The 1923 and 1925
... decorations for Saxony,
...avarian Ostmark, Halle-
...seburg, Hessen-Nassau,
... Magdeburg-Anhalt,
...ecklenburg-Lübeck, and
...vabia (the 1923 decoration
...nly for the last named).

... Party by the H.J. (Hitler-
...end = Hitler Youth Organis-
...n).

**The Pledge**
...n he is given his membership
..., the member will be solemnly
...n in. All new Party members
... have to undertake this Bind-
...Oath, regardless of whether
... belong to the S.A. or the
... The Binding Oath is ad-
...istered by the Local Branch
...der or the Base Leader during
... meeting of Party mem-
... In the course of a brief
...ess, he will outline the duties
...he Party member and stress
... significance of the oath of
...giance. Then he himself will
...k the words of the oath of
...giance, sentence by sentence.
...ll view of the National flag,
...e to be sworn in will repeat
...pledge, sentence by sentence,
...le raising their right arm in
... German Salute. The text of
... oath of allegiance is as fol-
...:

... pledge allegiance to my
...ührer Adolf Hitler. I promise
... all times to show respect and
...edience to him and to any
...aders he may appoint for me."
... handing over of the member-
... book by the Local Group
...der will take place in solemn

style during the meeting of Party
members, accompanied by the
words:

"In the name of the Führer I am
handing over to you your membership book. Remain as loyal
to the Party as you have been
up to now!"

### (3) Withdrawal
Membership lapses through
death, through voluntary withdrawal, through individual expulsion, and through expulsion
of whole Blocks, Cells, Bases, or
Local Branches. Voluntary withdrawals, caused almost invariably by personal grievances
or alleged slights, prove that the
person concerned is no National
Socialist. Such a loss does not
render the Party any poorer; on
the contrary, it can only gain by
it. A true National Socialist will
never withdraw voluntarily, because for him National Socialism
has become his purpose in and his
way of life. If the withdrawal
takes place in order to forestall
expulsion, the regular legal proceedings of the Party will nevertheless have to be carried out.

In connection with appli-
cations for expulsion, it will be
necessary to exercise the utmost
care and the highest sense of
responsibility. Expulsion is the
most severe punishment the Party
has. Today it means loss of livelihood and loss of all personal
standing to the person to whom
it is meted out.

Members *will* be expelled
(a) if they commit dishonourable acts, or if the fact that
they committed such acts in
the past comes to light;
(b) if they act contrary to the
aims of the N.S.D.A.P.; and
(c) if by their moral behaviour they give offence to the
Party and to the general
public and thereby harm the
Party.

Members *may* be expelled
(a) if within a Local Branch,
a County or an Adminis-
trative District they have
repeatedly been the cause of
bickering and quarrelling;
(b) if, in spite of reminders,
they are three months in
arrears with their membership fees, without having
tendered an apology; and
(c) because of lack of
interest.

Should there be mitigating circumstances, a warning may be
decided upon in place of expulsion
and, should the occasion arise,
the loss of the right to occupy
posts in the Party administration

for the duration of up to three
years.

Based on a legally valid
decision of a Party Tribunal, the
following persons are qualified
to order expulsion:
(a) the Local Branch Leader
(b) the County Leader
(c) the Administrative District Leader
(d) the Führer.

In the first instance, the expulsion will be executed by the
Leading Functionary to whose
administrative area the Party
Tribunal making the application
belongs.

The Party Tribunals have only
the right of application for expulsion. They must send this
application to the accused and
to the Leading Functionary responsible. Both have the right to
lodge an appeal within a period of
eight days. This appeal has the
effect of deferring judgement. A
Leading Functionary may execute an application for expulsion
by the Party Tribunal only if the
Party Tribunal informs him that
the accused has not made use of
his right to lodge an appeal. In
urgent cases the expulsion may
be carried out by the Leading
Functionary in agreement with
the Chairman of his Party Tribunal.

Objection against this procedure is allowed within eight
days. However, this objection
has no deferring effect. In every
case where an objection is being
lodged, Party legal proceedings
will have to be carried out. If in
the course of these proceedings
the expulsion is confirmed, the
accused must be informed by the
Leading Functionary that the
expulsion has become final. Final
judgement in all matters concerning expulsion rests with the
Führer. It is he who has authority, in agreement with the
Supreme Party Tribunal, to order
the expulsion of complete Local
Branches. In that case, their
assets go to the N.S.D.A.P.

### (4) Re-admission
As a rule, for Party members who
left after January 1, 1932, whether
they left of their own accord or
through expulsion, re-admission
into the N.S.D.A.P. is out of the
question. In principle, re-
admission of an expelled Party
member will only take place in
agreement with the local Party
Tribunal. Extensive leniency
should be exercised with expelled
persons as far as is compatible
with the standing and the honour
of the Party.

### (5) Transfer
Every Party member must know
that members of the N.S.D.A.P.
are obliged to notify their local
Political Office of all changes of
address and of personal status,
including temporary changes.

### (6) Duties of a Party Member
A National Socialist's commandments:

The Führer is always right!
Never offend against discipline!
Never waste your time in idle
gossip or in complacent criti-
cism, but lend a hand and work!
Be proud, but not conceited!
Let the (Party) programme be
your dogma; it demands your
utmost commitment to the
Movement!
You are a representative of the
Party, let your behaviour and
appearance be determined by it!
Let loyalty and selflessness be
your highest precept!
Be a loyal comrade, you are
then a true Socialist!
Treat your fellow citizens as
you would be treated!
In battle, be tough and silent!
Courage is not the same as
brutality!
What is useful to the Move-
ment, and thus to Germany, i.e.
your country, is right!

If you act according to these
commandments, you will be a
true fighter for your Führer.

### (7) Rules of Conduct for
**Members of Local Branches**
The following rules of conduct
are to be made known to members
of both sexes, to be thoroughly
memorised:

Make the work of Political
Leaders easier by discharging
your duties promptly.

If you are a female Party
member, take part in the work of
the N.S. Women's Guild. There
you will find tasks awaiting you.

Do not buy from Jews!

As a token of consideration for
the health of speakers and Party
Members, refrain from smoking
at Party meetings.

Do not become the mouthpiece
of political enemies by spreading
false rumours.

To be a National Socialist
means to set an example!

### (8) The Wearing of Badges
**and Uniforms by Party
Members**
(1) When in civilian clothes, a
Party member wears his Party
badge.
(2) After two years' membership,
a Party member is entitled to
wear a brown shirt with his

civilian clothes.

(3) Party members are allowed to wear uniforms or parts of uniforms of Political Leaders, the S.A., the S.S., the N.S.K.K. (the transport corps), and the H.J., with or without badges, only when they belong to one of the above-named units and possess a pass to that effect.

## Who is entitled to issue Assessments?

Unless requests are made by higher-ranking departments of the Party, political assessments and personal character references may only be issued by Leading Functionaries from the rank of District Leader upwards.

For official or semi-official purposes as well as for the purpose of planned distribution of labour such references are to be given as a matter of principle. In all other cases the giving of references is at the discretion of the Leading Functionary.

## Passport Photographs

Members of the N.S.D.A.P. or members of their units and of associated formations are not allowed to use passport photographs showing the holder of a pass in party uniform including section badges.

## Conversations with Foreigners

All Party members are forbidden to hold conversations about foreign affairs with foreigners. The authority to do so belongs solely to Führer appointees.

## Correspondence with Foreign Countries

All correspondence with foreign groups of the N.S.D.A.P., their associated organisations, or with Political Leaders or Party Members must be conducted via the management of the German Foreign Institute, Berlin.

## Private Correspondence

In connection with private correspondence, in particular with German nationals abroad, the use of official stamps, notepaper and envelopes of Party departmental offices is not permitted.

## Qualities a Party Member holding a Leading Position is expected to possess:

His leading position will be acknowledged only if the Party member is outwardly and inwardly unblemished.

If he does not behave in an obsequious manner to his superiors,

if he does not give himself airs with his subordinates,

if at any time he has the courage to speak the absolute truth,

if he is too much on the alert ever to be misled.

Further, leading Party members in the Movement should distinguish themselves by endeavouring

to distinguish soundly between right and wrong,

to practise self-control,

to prepare their plans thoughtfully,

to carry out their tasks thoroughly,

always to keep their pledged word,

never to promise anything they cannot keep,

to be straightforward,

to win the love and respect of others through their behaviour.

## Leading Party Members in the Life of the Local Branch (or of the Base)

Political Leaders, Leaders of Units, Party members holding high office in the service of the State, and full-time Party workers who are not included in the Local Branches at their place of residence, but who belong to the Section *Gauleitung* or to the Local Branch *Braunes Haus* (Brown House), are to consider it their natural duty to take part in the life of the Local Branch at their place of residence. They are to attend the functions of their Local Branch and, unless they are employed in leading posts in the Party Organisation, they are, if possible, to serve actively in the Local Branch at their place of residence.

In this connection, it is a matter of course that Junior Leaders in the Party who have as their subordinates Party members occupying, for example, high-ranking Government posts, may give orders to them only in their capacity as Party members, and may not abuse the Party authority conferred upon them to exert any influence whatever on their State and other functions.

## 3. Aims

### I

Through efficient distribution of activities, a leading Party member working in an honorary capacity should be enabled thoroughly and conscientiously to carry out his Party activities, including those in sections and associated organisations,

*Important Party banners:*
△ *The banner of the* Kreis *of Munich . . .*
△▷ *. . . and that of the* Ortsgruppe *of Altdorf.*

without having to neglect his Family and his Job.

Attempts should therefore be made to reduce as far as possible the fields of action of the individual so that the above principle may be taken into account.

### II
### The Party's Tasks are solely ideological

Attempts must therefore be made gradually to transfer all those technical tasks which during the upheaval of organising the Reich are still being carried out by the Party, to the associated organisations or, if expedient, to Government administration. If necessary or possible, orders should be issued by the individually responsible office of the National Executive.

The Party itself as instrument of ideological education has to become the leading corps of the German people. The leading corps is responsible for the complete penetration of the German people in the National Socialist spirit and for overcoming dependence on internationally orientated forces, which is still partially rooted in the people.

Furthermore, it will be the duty of this leading corps to see that the technical and specialist tasks which are being carried out in associated organisations as well as in Government administration are in fact accomplished in alignment with National Socialist thinking.

## 4. The Political Leader

The basis of Party organisati the principle of leadership. community cannot rule i either directly or indirectly. ever is best fitted for such should be a leader. Such a will be supported by the c dence of the people. All Pol Leaders are held to have appointed by the Führer and answerable to him; towards subordinates they enjoy ful thority. What matters in selection of Political Leade to place the right man in the post. The offices of the Party to such a degree that the accu selection of leaders requires siderable knowledge of hu nature as well as long experie Age and social position are ir vant, character and apti alone being decisive in the s tion of leaders.

In principle, it has to be served that only he who has trained through undertaking painstakingly detailed wor our Party is entitled, if suit for the purpose, to lay clai higher posts. We can only use of leaders who have wo their way up from the ranks. Political Leader who devi from this principle shoulc removed or relegated for training to less important sph of action (i.e. as Block or Leader).

Let every Political Leade member at all times that le

does not simply bring with
~~e~~ater rights, but that, first
~~f~~oremost, it imposes greater
~~o~~nsibility.

~~i~~s the first duty of a Political
~~d~~er, in his personal bearing
~~i~~n his conception of duty, as
~~w~~as in his private way of life,
~~~~ a shining example. Let him
~~co~~nscious of the fact that more
~~~~ is done by the bad example
~~a~~ Political Leader than can be
~~m~~ up for by a hundred and one
~~mu~~nitions. Invariably, Cells,
~~c~~ks, Bases, or Local Groups
~~are~~ the mirror image of their
~~Lead~~ing Functionary. Whoever
~~fails~~ to do his duty in his home
~~town~~ or place of residence, will
~~fail e~~lsewhere.

~~Hi~~s second duty is absolute
~~justi~~ce. Nepotism must not be
~~toler~~ated. Whoever sits upon able
~~Part~~y members because he is
~~afrai~~d they might outshine him,
~~is a~~ despicable wretch and a
~~detri~~ment to the Party. The
~~Lead~~ing Functionary should not
~~wish~~ to do everything single-
~~hand~~ed. He must be guide, super-
~~viso~~r, and arbitrator. In a nut-
~~shell~~: the very life and soul of it
~~all. ~~Because he cares for his
~~grou~~p-in many cases his own
~~crea~~tion-the Political Leader
~~must~~ immediately extinguish any
~~spar~~k which might cause a con-
~~flagr~~ation. He must anticipate
~~and ~~not be caught napping. For
~~thes~~e reasons he must not over-
~~burd~~en himself with laborious
~~deta~~ils.

~~An~~y position of leadership de-
~~man~~ds a considerable measure of
~~know~~ledge and ability. That is
~~why ~~every Political Leader has to
~~work~~ on educating himself con-

tinuously. That is why the Party
considers it to be its chief task to
make possible the continuous
training of all Political Leaders.
It is not his commission which
makes a leader, but the fact that
his followers may look up to him
in every respect. Not every
Political Leader can be a good
speaker, and yet he must be a
preacher and a propagandist for
the Idea.

Every Political Leader must
have a strong personality. Do
your duty in the place your Führer
allocates to you. If you are a
front-line soldier, you cannot be
a general staff officer, and *vice
versa*. Take care of your job, and
do not take on more tasks than
you are able to perform; but carry
those you have accepted to completion. If the Political Leader
wants to perform the tasks
assigned to him correctly and
thoroughly, he must not fritter
away his powers. That is why
membership of non-Party societies, and, in particular, taking
part in their activities, is undesirable.

Each public appearance of the
Party and, similarly, every internal function, such as discussion groups, indoctrination
evenings, meetings of Party members, etc., must be most carefully
prepared. When giving orders,
give them clearly, concisely and
accurately. Never say: "I think ...
one ought to ... it is advisable ...".
Your opinion is immaterial; on
the other hand, every one demands to know what you want.
Only then may you call every one
to account, only then will there
be no uncertainty.

Bear this in mind: whoever
cannot obey, will never be fit to
give orders. Never put your own
personal standing first. There is
only one standing, namely that of
the Movement. Carefully culti-
vate comradely relations with all
other sections of the Party.

### The typical Political Leader

From what has gone before, there
emerges a picture of the typical
Political Leader. The Political
Leader is not a civil servant, but,
at all times, the political representative of the Führer. He must
see and think clearly. In times of
national crisis, he must stand
firm as a rock and obey orders
implicitly. By means of Political
Leaders we are building up the
political management within the
State.

The Political Leader must be
preacher and soldier at one and
the same time. He may never
become a bureaucrat, he must
always work with the people and
for the people. He must be an
example.

Reason is the product of instinct and intelligence. It is not
absolutely necessary for the
Political Leader to possess detailed technical knowledge: he
has competent officials for that
purpose; but his judgement must
be superior. The typical Political
Leader is not characterised by his
office. There is no Political Leader
of any one Party organisation,
but only

**a Political Leader of the
N.S.D.A.P.**

### The Swearing-in of Political Leaders

The swearing-in of Political
Leaders takes place annually at
the same time as the swearing-in
of male and female leaders of the
Hitler Youth and its associated
organisations.
The formula of the oath is as
follows:

> "I pledge unswerving loyalty to
> Adolf Hitler. I pledge absolute
> obedience to him and to any
> leaders he may appoint for me."

The Political Leader feels indissolubly bound up with the
ideas and the organisation of the
N.S.D.A.P. He may not resign
from the post assigned to him
without the express consent of
his superior administrative office.

The oath will expire only with
the death of the person sworn in,
or with expulsion from the
National Socialist community.

Political Leaders require the
following personal documents:
   (*a*) personal questionnaire

   (*b*) curriculum vitae
   (*c*) family tree as proof of Aryan
      origin
   (*d*) extract from prison records
      (in case of criminal record)
   (*e*) two passport photographs.

### General Remarks concerning the Political Leader's Uniform

The Political Leader's uniform
has been developed out of the
realisation that political work
for Germany is based on soldierly
principles.

In creating it, the Führer has
clearly expressed his wish to
bring about a clear distinction
between the typical Political
Leader of the N.S.D.A.P. and
civilian politicians of former
parties and countries. The Political Leader is preacher and soldier
at one and the same time; he
represents that political leadership for which the German nation
has fought for 2,000 years.

The Political Leader should be
conscious of this lofty mission
when he wears his dress of
honour, awarded to him by the
Führer.

### Notes

Political Leader = *Politischer
Leiter*. Any person in a leading
position within the Party hierarchy.
Leading Functionary = *Hoheit-
sträger*. Alternative name for a
person in charge of Nazi Party
units.

## 5. Duty Parades

There exist Service *Section* duty
parades and Service *Area* duty
parades.

The following are Service Sections: Base Command, Local
Group Command, District Command, Regional Command, and
the Service Sections of National
Command.

Service Areas, on the other
hand, are: The entire area under
the control of Base, Local Group,
District, Region, and the Reich.

Duty Parades of Sections and
Areas will take place at Bases,
Local Groups, Districts, and
Regions.

### Service Section Duty Parade

(1) All Leading Functionaries are
obliged to hold a parade for all
Political Leaders of their Service
Section at least once a month, in
such a manner that, as far as
possible, place, day and time are
the same.
(2) If required, special parades
may be held.

(3) All Political Leaders attached to the Service Section, regardless of rank, are obliged to attend. Non-attendance at duty parades is permissible only on the strength of express leave of absence, or requires reasonable excuse.

It is desirable that senior leaders of the S.A., S.S., N.S.K.K., and the H.J., responsible for the Region in question, should be included in these parades.

(4) The purpose of a duty parade is as follows: the Section Leader is to be given an opportunity of meeting and talking to his closest colleagues outside their daily duties; of informing them–insofar as he considers this to be necessary–of his views, wishes, and suggestions; and, above all, of getting to know them as comrades.

Political Leaders should be able to see their Section Leader; to get to know and appreciate the work their comrades are doing; and to strengthen the ties of comradeship among themselves as much as possible.

(5) As a matter of principle, service dress is worn on duty parade.

(6) The organisation of duty parade. Duty parade consists of the following:

(a) Report to the Section Leader
(b) Report by office holders
(c) Comments and decisions, as well as a report on the political situation by the Section Leader
(d) Social gathering of comrades.

## Further instructions

(a) Report: A few minutes before commencement of duty parade, the officer in charge of training or, in his absence, the most senior office holder present, will order all Political Leaders to line up and ascertain the number of those present.

As the Section Leader, or his deputy, appears, the officer in charge of training will give the command "Attention!"; he then will walk up to the Section Leader, salute by raising his arm and report the number of those present, either "Political Leaders, all present and correct!" or "Political Leaders present! Absent with leave, Party Member X; absent without leave, Party Member Y." The Section Leader will thank him and command "at ease!"; then he will greet all Political Leaders with a handshake. Subsequently they will all sit down, in such a manner that

(in the case of larger staffs) members of the same office sit together.

(b) Then, one after the other, office-bearers (in Local Groups or Bases this includes Cell Leaders and, if expedient, Block Leaders) will report on their work, briefly and succinctly. If necessary, the Section Leader may order individual discussions.

(c) After receipt of reports, the Section Leader will summarise briefly the results of discussions. He will issue final instructions, and this will immediately be followed by a brief lecture on the political situation.

(d) Social gathering of comrades: gatherings after duty parade should not be held in the Section office rooms but elsewhere, since, as a rule, during the course of these gatherings, eating, drinking, and smoking take place. If the meeting place should be a public restaurant, conversations about internal Party matters will have to cease.

## Notes

The hierarchy of the Party was as follows:

Block = *Block*, the smallest subdivision
Cell = *Zelle*
Base = *Stützpunkt*
Local Group = *Ortsgruppe*
District = *Kreis*
Region = *Gau*

S.A. = *Sturm-Abteilung* (Storm Troopers or Brown Shirts)
S.S. = *Schutz-Staffel* (Security or Defence Squad, Black Shirts)
N.S.K.K. = *Nationalsozialistisches Kraftfahr-Korps* (National Socialist Motor Transport Corps)
H.J. = *Hitler-Jugend* (Hitler Youth Organisation)

# 6. Applied Disciplinary Power

## (1) Is disciplinary power necessary?

Every chief who has to carry out a task, for the execution of which he requires assistants and subordinate offices, must realize, above all else, that it is necessary, in order to solve problems, maintain discipline, and carry out normal duties, to direct the will inherent in every single assistant towards the execution of their relevant tasks.

In his consideration of the form in which the human will manifests itself, the task of the Political Leader is made easier by the fact that he deals consistently with

*Uniforms of Political Leaders:*
◄◄ *An* Ortsgruppenleiter *in service dress.*
◄ *A* Haupstellenleiter *of an* Ortsgruppe *or a* Stützpunkt *(Base) in service dress and greatcoat.*

assistants who, by dint of the leader concept, have been pre-trained to such an extent that they have learned to regard as necessary the subordination of personal advantages to the good of the community.

The release of an act of will requires a motive, an impetus, just as it is utterly impossible for a stone to fall down from a roof without impetus. Therefore, in order to give to a person's will a certain direction, it is necessary to present it with a motive which will allow him to work in the desired direction.

This he will pursue until a stronger motive will turn him away from his original direction. In other words, an assistant will co-operate in the execution of a task; in upholding manly discipline; in the service as a whole; until he considers something else to be more important.

This something else may be a motive which approaches him from outside; on the other hand, it may be something within himself, such as, for instance, personal indolence, or becoming habituated to a vice, or similar causes. However, each of those motives which are inclined to keep an assistant from the execution of his official duties, must be curbed by the holder of disciplinary power. This is achieved by a chief, once and for all, bringing his assistant to the irrefutable conviction that his allotted task is the most important thing which has been assigned to him to be carried out in the interest of the Movement.

An assistant who has not yet grasped that the general welfare is his own welfare, cannot be regarded as such. Inner motives may be countered only by forcing to a speedy retreat that stubborn pigheadedness (so well-known to soldiers) that frequently erupts on such occasions, by threatening exceedingly uncomfortable, even unpleasant, countermeasures.

The realization that there exist measures to deter forcibly any form of egotism wishing to act anti-socially, from doing anything of the kind, has, for thousands of years, proved to be the most effective antidote for any troublesome manifestations of

will, be they of selfishness or sloppiness.

## (2) Prevention of situations which may necessitate the application of disciplinary power:

The best motive to give to the human will is the effect of authority. **Authority is achieved by continually giving a good example.** The leader who, in open battle, storms ahead of his troops, will have much less cause for complaint about cowardice among the ranks of his comrades than one who gives orders to attack from a safe position, having not the least intention of leaving it.

If it should happen that hours of work need to be extended over and above normal working times, and if the Section Leader is himself the last man to leave the office, no murmurings are likely to be heard, but they *will* be heard when he himself sets a job of work and then goes home before it has been finished.

In the interest of comradely co-operation, it is of great importance to avoid having to apply disciplinary power. However, this can be achieved only through most strenuous and consistent efforts on the part of the chief, by giving, in his own person, an example worth striving for, on the one hand by a blameless life, that is to say by self-discipline, on the other hand by tireless execution of his duty.

But that is not by any means enough! Any chief not well-informed about the characters of his assistants will often arrive at individually wrong methods in the handling of comrades who are his subordinates. As wrong as the widely-believed fallacy that a horse may be broken in by means of curb and spur, is the assumption that, in principle, by peremptory and harsh conduct one will have equal success with all assistants.

Indeed no, only careful study of the disposition of every single assistant will enable the chief to act correctly at all times. And that, in turn, will spur on the desire to do one's duty and reduce the necessity of meting out punishment. This study of characters should most conveniently take place by means of private social gatherings; indeed, it is their true purpose. For, conversely, by means of social intercourse the assistant, in turn, will gain better understanding of his chief, namely when he cannot

3283

but perceive that his chief is a thoroughly good comrade, possessing far greater knowledge and ability than may be observed during daily office routine.

The best test of correct treatment of assistants is in the frequency with which disciplinary power has to be applied. The less often it puts in an appearance in well-functioning establishments, the more readily it is an indication that the chief knows how to handle his assistants psychologically correctly. It is better that actual punishment should be applied infrequently, for a knife that is seldom used keeps its edge. A penal law continuously applied quickly loses its educational value.

In order to carry out this pedagogic education of one's assistants, it is necessary that one should feel fully equal to one's job. The realisation that one has an advantage over each of one's assistants in respect of knowledge, ability, and capacity for work, is the most important basis for cordial co-operation between chief and assistant. And once that true comradeship has been achieved, everybody will anxiously guard against infringing any regulations, for, in that case, he will fear the anger of fellow workers more than the application of disciplinary power.

On the other hand, a chief's conceited and aloof conduct *vis-à-vis* his assistants demonstrates almost invariably that the chief is quite incapable, and his stand-offishness is nothing but a miserable fence which he has built round himself in order to hide his incompetence. Eighty per cent of pre-war class conceit was nothing other than fear, in case the man in the street should notice the puffed-up emptiness of so-called good society.

And yet, in the long run this fence is of no avail. Before long the assistant will have discovered that his chief knows less than he does himself, and at once his devotion to duty will diminish; at first, infringements against disciplinary regulations will occur, and presently conditions will prevail at the office which cannot but be called unpleasant. For that reason, if the head of a department should notice that he is not equal to his job, he should not attempt to stifle the justified criticism of his assistants with the help of disciplinary power, but he should resign instead. Then no one will reproach him, rather will they admire his cour-

age and readily transfer hi[m] more suitable post. In the event, that is to say w through the unpleasant ditions described above, su constant punishments, similar occurrences, a dr change of head of depart will be considered necessa higher quarters, he will, of co be regarded with justified picion.

We National Socialists are to giving our opinions fra and without diplomatic ac ments. This quality, praisewo in itself, must not be allow tempt us into committing following mistake. When c sponding with other, perhaps ordinate, offices, one may to forget that there an National Socialist does his Our sharp tone may induce to reply in like manner, and a brief exchange of letters, th will frequently have come to a pitch that disciplinary p will have to intervene.

Let everyone therefore a this principle: to proceed courteously as possible corresponding with other offices, including subordi ones. It is easily forgotten t harsh word on paper outwe the spoken word three time principle, letters written harsher than usual tone sh be released for despatch only or two days after dictation, even then only after rea them through once more.

It is gravely in conflict maintaining one's own sta[n] as holder of disciplinary pow that holder has two diffe ways of communicating others, being rude when the l is addressed to a subordi office, and wheedling writing to a superior.

Such people are called "[?] licking bullies". Their behav carries its own punishment, s it lends itself like nothing el putting assistants into secre position and to destroying comradeship.

**(3) Application of disciplir power:**

Before meting out punishn every punisher should ask self the following questions:
(i) Have I listened to both par the accuser and the accused
(ii) Am I in a sufficiently frame of mind myself to nounce a just punishment?
(iii) According to the cas question, is a corrective o exemplary punishment called

It is quite impossible to conn anybody without having
ned to his statement relevant
he case. Such proceedings
ld, after a very short time,
w open wide the gates to
rmers and their nefarious
vities. The quality of human
ctivity being defective, it is
sable always to examine carewhether the plaintiff may
have had personal grounds
ch could have slightly shifted
argument to the disadvantage
e accused.

The punisher will be well
sed to take good heed of the
ciple **never to pronounce
ishment immediately**, but
eep on the case before proncing judgement. That will
tribute a great deal towards
ctivity. Punishments pronced in the first flush of
er frequently have to be
nded later on, which does not
 to enhance the standing of
person holding disciplinary
er.

In meting out the sentence,
following should be taken
 of: **"Justice is the hardest
ue!"** (Schopenhauer). Aclingly, great pains should be
n not to assail the accused
ediately – whether found
ty or having admitted his
t – with the most severe
ns, but to try, through inction and pedagogically
ly chosen punishment to rein him from repeating his
nce. In particular, dismissal
 service should be applied
 in most severe cases, for we
 t realise that a person dissed from the Party and its
anisations because of an
nce will scarcely be able to
 a new sphere of activity
where in Germany.

eral remarks
eneral, it will be sufficient to
inister an appropriately
re reprimand to Party memor fellow citizens who have
mitted minor offences.
nce a punishment has been
ded upon, let it be carried out
out the least amendment, for
ill, after all, be pronounced
 after a carefully considered
gement has been arrived at.
action or mitigation of punment makes the punisher
ear inconsistent and, in the
 run, renders illusory the
ventive deterring effect of
al laws. On the other hand,
punisher and those working
 him should realize that

attacks on Movement and State,
which were obviously animated
by a contemptible way of thinking, invariably demand most
severe punishment.

A man authorised to mete out
punishment must be particularly
severe with himself. It is impossible to reprimand or punish
an assistant for an offence of
which, at all times, one is guilty
oneself. The following may serve
as an example: it is not possible
to reprimand one's subordinate
assistant X because he continually plunges his hands into his
trousers pockets when, while
reprimanding him, one puts
one's own hands into one's
pockets in agitation. This is
bound to arouse in X a feeling of
ridiculousness, and thus one will
have achieved the opposite of
what one had intended. To give
another example: an assistant
has been seen drunk in the street.
How is it possible for an office-
bearer to punish that man when
he himself, as is well-known to all
and sundry, indulges in the same
vice?

More than anyone else, therefore, the holder of disciplinary
power will have to justify the
great trust placed in him. Never
ever, in the execution of his
difficult and responsible office,
may he turn his gaze away from
our unique example, our Führer,
Adolf Hitler!

### Notes
Boot-licking bully: a free translation of the German *Radfahr-
ernatur*, the literal meaning of
which is "a person with a cyclist's
mentality". This is a colloquialism much used in German:
it describes – aptly – a person encountered not infrequently,
especially in Germany, who
cringes to those he considers his
superiors, while kicking those
whom he looks down upon, symbolically describing the attitude
and movements of a cyclist.
Fellow citizen: *Mitbürger* would
be the German equivalent of
"fellow citizen". The Nazi concept of *Volksgenosse*, used
throughout the text, has happily
no equivalent in the English
language and is thus untranslatable.

# 7a. Regulations concerning Complaints

Complaints may be lodged
(1) against a disciplinary decision; for instance, a reprimand, a suspension, or a dismissal from the office of Political Leader;
(2) if a Political Leader considers himself to have been injured or damaged in his service competence and authority;
(3) if a Party member believes his honour or his reputation to have been violated by actions on the part of other Party members.

Not included under (1) are judgements by Party Tribunals which have been executed by a Leading Functionary.

The Leading Functionaries of the N.S.D.A.P. or the respective responsible heads of departments are the only persons entitled to accept and deal with complaints concerning internal Party matters and Party leaders. They alone are responsible for integrity and justice in the Movement, and it is their duty conscientiously to examine, or to have examined, every complaint, whether made in writing or orally. Each case must be dealt with as speedily as possible. If the complaint is directed against a chief or a Leading Functionary, it has to be lodged with the next higher-ranking leader. Under no circumstances may the right of complaint be misused by narrow-minded people and by grousers for the purpose of unproductive arguments. Within the National Party Executive the correct procedure for complaints is via the competent departmental or head office director to the immediately superior National Director or the Deputy of the Führer.

Complaints may be made orally or in writing. Collective complaints by several Party members are inadmissible and will be punished. If any one incident should give cause for complaint to several Party members, it is up to each individual involved to make a complaint. All complaints should be made after calm and mature consideration only. If any one should, capriciously or against his better judgement, make a complaint which is based on an untrue assertion, he must expect to be disciplinarily punished himself. Should the investigation prove the complaint to have been justified, the fault which has come to light must be remedied forthwith. The head of a section is responsible for any

formal complaints within sectional purview and, in of complications, responsib rests with the Leading Func ary.

If a Party member believes his complaint has not been sidered at all, or insufficientl he is entitled to take his compl to the immediately superio ficial for settlement. The wa the Führer or to his Depu open to every Party member only if no settlement of his plaint has been forthcoming lower departments of the P that is to say, Local Gro District, or Regional director

It is strictly prohibited to a to State departments, or to vidual persons, in connec with complaints concerning ternal Party affairs or P leaders. In case of contraven expulsion from the Party have to be faced.

## Internal complaints
Insofar as technical disputes within an area, the decision with the immediately sup Leading Functionary. Insofa the Leading Functionary is self implicated in these disp and directions from a de mentally superordinate de ment regarding the matter come to hand, the decision with the next superordi Leading Functionary. For ample:

The Regional Administra of the N.S.V. has issued a partmental directive to the trict Administration of the N The District Leader respons disagreeing with the execu of the directive for his dist appeals to his District Adm trator. The District ministrator reports the ap to his Regional Leader wh departmentally his supero ate, who, in his turn, shoul insist in the execution of directive, will get in touch the District Leader.

If the District Leader sh persist in refusing to allow cution of the directive to proc the Regional Leader will de after hearing the Regional ministrator of the N.S.V. anc District Leader. If the Regi Leader should be satisfied the proposed measures are order, he will inform the Dis Leader that they should be lowed to proceed.

If the Regional Leader sh agree with the District Lea but the directive issued on part of the Regional Adm

*Leader candidate (Führer-*
*...rter) at Training Castle*
*...nsburg) in service dress.*
*...idates were mostly from the*
*...und destined for high posts*
*... Party.*

*... Amtsleiter of the Reich*
*...ime Party (or Central)*
*...tive (Reichsleitung) in*
*...ng out dress.*

...n of the N.S.V. corresponds
...a directive of the National
...nistration of the N.S.V., and
... National Administrator is
...e opinion that the directive
...ave to be carried out with-
...ail, then the National Ad-
...strator will try to reach an
...ment with the Regional
...er. Should agreement once
... not be reached, the Deputy
...er will decide after hearing
...National Administrator of
... N.S.V. and the Regional
...er.

...e right of appeal has become
...id if the dispute concerns a
...ure within an area, which
...not been decreed by the
...rtment of a superordinate
... In this instance, the Leading
...tionary of his own area has
...right of making the final
...ion.

...s

...onal    Director = *Reichs-*

...*J. = Nationalsozialistische*
...*swohlfahrt* (National Social-
...ublic or People's Welfare
...nisation)

## ...arty Meetings
## ...Public Functions

...ing Party Functionaries are
...nsible for fixing all Party
...ings and public functions
...ied by Party offices and af-
...ed organisations. They will
...thorised

...y the Local Group Leader,
... their importance does not
...d the scope of the Local
...p;

...y the District Leader, when
...importance does exceed the
... of the Local Group; and

...y the Regional Leader, when
... possess general political
...ficance for the Region.

...for the rest, the organisa-
...of meetings and functions
...take place according to the
...lations of the department re-
...sible for organisation and
...aganda.

...or to arranging demon-

strations of general political importance for the country, the
point of view of the National
Propaganda Chief must be sought.
Large meetings arranged with
lightning speed may take place
only with the approval of the
National Propaganda Chief.

When fixing a timetable for
their functions, District and Local
Group Leaders must take into
consideration functions planned
for their Region, and, similarly,
Local Group Leaders functions
planned for their District.

By the twentieth of each month,
Political Leaders and Administrators must inform their responsible Leading Functionary of
all functions planned for the
following month; subsequently
he will, by the twenty-fifth of each
month, fix and announce the
overall plan. All Local Group
Leaders must submit their plans
for functions to their District
Leaders in duplicate by the
twenty-seventh of each month,
who, by the last day of each
month, will pass on one copy of
these plans to the Regional Administration.

The current Leading Functionaries are obliged to inform responsible leaders of the S.A., S.S.,
H.J., and N.S.K.K., about dates
of functions, so that, when fixing
their duty rota plans, they may
enable members of the S.A., S.S.,
H.J., and N.S.K.K. to attend at
least important meetings.

Party Tribunals, internal
Leader Conferences, etc., are not
affected by these regulations.

With the help of these plans,
Regional Leaders, Regional Inspecting Officers, Central Office
Leaders, and Section Leaders of
the Regional Administration,
District Leaders, etc., will be
able to pay unannounced visits
every month to remote Local
Groups, in order to obtain a clear
picture concerning the state of
the organisation, the suitability
of Junior Leaders, and feeling
among Party members and fellow
citizens. The surprise appearance
in a remote Local Group of a
high-ranking Leader is possibly
of more important and more
lasting value than an important
speech at an important meeting.
Above all, every Political Leader
and Administrator will be on his
toes to keep his organisation
functioning smoothly at all times,
and not only when important
visitors are announced. Again
and again, procedure of this kind
has increased the trust of the
most humble Party member in
his high-ranking leaders who

# Political Leaders' Service Rank Insignia

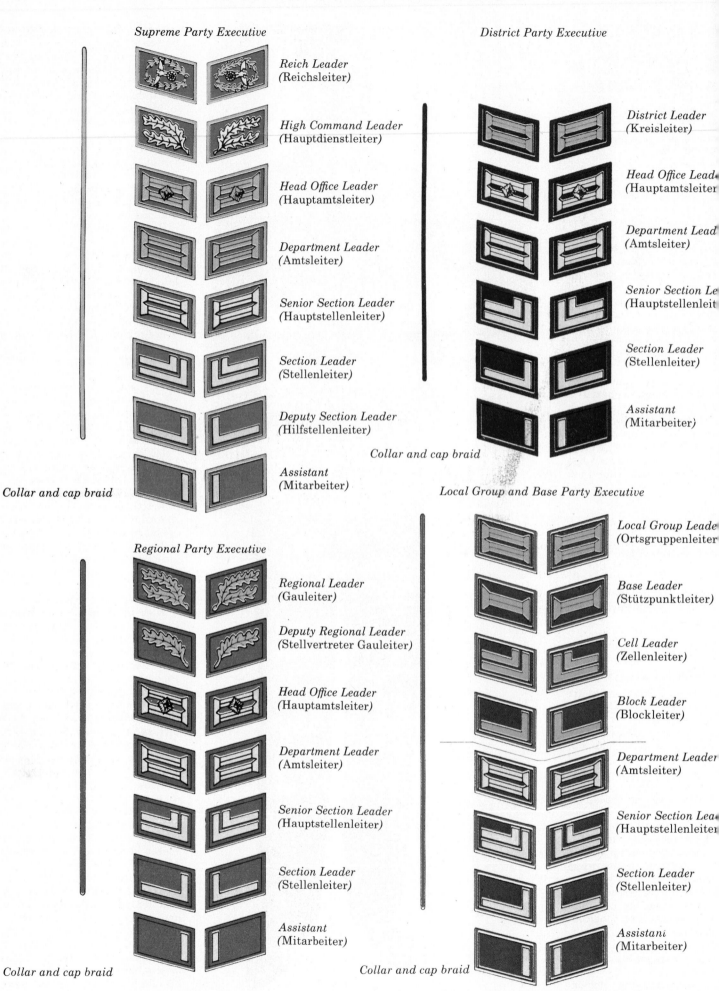

**Supreme Party Executive**

Reich Leader
(Reichsleiter)

High Command Leader
(Hauptdienstleiter)

Head Office Leader
(Hauptamtsleiter)

Department Leader
(Amtsleiter)

Senior Section Leader
(Hauptstellenleiter)

Section Leader
(Stellenleiter)

Deputy Section Leader
(Hilfsstellenleiter)

Assistant
(Mitarbeiter)

Collar and cap braid

**Regional Party Executive**

Regional Leader
(Gauleiter)

Deputy Regional Leader
(Stellvertreter Gauleiter)

Head Office Leader
(Hauptamtsleiter)

Department Leader
(Amtsleiter)

Senior Section Leader
(Hauptstellenleiter)

Section Leader
(Stellenleiter)

Assistant
(Mitarbeiter)

Collar and cap braid

**District Party Executive**

District Leader
(Kreisleiter)

Head Office Leader
(Hauptamtsleiter)

Department Leader
(Amtsleiter)

Senior Section Leader
(Hauptstellenleiter)

Section Leader
(Stellenleiter)

Assistant
(Mitarbeiter)

Collar and cap braid

**Local Group and Base Party Executive**

Local Group Leader
(Ortsgruppenleiter)

Base Leader
(Stützpunktleiter)

Cell Leader
(Zellenleiter)

Block Leader
(Blockleiter)

Department Leader
(Amtsleiter)

Senior Section Leader
(Hauptstellenleiter)

Section Leader
(Stellenleiter)

Assistant
(Mitarbeiter)

Collar and cap braid

*Service rank insignia for Political Leaders on active service:*
▽◁ *Head Office Leader of the Supreme Party Executive.*
▽▽◁ *Deputy Regional Leader.*
▽▷ *Department Leader of the District Party Executive.*
▷ *Senior Section Leader of the Local Group or Base Party Executive.*
*Political Leaders' honour weapons:*
▷▷ *The honour weapon, and* ▷▷▽ *holster for the honour weapon.*

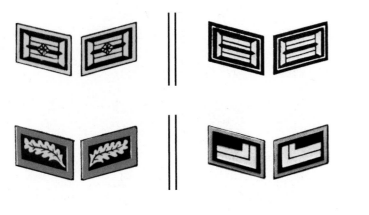

ht perhaps become strangers e should catch only a glimpse hem from afar at Regional ies, or read about them in his spaper.

hould the Leader of a supernate office be present, no ter whether he is there on y or as a guest, the function t be reported to him, in any e. If he wishes to take the r, he will make this known ing the report. The report will ays be addressed to the most h-ranking Political Leader ent. If, in an emergency, the der of a superordinate office rvenes in the management a conference of Political ders, or of a meeting of nbers of the Party or of one of affiliated organisations, he st do so by declaring: "I am taking charge of the management of this function."

hould two units of equal rank anise a meeting or conference, preparation and management be in the hands of the most or Political Leader. The cerate of appointment will decide ority. If both bear the same , seniority will have to be rmined by age.

ith reference to public demontions, meetings, parades, monies, etc., public liability rance in case of accidents have to be taken out. In this nection, the regulations of the National Treasurer of the N.S.D.A.P. will have to be taken into consideration well before the event.

**Notes**
Local Group Leader = *Ortsgruppenleiter*
District Leader = *Kreisleiter*
Regional Leader = *Gauleiter*

# 8. Prospective Leaders and their Selection

During our Time of Struggle there existed in the N.S.D.A.P. no problem of prospective leaders as it does today. The Struggle was the most effective means of selection. Whoever did not possess unshakeable faith in the truth of our Führer's idea, as well as the fanatic will to be victorious, in addition to the general qualities of leadership demanded, was unable to stand his ground as leader in the Struggle and in that way was automatically eliminated. Besides, the Party had no well-paid posts to bestow, and its adherents in their bourgeois posts were frequently subject to persecution. Thus it was that only those Party members assumed positions of leadership who were imbued with the spirit of sacrifice and ready to toil at the work of the Führer, utterly dedicating their entire strength to their task.

With the Assumption of Power by the Party, the selection of leaders through trial in battle ceased, naturally. And yet, it is essential that the leadership of the Party should continuously keep up its former fighting strength and buoyancy, for what is at stake is the task of safeguarding and of firmly consolidating what has been won by hard struggle. There has therefore arisen the question of prospective leaders which, especially as far as the higher-ranking, specifically political Party leadership is concerned, is to be solved as follows.

(1) Leading Functionaries, and in particular Regional Leaders, have been instructed to devote the utmost attention possible to prospective leaders.

(2) Special castles, called *"Ordensburgen"*, have been created. In these castles, valuable Party members from all regions undergo three years' training as prospective leaders. Party members must be aged 25 to 30 and represent an élite, racially, physically, and mentally. In this connection, their previous occupation is immaterial. They are chosen by the National Chief of Organisation at the suggestion of their Regional Leader in conjunction with the Head Office for Public Health. Among the sub-jects taught are History, Social Politics, Philosophy of Life, every kind of sport, as well as Deportment, etc. If necessary, training will be continued until trainee leaders can be released into the Regions as fully-trained Political Leaders.

(3) In the Regions, it is desirable that at first these Party members should be employed as Local Group Leaders, and that subsequently they should, as and when possible and necessary, work their way through all ranks of Political Leadership. These Party members will undergo continuous assessment of their abilities as Political Leaders.

(4) It is intended that Political Leaders thus trained should form a replacement nucleus for the higher-ranking and more directly politically active Party leadership.

However, attention will have to be devoted not only to future training for prospective leaders, but just as much attention will have to be given to effective utilisation of Political Leaders already serving. In that connection the following regulations exist:

(1) Higher Party leadership should be supplemented solely with Party members who have already proved their mettle in Local Groups, Districts, and Regions.

(2) Accordingly, only those Party members may be proposed by the Führer for posts as Deputy Regional Leaders who previously have held office as Local Group Leaders or District Leaders, or Local Group Administrators or District Administrators; it is most desirable that, in addition, they should also have held office as particularly politically active Regional Administrators.

(3) The following are deemed to be particularly politically active Regional Administrators: The Regional Secretary, if he deals with the entire business of the Regional Executive on behalf of the Regional Leader; the Regional Director of Organisation; the Regional Director of Personnel; the Regional Director of Training; the Regional Director of Propaganda; and the Regional Inspecting officers.

(4) Those Regional Directors mentioned under (3), from whose ranks, as from the ranks of District Leaders, are to emerge Deputy Regional Leaders, may only be proposed for approval of nomination for office, if they have been previously active as Political Leaders at Bases, Local Groups, or District Executives. Until further notice, only those ·Party members may be employed in offices listed under (1) who joined the Party not later than the Assumption of Power and who previously had been working actively either politically or in one of the organisations of the Party.

(5) Where from the point of view of personnel policy it can be justified, honorary District Leaders may be made full-time District Leaders, or replaced by full-time District Leaders.

(6) In order to bring continuity to the work of District Executives which, according to trends of development, must be regarded as very important areas, and also in order systematically to create prospective personnel for the offices of District Leader and for work in Regional Directorates and, beyond Regional Executives, in the National Executive, at least one full-time District Administrator will have to be appointed in District Executives. These District Administrators who may, in addition, hold one of the offices of the District Executive mentioned under (3), will have to be carefully selected by District Leaders: (a) they should have worked actively in a Local Group; (b) they should have be-belonged to the S.A., S.S.,

N.S.K.K., or H.J.; and (c) they should have shown potential for growth. In making this selection, care must be taken to avoid favouring the old. That is to say that, as far as possible, Party members who are young in years should be selected for the post of full-time District Administrator. However, it is a condition that they should have joined either the Party or the H.J. prior to the Assumption of Power.

Where financially possible, as for instance in larger Districts or Urban Districts, several full-time District Administrators should be employed.

(7) It is the duty of Regional Leaders to see to it that District Leaders, and in. particular full-time District Administrators, are enabled to gain as much experience as possible by transfers within their Regional area and also by temporary secondment to Regional Executive. However, continuity of work of District Executives must not be allowed to suffer on account of these arrangements.

(8) Just as it is possible for a District Leader to become Deputy Regional Leader without first having been Regional Administrator, it is also possible that a Local Group Leader may become District Leader without first having been District Administrator. Local Group Leaders should be re-assessed regularly to ascertain to what extent they may be considered as replacements for retiring District Leaders.

(9) Broadly speaking, Regional Leaders and District Leaders must devote their utmost attention to the question of replacement of personnel right down to Bases and Local Groups.

(10) In the interest of systematic training of prospective leaders who are closely tied to their people (*volksverbunden*), careful attention to the above regulations is absolutely essential. Regions have the opportunity of selecting from among their tens of thousands of Party members those prospective leaders who, passing from Block and Local Group to Regional Executive, may be able, during temporary or permanent activity in the National Executive, to make good use of their experience gathered in every office in closest contact with our most humble fellow citizens, for the benefit of Movement and people.

At the same time, the selection of the very best human material

respect to character, ...evement, and experience is ...in the interest of work in the ...ons.

...rsonal connections, relation-...s, origin, and standing must ...r be allowed to play a part in ...election nor in the training ...rospective leaders in the ...y.

*Political Leaders:*
◀ *Section Leader of a Local*
*Group or Base in service dress*
*with pack.*
▷ *Senior Section Leader of a*
*District Party Executive in*
*service dress with greatcoat*
*and pack.*
▷ *Items of Political Leaders'*
*service equipment.*

The National Director of ...anisation, on behalf of the ...ty Führer, will supervise the ...ution of the above regu-...ns.

## H.J. as source of ...pective leaders

...der to safeguard from among ...H.J. valuable, trained pros-...ive leaders for the Party, ...able members of the Hitler ...th may be assigned to Leading ...ctionaries from Local Group ...der upwards for the purpose ...aining.

...uring their period of second-...t to Party service, members ...e Hitler Youth are excused ... service in the H.J. The ...ction of youths will be under-...n jointly by the Leading ...ctionary and the H.J. Leader ...harge. Care will have to be ...n to select youths from all ...ors of the community.

...ter 12 to 18 months' training, ...ng which time members of the ...er Youth must be made con-...ant with all official duties, ... will be detailed for attending ...gional School for Leaders. On ...pletion of his training, a ...iled certificate of aptitude ...be made out for each member ...e Hitler Youth, to be kept at ...respective personnel office. ...sequently, members of the ...er Youth thus trained will be ...gned as Block Leaders to ...al Groups; it is desirable that ...r they should be promoted ...rding to aptitude and oppor-...ty.

... general, in addition to the ...lations on selection recorded ...ve, a process of selection will ...stablished automatically be-...se of the fact that from his ...iest days, every German ...w citizen will be included in

the Party, the Party guiding and educating him.

The first occasion on which they are thus gathered together is in the *Jungvolk*, whence the young people are transferred to the Hitler Youth. A member of the Hitler Youth will then enter the S.A., the S.S., or the N.S.K.K., or he will co-operate in the work

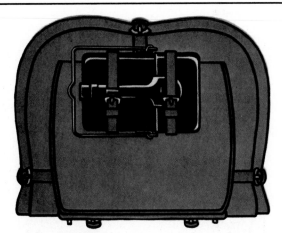

*Pack with blanket, groundsheet, and mess tin*

*Whistle lanyard for Training Leader (Ausbildungsleiter)*

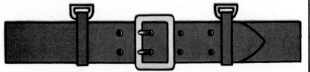

*Belt with double pin buckle and two D rings.*
*60-mm wide*

*Bread bag and water bottle*          *Message pouch*

of affiliated organisations of the Party. After completion of his Labour Service and military service, the soldier will return for duty in the Party or its affiliated organisations.

The following will be the criteria for the Party, including all its organisations, for selecting the corps of leaders:

Character
Frankness
Honesty

Tidiness
Perceptiveness
Qualities of Leadership
Community Spirit
Reliability
Sense of Justice
Independence of Thought
   and Deed and of
     General Knowledge
Courage and Determination

**Notes**
The Time of Struggle = *die Kampfzeit*, a Nazi concept referring to the time before
The Assumption of Power = *die Machtübernahme* on January 31, 1933
*Ordensburgen:* These castles were created in imitation of the castles of the Teutonic Knights who in the 14th and 15th Centuries colonised and conquered Prussia.
Regional Administrator = *Gauamtsleiter*
Regional Secretary = *Gaugeschäftsführer*
Regional Director of Organisation = *Gauorganisationsleiter*
Regional Director of Personnel = *Gaupersonalamtsleiter*
Regional Director of Training = *Gauschulungsleiter*
Regional Director of Propaganda = *Gaupropagandaleiter*
Regional Inspecting Officer = *Gauinspekteur*
*Deutsches Jungvolk* = German Youth, a section of the Hitler Youth for boys between 10 and 14 years of age

# 9. N.S.D.A.P. Organisation

"The Party has been created by the Führer from the realisation that if our people are to live and walk towards a new Golden Age, they will have to be led according to an ideology which is true to our German nature. This ideology requires men who rise above the average, that is to say, men who, through self-discipline and self-control, through achievement and greater insight, surpass all others. Consequently, the Party will always have to represent a minority, the Order of National Socialist ideology, comprising the leadership of our people.

"For that reason, the Party consists solely of fighters, ready to undertake anything and to risk their all for the realisation of National Socialist ideology. Men and women to whom service to the people is their first and most sacred duty."

The N.S.D.A.P., being the German people's Order of Leadership, entirely dominates public life everywhere, whether–seen from the point of view of organisation–they are affiliated organisations, or organisations of the State administration, etc. In the long run, it will be impossible for leaders to remain in responsible posts anywhere, unless they are recognised by the Party. Moreover, in future suitable conditions for the systematic selection of leaders will be created by the Party.

When forming new National Socialist organisations, the following principles should be borne in mind:
(a) the Führer principle
(b) subordination to and integration with the overall organisation
(c) regional unity, and
(d) giving expression to practical community spirit.

**The Führer principle**
The Führer principle presupposes a pyramid- shaped organisational structure, in detail and as a whole.

At its top stands the Führer.

He appoints the leaders required for the individual spheres of action of the National Directorates of Party and State.

Thus the terms of reference for the purpose of the Party have been clearly outlined.

It is an Order of Leadership. Moreover, it is responsible for the spiritual, ideological, and National Socialist alignment of the German people.

The right to organise men for their own sake stems solely from such reasons.

Hence follows, in addition to the inclusion of men and women in the organisations of the Party, namely the S.A., the S.S., the N.S.K.K., the H.J., the N.S. League of Women, the N.S.D. Students' Association, the N.S.D. University Lecturers' Association, the justification for subordinating to the Party organisations concerned with public welfare.

The National Socialist structure of leadership is already clearly shown here.

Every single organisation is in the care of an office of the N.S.D.A.P.

In every instance, the leadership of each single organisation is supplied by the Party.

The National Director of Organisation of the N.S.D.A.P. is simultaneously leader of the D.A.F. The N.S.B.O. gives organisational support to the D.A.F.

The Director of the Head Office for Public Welfare is also Director

◄◄ *Bandmaster of a "Bandsmen's Squad" of a Regional Party Executive in service dress.*
◄ *Bandsman of a "Bandsmen's Squad" of a Regional Party Executive in service dress.*

of the N.S. People's Welfare.

The same relationship exists between
(i) the National Department of Justice (*Reichsrechtsamt*) and the N.S. Lawyers' Association (*Nationalsozialistischer Rechtswahrer-Bund*)
(ii) the Central Office for Public Health (*Hauptamt für Volksgesundheit*) and the N.S. Medical Association (*Nationalsozialistischer Aerztebund*)
(iii) the Central Office for Education (*Hauptamt für Erzieher*) and the N.S. Teachers' Association (*Nationalsozialistischer Lehrerbund*)
(iv) the Central Office for Civil Service (*Hauptamt für Beamte*) and the National Association of Civil Servants (*Reichsbund der deutschen Beamten*)
(v) the Central Office for War Victims (*Hauptamt für Kriegsopfer*) and the N.S. War Victims Welfare (*Nationalsozialistische Kriegsopferversorgung*)
(vi) the Department of Technical Science (*Amt für Technik*) and the N.S. German Technical Association (*Nationalsozialistischer Bund deutscher Technik*)
(vii) the Eugenics Office (*das Rassenpolitische Amt*) looks after the National Association of families with three or more children (*Reichsbund der Kinderreichen*)
(viii) the N.S. Women's League and the German Women's Service

Moreover, the Central Office of the N.S.D.A.P. for Agrarian Policy (*Reichsamt für Agrarpolitik der N.S.D.A.P.*) is closely connected with the National Agricultural Board (*Reichsnährstand*), a Government Department. Here, too, indirect supervision and unity of leadership are ensured.

The understructure of all affiliated organisations, as well as all Party offices, is based not only on the National leadership, but also on lower organisational levels, namely on the Regions, and then on the Districts, and furthermore, if expedient, on Local Groups or Bases. In addition, with the N.S. League of Women, the D.A.F. and the N.S.V., this also applies to Cells or Blocks. In Local administrative areas, in District sectors or District squads, which geographically correspond to Local Groups or Bases of the Party, members of affiliated organisations will automatically be included.

## The Führer principle. Subordination to and integration with the overall organisational structure

However, the leadership structure would be split up if all organisations or affiliated bodies, from the smallest unit to National leadership, as far as their respective structure was concerned, were to be completely independent, and subordinate only directly to the Führer at the top.

If one takes into account the four chief areas, (Reich, Region, etc.) the situation might be compared to a four-storied house, all of whose posts and walls go right up to the roof, without shoring and connections on each floor.

Furthermore, it would be incompatible with the National Socialist Führer idea, which presupposes a complete sense of responsibility, to assume that, over and above his technical and practical responsibility, the leader of an organisation or of an affiliated body would be in a position to guarantee, from the point of view of National Leadership, the political and ideological attitude of all junior leaders down to the smallest unit.

Besides, the completely detached status of each organisation would involve each single organisation having to establish its own offices for organisation, personnel, and training. This in turn would, with the best of good will on the part of all National Leaders, Central Office chiefs and administrative leaders, in charge of the National Leadership of the Party, lead to a situation where, in the course of time, in every case, differences would arise, which, at a later date, would bring about a state of completely different systems in regional, vertical, personal, etc. respects, within the National Socialist régime.

For that reason, organisations such as the N.S. German Students' Association, the N.S. Women's League, the N.S. German University Lecturers' Association, affiliated bodies and their leaders, while, starting from the bottom, they are subordinate to the next superordinate office within their organisation, are, in the sovereign areas of the Party, disciplinarily subordinate to the responsible Leading Functionary of the N.S.D.A.P., that is to say in respect of organisation, ideology, politics, supervision, and personnel.

In this way, all organisations will be securely moored to the structure of the Party, and in all areas a firm connection with the Leading Functionaries of the N.S.D.A.P., commensurate with the National Socialist Führer principle, will have been created. The National Socialist structure of organisation will always stay alive and flexible. As it becomes expedient to do so, we shall extend the organisation, but, at the same time, we shall summon up courage, should the situation result in displacements, to reduce individual fields of duties, if necessary, or alternatively, to undertake the disbandment of individual sections of the organisation. The foundation, however, will remain untouched forever.

### The practical expression of community spirit

If we National Socialists would wish to spread the National Socialist idea of solidarity among the people to replace liberalistic mentality, we shall have to build upon the community of the family, and in that way we shall achieve **the fellowship of the people.** Fellowship of the people, however, cannot be represented by any one class or section.

A spirit of fellowship is not proved merely by the fact that one feels "compassion" for other sufferers, and is prepared to dispense "charity".

Furthermore, we shall have to recall the pronouncement of the National Director of Organisation of the N.S.D.A.P., in which he said that we should "follow the proclamation of the idea of fellowship of the people by practising that fellowship".

Hence follows the task of bodies affiliated to the N.S.D.A.P. Starting from the clear realisation that it is fundamentally wrong to organise people for technical reasons, and turning away from Ottmar Spann's idea of different "orders", the Party has set about the problem of the idea of fellowship in the field of organising men, and it has solved that problem by creating the National Socialist fellowship organisation, called "The German Labour Front" (D.A.F.).

In the German Labour Front, the fellowship spirit is practised at the place of employment. In their professions and on the shop

floor, factory workers, employers, civil servants, and office workers form one single community of staff and management. The establishment is an integrated whole.

As in the field of family life, the idea of community spirit has been made secure in office and factory.

In addition, there is a revolutionary new creation, namely the care of men and women by the department of the D.A.F., entitled "The N.S. Association 'Strength through Joy'".

Here, once again, the community spirit is being practised.

### Notes

N.S. League of Women = *N.S. Frauenschaft*
N.S.D. Students' Association = *Nationalsozialistischer Deutscher Studentenbund*
N.S.D. University Lecturers' Association = *Nationalsozialistischer Deutscher Dozentenbund*
National Director of Organisation = *Reichsorganisationsleiter*
German Labour Front = D.A.F.: *Deutsche Arbeitsfront*
the Administrative sub-division of the German Labour Front
Head Office for Public Welfare = *Hauptamt für Volkswohlfahrt* =
N.S.B.O.: *Nationalsozialistische Betriebszellenorganisation*

orders: the word is to be understood here in the sense in which it was used in Victorian times, i.e. "the lower orders".
Strength through Joy: Although this has become the accepted translation for *Kraft durch Freude*, perhaps on the analogy of Schiller's *An die Freude*, which is "Ode to Joy" in English, it would be more accurately translated as "Strength through Pleasure" or "Enjoyment" or even "Happiness". The aim of this organisation was to take charge of everybody's leisure time, by providing organised amusements, entertainments, and holidays for the workers, under the supervision of the Party.

## 10a. The Block: smallest subdivision of the N.S.D.A.P.

**Organisation:** The household: The household is at the bottom of the chain of communities; it forms the basis of the systems of Blocks and Cells. A household is the organisational joining together of all fellow citizens living in the same dwelling, including lodgers, domestic help, etc.

*Nazi Party badges. From top to bottom these are:*
*National insignia (Hoheitszeichen) of the old pattern;*
*Party badge (Partei-Abzeichen);*
*National insignia of the new pattern;*
*S.A. badge as worn on civilian clothes;*
*S.S. badge as worn on civilian clothes; and*
*N.S.K.K. badge as worn on civilian clothes.*

*Example*: Residing on the floor, at 20, Senefelderstr the Müller family, consisti four members, in addition t lodger and one domestic the latter, although living i same house, occupying her room not on the same fl form
**one Residential Commu one Household.**
Whether or not the lodger his own board is, in this con completely immaterial.

### A N.S.D.A.P. Block consis of 40 to 60 Households
Whether the number of h holds included in a Bloc nearer the upper or lower depends on the density of lation or on local condition the area.

The combination of house to form a Block will be ca out down one side of the st in the case of houses for polygons (geographical trian squares, rectangles, etc.), it be carried out according to course of the street, skirting t polygons.

The size of the scheduled must be such that it gives t responsible Political Leader to Administrators and War an opportunity of thorough comprehensive canvassing.

### Personnel
(a) A Block Leader is the junior Leading Functionar the N.S.D.A.P.
(b) Selection: A Block Le must be a Party member. should be chosen from ar the best Party members wi his Local Group. His service is:

### Block Leader of the N.S.D.A.P.
(c) Subordination: In his L Group, a Block Leader is d plinarily subordinated to the Leader. In a Base, the B Leader, in case there are no C is subordinate directly to Base Leader.
(d) Nomination: A Block Le is nominated by the Local Gr Leader or the Base Leader.
(e) Appointment: After a pe of probation and productio the prescribed personal d ments (proof of Aryan ance up to and including gr parents), and three to four mo after his provisional app ment, he will be officially pointed Block Leader by competent District Leader.
(f) Rank: The Block Leader h

3294

ervice rank of Block Leader
...e N.S.D.A.P.; service uni-
...of a Political Leader; Local
...p tabs with gold corners;
...buttons, twin-tongued
...le, and cap cord.

**...s and Responsibilities**
...ck Leader is responsible for
...ccurrences in his area re-
...g to the Movement; he is
...answerable to the Cell
...er, or, if in a Base, possibly
...tly to the Base Leader. The
...arge of the following duties
...cumbent upon him. At least
...a month, the Block Leader
...call a meeting of his disci-
...rily subordinate fellow
...ers, or, as the case may be,
...k Administrators, during the
...se of which reports are given
...ctivities and on situations
...untered. On this occasion,
...eans of discussion and agree-
..., directives for future work
...ld be laid down.
...e Block Leader decides upon
...asks planned for the future.
...ecial cases, special meetings,
...and above regular dis-
...ions, may be held. In this
...ection, it is immaterial
...her the meetings take place
...restaurant or at a private
...lence. (It is most advisable
...e different private residences
...rn).
...Block Leader acts as leader
...nd adviser to, all Block Ad-
...strators, etc., and Party
...bers working in his Block

...e has to act in an enlighten-
...mediating, and helpful cap-
...y, in accordance with the
...ciples of the Movement. He
...o see that people who spread
...ours are traced, and to re-
...them to the Local Group or
...Base, as applicable, so that
...uthorities may be informed.
...ot only must a Block Leader
...preacher and champion of
...ional Socialist ideology with
...ect to those Party members
...fellow citizens entrusted to
...political care, but he must
...work to achieve the practical
...peration of Party members
...nging to his Block area, and,
...he case of their exceptional
...tude and achievement, to in-
...uce them to the Leading
...ctionary.
...gain and again, the Block
...der should draw the attention
...arty members to their special
...es towards State and People.
...arty member should not only
...contributor of membership
..., but an active comrade-in-
...s and a propagandist for the

*Nazi Party badges. From top
to bottom these are:
Honour badge (*Ehrenzeichen)
*of the* Hitlerjugend *or Hitler
Youth;
Hitlerjugend *badge;*
Deutches Jungvolk *badge;
and German Students' League
(*Deutsches Studentenbund)
*badge.*

Movement (decoration of houses
with flags, attending of Party
meetings, co-operation, willingness to make sacrifices, etc.).
Every Party member is obliged to
co-operate and may be called on
to give his support at any time.

The collection of membership
fees on behalf of the N.S.D.A.P.
will be undertaken by the Block
Leader.

Although the payment of
membership dues represents a
debt to be discharged at the
domicile of the creditor, prompt
collection of dues from every
Party member affords the best
possible opportunity for the Block
Leader to make and keep up the
required personal contact with a
fellow Party member. In handling
the collection of membership dues
it is the Block Leader's duty
strictly to adhere to the instructions issued.

The card index recording membership dues, which the Block
Leader is obliged to maintain and
keep up to date, has to be left
under lock and key and access to
it may be afforded to no one except
competent Political Leaders. In
addition, the Block Leader will
keep a record concerning each
household.

As with all Political Leaders,
Administrators, and Wardens,
incessant training, education,
and instruction, manly discipline
and exemplary bearing, not only
on duty, but also in his private
life, are, particularly for the Block
Leader, the presupposition for
the accomplishment of his tasks
and his weighty responsibility.
On request, he must lend a hand
in training, education, and functions duties, just as he will see to
the participation of subordinate
Political Leaders, Administrators, and Wardens, should he
be ordered to do so.

When wearing service uniform,
the Block Leader should apply
himself at all times to displaying
exceptionally correct bearing,
cleanliness, and strict adherence
to regulations concerning uniforms. It is the aim of the Block
Leader to succeed in persuading
the sons and daughters of the
families in his Block area to join
the relevant units of the H.J., the
S.A., the S.S., and the N.S.K.K.,
as well as relevant affiliated
bodies, such as the D.A.F.; and
to see that National Socialist
functions, demonstrations, and
ceremonies are attended.

In brief, the Block Leader is an
incessantly toiling activist and
propagandist of the Movement.
He has to observe and pay daily

attention to bars imposed on
members, and to relevant regulations of the Party, its offices,
formations, and associations. A
Block Leader has to guide and
supervise the activities of the
Block Administrators and existing helpers. In principle, a Block
Leader must attend to his official
duties verbally or, as the case
may be, accept and pass on mes-
sages verbally. Communications
in writing will take place only in
the case of absolute expediency
or necessity.

Upon Party members being
newly admitted, their application
form passes through the Block
Leader's hands.

**Notes**
Administrators and Wardens =
*Walter und Warte.* Note the
alliteration, giving the phrase
that authentic Germanic flavour.
A debt to be discharged at the
domicile of the creditor: the
German word used in *Bring-
schuld.* This is a strictly legal
term, the English equivalent for
which has been used in translation, in order to emphasise the
ludicrous way in which this
weighty expression has been misused to describe the process of
paying one's membership dues.

**The House Notice Board
of the N.S.D.A.P.:**
In every apartment house (corresponding to a house group) a
House Notice Board will be fixed
in a clearly visible place (at
ground floor level), according to
the regulations listed. In settle-
ments and villages with normally
not more than one to three
families per house, it is advisable
to put up House Boards at Parish
Information Boards, Party press
showcases, etc., or at any other,
clearly visible, places.

The Block Leader is responsible
for keeping the House Notice
Board in good order; this includes
putting up or removing announcements and notices, as well as
keeping in order directions and
personal denominations affixed.

**Behaviour towards Fellow
Citizens:**
Work in Blocks of the N.S.D.A.P.
presupposes an exceptional
measure of tact, knowledge of
human nature, care, and empathy
towards one's fellow citizens. Any
insolently peremptory behaviour
and, similarly, any ingratiating
behaviour, can do nothing but
harm, whereas matter-of-fact behaviour, making plain one's concern for the fellow citizen under

one's care, is, for the most part, the sole means suitable to create, strengthen, and consolidate a relationship of trust with the fellow citizen.

In this connection, it is a matter of course that pride, a stainless way of life, propriety and correctness are prerequisites to the position of trust as Block Leader and Block Administrator, conferred upon a man on the part of the Party.

(*a*) A Block Leader spreads National Socialist propaganda. Gradually, he will awaken the understanding of those forever dissatisfied people for measures and laws of the National Socialist Government which have often been merely misinterpreted and misunderstood. He should invite fellow citizens to put questions to him; point out to them that they are welcome to unburden themselves to him freely; but, for the rest, should the occasion arise, urge them to be discreet concerning idle chatter with regard to other fellow citizens. Should complaints and belly-aching make themselves heard, it is by no means his job to agree in order to demonstrate his solidarity, but he must, in every case, endeavour to think positively and as one affirming life, and accordingly, by his confident attitude, exert an influence on the men and women in his care.

(*b*) Insofar as enquiries cannot be dealt with by the Block Leader, information should be given as to the place at which the problems in question could be attended to. (Office of the N.S.D.A.P.) Questions will only be answered when the correct answer is known, otherwise the answer will be put off until the proposed visit to the N.S.D.A.P. office. It is not to anyone's discredit if he admits openly that, at that moment, he is unable to answer a question clearly. On the other hand, it *is* to one's discredit if the questioner notices that one's answers are superficial and hasty.

(*c*) Any information given is not legally binding.

(*d*) The utmost discretion in all things is a precondition for winning the confidence of all fellow citizens. Anything which comes to the knowledge of a Political Leader in the execution of his Party duty, comes under the heading of "Official Secret" which he has to guard absolutely against everyone.

The following example is quoted to illustrate a Block Leader's field of duty, its peculiar aptness accounting for the great detail and comprehensiveness of narration.

The family N.N., living in rather wretched circumstances, and consisting of the father, an unskilled labourer, the mother, an adult son, and three daughters, aged 14, 8, and 2, suddenly loses its breadwinner through death.

The competent Block Leader (or, where suitable, the Block Administrator or Block Helper, if any) betakes himself to the widow in order to offer her his help and advice:

He informs the D.A.F. Block Administrator so that the previous contractual working conditions of the head of the family may be ascertained in order to apply to the previous employer of the head of the family for possible special assistance, or to persuade him to grant such assistance.

On that occasion he may ask for and be given information about the adult son's earning potential, since he will be temporarily the breadwinner of the family, in order to consider possibilities of how his earning opportunities may be improved.

He will help the widow in obtaining whatever legal aid is necessary in connection with insurance claims.

He will ascertain which social security or accident assurance institutions are obliged to make disbursements in this case, in order to assist the widow.

He will enquire after the state of health of the children who are minors, so that, if necessary, he may arrange for the help of the N.S.V. (and the Office for Public Health) via the responsible Block Administrator of the N.S.V.

Moreover, he will ascertain what arrangements may be made for the two school-age daughters, by making them join the B.D.M. or J.M., to work in the spirit of the Führer's youth education; and, in order to alleviate the widow's domestic cares, he will concern himself with obtaining sponsorships for membership fees and free supplies of service uniforms and equipment for both girls.

He will arrange for the widow to be looked after in purely womanly matters by the N.S. Women's League, which for example, will see to it that the 14-year-old girl, who will be leaving school shortly, will either remain at home to help her mother in the house, or, according to what is more advisable, be

*Political Leaders' vehicle standards and pennants:*
Top line: *Reich Leader's standard (*left*) and the pennant for a Senior Service Leader (*Hauptdienstleiter*), Senior Department Leader (*Hauptamtsleiter*), and Department Leader (*Amtsleiter*) i the* Reichsleitung.
Second line: *Regional Leader's standard and the pennant for a Deputy Regional Leader (*Stellvertreter Gauleiter*) and Department Leader in a* Gauleitung.
Third line: *District Leader's standard and the pennant for a Department Leader in a* Kreisleitung.
Fourth line: *Ordinary Party standard and pennant.*

ed to serve her compulsory
of domestic or agricultural
so that immediately after-
and up to her marriage,
ay be directed to a suitable
tunity of earning money.

will endeavour to remedy
isfactory living accommo-
n.

will arrange for the son to
e a member of the D.A.F.

will put the son, who is
orked but otherwise
hy, in touch with the K.d.F.
Warden, so that the possi-
of a cheap holiday may be
ssed.

efly, he will make himself
dential adviser and helper of
amily in the tragic loss of
father, with all their daily
les and care, and in this way
ll become the intermediary
een the people and the Move-

e deserving and modest poor
d be reported to the N.S.V.
nistrator for special care.
a piece of good advice may
to convince a fellow citizen
honest endeavour to create
te of Social Justice. The trust
to him, he will have to
y by obtaining help and
e, either in person or in
ation with the office of Party
ate responsible.

ofar as the sale of pam-
s, badges, admission tickets,
has been stipulated, the
Administrator, Block
er, etc., may under no cir-
tances whatever become im-
nate towards fellow citizens
Party members.

principle, Political Leaders
w the rank of Cell Leader are
ed to communicate not in
ng, but verbally only.

es
M. or *Bund Deutscher Mädel*
erman Girls' Association.

or *Jungmädel* = literally
ng Girls", corresponding –
e only – to Brownies.

cadre member, or an official,
e National Socialist
ents' League or N.S.
tscher Studentenbund.

## Block Helpers
The following is recommended to all Regions to be carried through voluntarily: Over and above the arrangement outlined above for linking 40 to 60 households in one Block, it is recommended that, within any one Block, House Attendants or Block Helpers should be appointed to help out.

## Tasks and Responsibilities of Block Helpers
(a) From time to time, Block Leaders may call in Block Helpers, if they have been found suitable, to assist them in their work.
(b) On behalf of the Block Leader, Block Helpers will take charge of the House Notice Board, being responsible for the display of announcements, etc.
(c) If instructed to do so, Block Helpers will take part in discussions arranged by the Block Leader.
(d) Block Helpers will attend functions arranged by the Party, especially training evenings and any training courses provided, as well as duty parades.
(e) Insofar as the local leader of the National Air Defence League was consulted at the time of the appointment of Block Helpers, and if, in consequence, they should, at the same time, be House Wardens of the National Air Defence League, any tasks laid down on the part of the National Air Defence League will be incumbent upon the Block Helpers.

In their service area, Block Helpers are regarded as trusted representatives of the N.S.D.A.P. and its organisations. Block Helpers should endeavour to fortify themselves ideologically; towards fellow citizens they should, at all times, do their best to behave consistently with the dignity of the Party. Confidentiality concerning official matters has to be strictly observed.

## Block Administrators
Insofar as sections or affiliated bodies of the Party have developed their organisation to include the formation of Blocks, a Block Administrator is to be appointed.

## Selection
The Block Administration will be run by the most suitable Party member from among the inhabitants of that particular Block Administration. If, within a Block

Administration, no Party member can be nominated for this task, the fellow citizen deemed most suitable will have to be appointed. It is, of course, essential that he should be politically reliable and of Aryan blood. The Block Administrator of the D.A.F. must be a member of the D.A.F. His service title is *Blockwalter*.

### Tasks and Responsibilities

(*a*) A Block Administrator will take part in the regular or extraordinary discussions, ordered by the Block or Cell Leader, or the Local Group or Base Leader.

(*b*) Insofar as special operations render this necessary, the Block Administrator has the right to apply to the Block Leader for an extraordinary meeting of all Block workers. Insofar as the Block Leader has named place and time, the Block Administrator making the application is obliged to inform all other Block Administrators, etc. accordingly, on behalf of the Block Leader.

(*c*) The Block Administrator will visit regular training evenings or training courses, as provided, as well as duty parades.

(*d*) He is responsible for work assigned to him by the Cell Administrator in authority.

(*e*) The Block Administrator will have to keep his Block Leaders as well as his Cell Administrator informed about his activities.

(*f*) In general, Block Administrators are not allowed to correspond with Block Leaders and Cell Administrators.

## 10b. The Cell

### Organisation

A Cell is composed of four to eight Blocks. A Cell Leader is the next highest Leading Functionary of the N.S.D.A.P.

### Tasks and Responsibilities

The tasks of a Cell Leader correspond by analogy to the tasks of the Block Leader. As the Block Leader is authorised and responsible for all events in his area affecting the Party, the Cell Leader is authorised and responsible in greater measure for the area of all Blocks under his authority.

In particular, he will have to render to his Local Group Leader valuable and active support in respect of training and political work. It will be necessary therefore that he keeps his Local Group Leader informed about all events of importance to the Party. A Cell

Leader will supervise the w
Block Leaders and Cell Ad
trators, if necessary interv
in order to help; he wi
responsible for seeing that
Leaders are not appoint
name only, but that they i
strive to accomplish their t

With permission of the
Group Leader, an experi
Cell Leader may or should
Cell Evenings for all fellow
zens in his service area. It i
intended that on these
Evenings spirited lectures s
be given, but that, for insta
chapter from Adolf Hitler's
*Kampf* should be read. S
quently, by means of ques
and answers, a so-called
cussion Evening will be orga
on the lines of Block Leade
Cell Leader discussions.
Cell Evenings may be enhanc
a dignified manner by commu
singing and musical renderi

The arrangements for si
evenings may be entruste
Local Group Leaders or
Leaders to particularly ex
enced Block Leaders for the
fit of fellow citizens in their
Permission for this purpose
only be given, however, if
is incontestable evidence
the Block Leader will prove e
to the organisation of suc
Block Evening.

### The Cell Administrator

A Cell Administrator should
Party member. He may, in
ceptional cases, be a non-P
member. Political and pers
reliability are, of course,
sential.

A Cell Administrator of
D.A.F. must be a member o
D.A.F. His service title is *Ze
walter*.

### General Regulations

**Questions:** All fellow wor
within Blocks and Cells are
pected to answer questions on
part of fellow citizens and P
members only if they are
position to answer these ac
ately. Otherwise a reply will
to be deferred until an op
tunity should present itself ag
and in the meantime, the Lea
Functionary or Administrato
the Local Group, who is qual
to make a reply, will have t
consulted.

**Sale of Admission Tick
etc.:** Just as no higher-ran
office is permitted to send
mission tickets, pamph
badges, etc. to Local Grou
Base Control with the inst

*ning School uniforms:*
*member attending a course*
*ttached units of the Nazi*
*ty.*
*member of a Regional*
*ning School.*

that they must all be sold,
absolutely forbidden that,
he part of Local Group or Base
trol, admission tickets, pam-
ts, badges, etc., be handed to
and Block Leaders or Cell
Block Administrators with
express instruction that they
have to be disposed of in their
rety.
lock Administrators, etc., are,
rally, expected to try to dis-
of the tickets, etc., handed
em. However, they are under
circumstances allowed to be-
importune towards fellow
ens and Party members.

**ff Records:** No detailed staff
rds will be kept on the part
ell and Block Leaders con-
ing Block Leaders, Block
ministrators, and Cell Admin-
ators, etc. If it becomes neces-
, Cell or Block Leaders may
llowed inspection of the per-
al records of their Local
up or Base Leader.

**agreements:** In the case of
greements and enmities, a
lement will have to be under-
en by means of personal ex-
nge of ideas; alternatively,
Leading Functionary who is
t in seniority will give a
sion. Insofar as measures and
imands should prove neces-
y, these will have to be ad-
istered to the person con-
ned in private, and never in
presence of other fellow
kers.

**te**
ional Air Defence League =
*chsluftschutzbund*, the Ger-
n Civil Defence organisation.

# N.S.D.A.P. Local Groups

### The Area defined
area controlled by a Local
up comprises one or more
munities. If necessary, towns
y be divided into several areas.
principle, Local Group boun-
ies should not cut across com-
nity boundaries.
A Local Group comprises a
imum of 50 Party members; it
y not exceed 500 Party mem-
s. The maximum number of
seholds in any one area, per-
ssible only in exceptional cases,

is 3,000. No lower limit on the
number of households per Local
Group has been fixed.
(*b*) The units upon which the
organisation of Local Groups has
been based, are rated according
to the following upper or lower
figures:

House Group = 8 to 15 House-
   holds
Block = 40 to 60 Households
Cell = 4 to 8 Blocks

### (2) The Local Group Leader
As Leading Functionary he has
authority for all expressions of
Party will; he is responsible for
the political and ideological
leadership and alignment of the
area under his control. The Local
Group Leader is immediately subordinate to the District Leader in
authority. Subordinate to the
Local Group Leader within his
area, as far as discipline is concerned, are all Political Leaders
and Party members as such.

Party members receiving appointments as Leaders will be
sworn in by the Local Group
Leader in the setting of a duty
parade. Final appointments as
Political Leaders will have to be
made by the Local Group Leader
on the occasion of a public
meeting of the Local Group. The
swearing in will take place in
solemn manner by means of a
handshake, while for a brief
moment the consecrated sovereign flag is lowered onto the
clasped hands.

Upon issue of a membership
card, provisional admission into
the Party has taken place (see
discourse on "The Party Member", paragraph 2, "The Pledge").
During the course of a solemn
members' parade, in full view of
the sovereign flag, the membership book will be handed over by
the Local Group Leader. In the
introductory remarks of his brief
address, the significance of Party
membership will be explained.
At the same time, emphasis will
be put on the fact that membership of the Party is meant as
preparatory to later activity in
a service post of the Party's
organisation. It is therefore the
duty of a Party member to prepare himself unrelentingly, by
training, self-discipline, and ideological attitude, for his future
duties; final admission into the
National Socialist German
Workers' Party embodies at the
same time the obligation to comply with every call by the Party.

Over and above all technical
and political tasks, a Local Group
Leader must be example, adviser

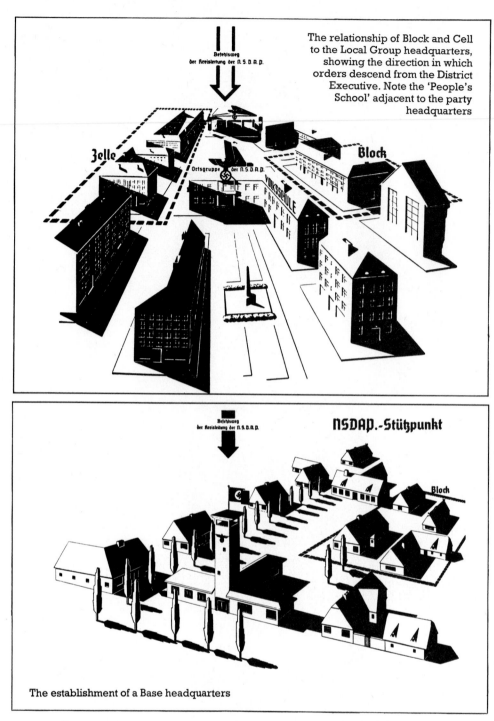

The relationship of Block and Cell to the Local Group headquarters, showing the direction in which orders descend from the District Executive. Note the 'People's School' adjacent to the party headquarters

**Zelle**

**Block**

The establishment of a Base headquarters

**NSDAP.-Stützpunkt**

**Block**

*The Nazi* Ortsgruppe *or Local Base (top) and* Stützpunkt *or Base (bottom). In the first the relationship of the two lowest levels in the Nazi administration, the Block (Block) and the Cell (Zelle), to their immediate superior, the* Ortsgruppe, *is immediately apparent. It is easy to imagine how the Party could keep its eyes on the activities of even the smallest elements of the new "pan-Teutonic" fellowship or community.*

points in which Base differs Local Group are
(*a*) smaller membership;
(*b*) in suitable cases, one Poli Leader holding more than post; and
(*c*) limited formation of Cell Regulations for Local Gr apply correspondingly to Ba

## 12. The District Executi

The District Executive is most subordinate office of Party with a full-time s Within the area under his trol, the District Leader is sponsible for the entire polit cultural, and economic dev ment of all manifestations of according to National Soci principles. If not other stated, the designation "Distr has, at all times, to be taken a ferring to the Party Distric opposed to the State Adminis tive District.

**The District Leader**

The District Leader is dire subordinate to the Regi Leader. Technical direct issued by the Regional Adm trator are binding for the Dist Leader. He will carry out gen technical directives, taking consideration the special na of his area.

The following are disciplina subordinate to the Dist Leader: all Political Leader his staff, as well as Local Gr and Base Leaders of the under his control.

The District Leader is wh responsible to his Regi Leader for the political and i logical education and alignm of Political Leaders and P members, as well as the p lation in the area under control.

## 13. The Regional Execu

The Regional Executive Regional Leader and his Regio Staff) has the job of politic leading a certain part of country and of acting in a pol forming capacity. Within the a under his control, the Regio Leader is responsible for entire political, cultural, and nomic development of all mani tations of life, according National Socialist principles.

**The Area Defined:** The Reg constitutes the incorporatio a number of Party Districts.

and comrade. He must see to it that strict secrecy is observed by his Political Leaders concerning all official incidents brought to their notice, and to set a good example himself in this respect.

**(3) The Local Group Flag**
Upon application by the District Leader, the Local Group may be granted the right to carry a sovereign flag by the Regional Leader. The sovereign flag is the

sacred symbol of the Local Group (or of the Base). It is on it that a Party member is pledged.

It will receive a place of honour at the Local Group (or Base) office. Insofar as no dignified place can be given to it, the District Leader will decide where the sovereign flag should have its place of honour. The sovereign flag may only be displayed at Party functions.

The Local Group or Base

Leader will appoint a serving Political Leader and entrust him with the honourable office of flag bearer. Only exceptionally deserving Political Leaders may be installed as flag bearers. The flag bearer must be conscious of the significance of his task. He honours the motto: "Man may fall, but the flag stands forever". Like the Local Group, the Base is an independent area under local control. The essential

rcation of its boundaries
be carried out, according to
Führer's directions, by the
tor of Organisation.

## he Regional Leader

Regional Leader is directly
rdinate to the Führer, or to
Deputy Führer acting on the
er's behalf. He is appointed
te Führer.

e Regional Leader bears
all responsibility to the
er for the area entrusted to
control. Rights, duties, and
res of authority of the
onal Leader arise mainly
his commission, granted by
ührer, and for the rest, from
lations laid down in detail.
e Regional Leader bears
all responsibility to the
er for the political and ideo-
al education and alignment
olitical Leaders, Party mem-
as well as the population.

## he Deputy Regional
der

hrough unforeseen circum-
ces, the Regional Leader is
lly prevented from the exe-
on of his duties as Regional
ler, the Deputy Regional
ler will take over all rights
duties of the Regional Leader
l relevant instructions from
Führer or Deputy Führer
e to hand.

te principal sphere of activity
te Deputy Regional Leader is
lieving the Regional Leader.
s the Regional Leader's con-
itial aide, receiving his in-
ctions from him. From this
idential relationship evolve
luties and rights.

*The relationship between
Kreis (District) and the* Gau
*ion). The illustration uses
Kreis of Pforzheim and the
of Baden to give reality to
example. Orders are
smitted from the* Gauleitung
te Kreisleitung, *and thence
her down the chain of
mand to the* Ortsgruppen
Stützpunkte.
*he relationship between the
leitung (Regional Party
cutive) and the* Reichsleitung
preme Party Executive). *The
here illustrated is Saxony,
its headquarters in
sden. In all there were
Gauen.*

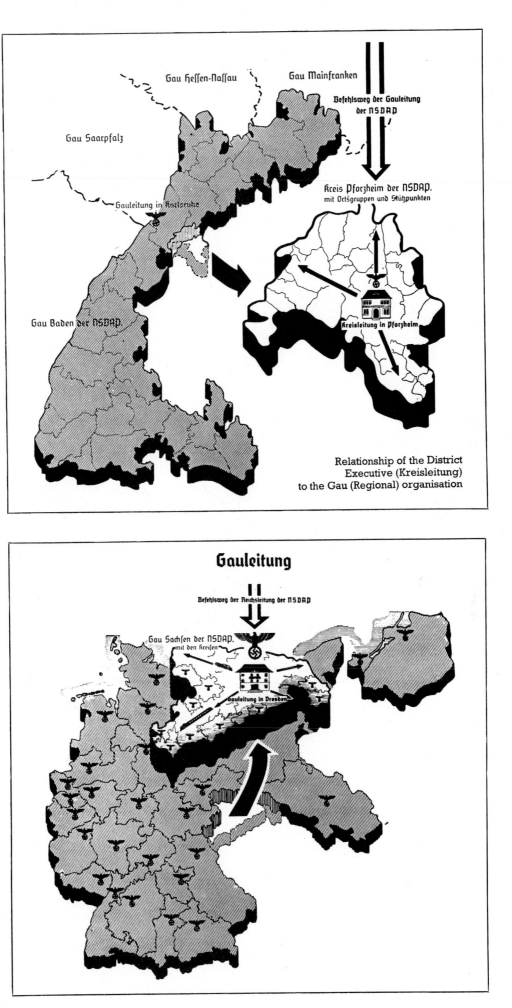

Relationship of the District
Executive (Kreisleitung)
to the Gau (Regional) organisation

3301

### (3) The Regional Inspecting Officer

The Regional Inspecting Officer is a representative of the Regional Leader. On behalf of the Regional Leader or his Deputy, it is his task to look into complaints, to carry out investigations, and to perform all kinds of special assignments.

All applications and complaints received by the Regional Executive either from the Deputy Führer or from other Party or State offices, as well as from public and private quarters, will be handled by the Regional Inspecting Officer.

It is the duty of the Regional Inspecting Officer to listen to callers visiting the Regional Offices in connection with complaints of one kind or another, and to prepare a report about the matter.

**The Foreign Section:** It is the task of the A.O. to win over German citizens abroad and also those employed at sea, to the National Socialist philosophy of life, and to keep alive, across class, profession, and creed, the idea of a Fellowship of the People in every single German national living abroad.

**Notes**

Regional Leader = *Gauleiter*
Regional Inspecting Officer = *Gauinspekteur*
A.O. = *Auslandsorganisation* (Foreign Section)
Fellowship of the People = *Volksgemeinschaftsgedanken*

## 14. The Central Executive

The N.S.D.A.P. represents the political conception, the political conscience, and the political will of the German nation. Political conception, political conscience, and political will are embodied in the person of the Führer. According to his directives, and conforming to the programme of the N.S.D.A.P., the German people's political aims will be guided and determined by the organs of the Central Executive. The threads of organisation of the German people and of the State meet in the Central Executive. Through the appointment of the Deputy Führer as Minister of the Reich, and through special administrative regulations, the penetration of the governmental apparatus by the political will of the Party has been ensured. It is the task of individual organs of the Central Executive, by means

of their sub-sections in the Regions, etc., to remain in the closest possible touch with the life of the people. What is observed in the Front of Battle should be compiled by the offices of the Central Executive for evaluation.

The Central Executive's structure has been planned in such a manner that the way from the most subordinate Party offices to the top makes possible the transmission of the smallest fluctuation and change in the temper of the people, and that, in turn, the moulding of will in the Central Executive brought about thereby reaches the Party's furthest command post, swiftly and unequivocally.

The Central Executive takes care, too, that reports of popular feeling should be passed upwards speedily and uninterruptedly, and that the will of the Führer should reach the outermost areas; exactly as with the healthy organism of a tree whose roots absorb nourishment from the soil, directing it to the leaves, whereas the nutritive juices formed in the leaves are sent down to the furthest roots. This interplay ensures an ever-renewed absorption of strength and an ever-increasing anchorage through the roots, and permits the crown

to spread ever more widely, to strive higher and higher and yet to defy wind and weather.

Since the National Socialist Movement evolved from within the people, it is first and foremost the task of the Central Executive to watch carefully that the strong roots of the Party, namely its bond with the people, should not wither away.

A further essential task of the Central Executive is the safeguarding of a first-class selection of leaders. The Central Executive must take care to see that in all spheres of life there exists a leadership which stands unswervingly for National Socialist ideology, working for its dissemination with all its energy.

In addition to the great general tasks which devolve upon the Central Executive, it will also have to ensure that all offices of the Party are properly organised. The National Director of Organisation, therefore, will exercise constant vigilance over the organisation of the entire Party apparatus to prevent a bureaucracy which might paralyse the Party's striking power from springing up. It is the supreme task of the National Director of Organisation always to maintain a sharp-edged sword for the Führer.

It is the purpose of the in[...] organisation of the Centra[...] ecutive to carry out the a[...] named tasks. The number [...] offices has been so calculate[...] all aspects of public lif[...] represented in the Centra[...] ecutive.

## 15. The Führer

It was his awareness of t[...] plorable state of affairs i[...] war Germany, preventing [...] did the development of a ge[...] community of the people [...] front-line experience of the [...] War with its spirit of com[...]

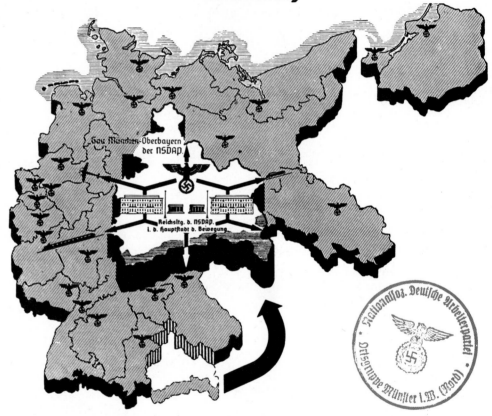

**Reichsleitung**

△ *The* Reichsleitung. *This, t[...] Party's government, was base[...] Munich in the* Gau *of Munic[...] Oberbayern. It will be remembered that the Nazi movement had started in Munich, and so its headquar[...] remained there.*

; and his loathing of a post-
Germany which was traitor-
y pacifist, that decided the
rer to enter politics and to
te for the German people a
state which, for centuries to
e, would safeguard their le-
mate vital interests.
order to achieve this end, the
rer created the National
ialist German Workers' Party.
imbued it with his spirit and
will, and on January 30,
, he seized power with its
. The will of the Führer is the
ty's supreme law. As the
vement's supreme Leading
ctionary he exercises the
t of pardon within the juris-
ion of the Party.
y a law of August 1, 1934,
cerning the head of state of
German Reich, the offices of
ch President and Reich
ncellor were merged. As a
lt, the former powers of the
ch President were transferred
the Führer, and now Reich
ncellor, Adolf Hitler. This
placed the leadership of Party
State into the same hands.
he Führer's wish the law was
mitted to a plebiscite, held on
ust 19, 1934. On that day, the
man people chose Adolf Hitler
be their sole leader; he is
onsible only to his own con-
nce and to the German people.
side the Party the Führer is
ressed as "My Führer"; on
ial, state and other occasions
"Führer and Reich Chan-
or".
o assist him, especially in
stions of Party policy, the
rer has appointed a
**Deputy Führer**
, in order to safeguard the
est co-operation between
ty organs and public authori-
, is a member (i.e. a Minister)
he Government.
addition, the Führer has
rusted
**eich Executive Directors**
hin the Reich Central Execu-
e of the N.S.D.A.P., with the
lementation of specific Party
ks.

## The Deputy Führer

e bearing of a National Social-
his demeanour and his re-
ionship with other Party
mbers and with fellow citizens
supported by self-confidence
sound self-assurance, ac-
red during the Struggle for
wer. This self-confident
neanour which a National
cialist draws from the fact that

the rules by which he lives are
firmly anchored in his ideology,
will impress others as genuine
and natural only if it is free from
any petty thirst for power and
from any nervous tendency to
regard as a threat to one's own
job any fellow Party member who
can accomplish more than oneself in some field of activity or
other.

No leading Party member, because at some time his personal
feelings might have been hurt,
must let himself be carried away
to pass an unfair judgement on
a subordinate Party member.

Leadership presupposes men
who follow readily, and that they
will do so as long as they are
conscious that their leader is a
National Socialist to whom
leadership means, not satis-
faction of his own lust for power,
but service to the Movement and
commitment to his men. A junior
leader who, from a feeling of petty
jealousy, is ready, at the drop of
a hat, to regard as his enemy
anyone whose task impinges on
his own; who insists on his authority because he fears a cur-

tailment of his position; has an
altogether discreditable attitude,
for it destroys the inner unity of
the Movement. Posts have not
been created to provide jobs for
Party members, but for them to
serve the cause of National
Socialism. In this service there
must be no petty and selfish
desires. Only close co-operation
in comradely solidarity with all
those who serve the Movement
will ensure the success and the
inner strength of the Party.

## 17. The Deputy Führer's Staff

After the Assumption of Power
by the National Socialist Movement, the Führer, in consequence
of the extraordinarily heavy demands made on him by affairs of
state, was obliged to appoint a
deputy for the leadership of the
Party; the head of the Central
Political Committee of the
N.S.D.A.P. was appointed to this
post. This appointment by the
Führer has placed an exceptional

▲*The Führer's personal
standard.*

degree of responsibility on his Deputy. The Assumption of Power had compelled the Party to second a large proportion of its best men to the State. Although these men did in part continue with their Party duties, they were no longer able to place their entire working capacity at the disposal of the Movement, especially as the re-building of the State demanded tremendous energy and personal effort. The Deputy Führer was thus forced to re-align the Party and to mobilise fresh forces. The organisations and affiliated bodies of the N.S.D.A.P. required a uniform political leadership.

Thus, at any given time, as instructed by the Deputy Leader, it is the main task of the staff, under the direction of the Chief of Staff, to bring the Regional Executives (*Gauleitungen*) of the N.S.D.A.P., as well as its organisations and affiliated bodies, into unified political alignment and to issue political directives to them. By order of the Führer, a further task of the Deputy Führer's staff is to take part decisively in legislative work of State authorities and in staffing them in accordance with National Socialist ideology.

## 18. The Chief of Chancellery of the Führer

The Führer's Chief of Chancellery heads The Private Chancellery Adolf Hitler, and the Führer's corps of adjutants. Here all Party matters received directly by the Führer are dealt with (provided they do not come under the competence of other offices), especially matters concerning Party members and applications for pardons in respect of sentences passed by courts of justice or Party courts.

## 19. The National Director of Organisation of the N.S.D.A.P.

The National Director of Organisation has been appointed by the Führer to deal with all organisational questions of the Party, its organisations and affiliated bodies.

In an ordinance dated May 12, 1934, the Deputy Führer has outlined in greater detail the scope of the National Director of Organisation. Accordingly, orders and measures initiated by Reich Directors as well as by all offices of the Central Executive, which concern Party organisation or which may affect it, must be discussed with and approved by the National Director of Organisation before publication or implementation. Any plan or order of the kind described above requires the counter-signature of the National Director of Organisation. Unless agreement, documented by countersignature, has been reached prior to the measures detailed above coming into force, all orders of the kind described are null and void. Further, by a decree dated October 20, 1934, the Deputy Führer, in order to prevent contradictory comment by Party offices, organisations or affiliated bodies, has given exclusive authority to the National Director of Organisation to issue compulsory directives and orders concerning all questions of organisation. The sovereign rights of Leading Functionaries, and the independence of the S.A., S.S., N.S.K.K., and H.J., in matters concerning their own organisations, are in no way affected by this decree.

In his capacity as National Director of Organisation, this officer is, at the same time, Reich Director of Indoctrination and Reich Director of Personnel. In the execution of his various tasks, he uses the services of his Chief of Staff and Official Adviser who, on his behalf and as instructed by him, will direct the following offices:

Central Office for Organisation
Central Office for Indoctrination
Central Personnel Office.

In addition, Official Advisers will direct the following offices on his behalf:

Central Staff Office
Central Office of the N.S.B.O.
Central Bureau for the Organisation of National Party Rallies
Central Bureau for Trade and Commerce.

In addition, the following offices which are politically subordinate to the Deputy Führer are in matters of administration, organisation, personnel and discipline, directly subordinate to the National Director of Organisation:

Central Office for People's Welfare
Central Office for Public Health
N.S.D. Students' Association
N.S.D. University Lecturers' Association

*The uniform of a* Mann *(Man), the lowest rank, in the* National sozialistische Betriebszellenorganisation *or N.S.B.O., the cell organisation of the* Deutsche Arbeitsfront *(German Labour Front) in commercial and industrial undertakings.*

ntral Office for War Victims
ntral Office for Civil Servants
ntral Office for Education
ntral Office for Local Govern-
nt
partment of Technical
ience.

, as shown by the above list,
competence of the National
ctor of Organisation is not
ed to matters of organisation
e narrower sense of the word.

petence:

range of duties regarding
onnel policy, indoctrination
organisation from an inte-
ed whole. Inclusion and in-
oration of Party members in
ell-regulated indoctrination
m is prerequisite for an
ent personnel policy. Only
dequate indoctrination will
ing Functionaries, and on
behalf personnel depart-
s, be in a position to pursue
uccessful personnel policy.
in turn is prerequisite for
reation of an efficient organ-
on.

the *Ordensburgen* of the
D.A.P. valuable Party mem-
from all Regions undergo
to three years' thorough and
ptionally exacting training
r the supervision of the
onal Director of Organis-
.

order to achieve unity among
ing Party members and in-
sed excellence as well as
ngth of mind especially
ng Leading Functionaries,
National Director of Organ-
on will summon District
lers (and Local Group or
Leaders) and Regional Ad-
strators to the *Ordens-
en* at regular intervals; this
addition to regular Regional
ler Conferences. At these con-
nces, leading figures of Move-
t and State will speak about
tasks.

ie Führer will himself speak
nese gatherings, and fellow
y members will have an op-
unity of meeting the Führer.
nce every year the three hun-
most senior Political Leaders
be invited by the National
ctor of Organisation to en-
travelling together through
of Germany's Regions. These
neys serve to strengthen the
ls of comradeship among
ran fighters, and their ties
their fellow citizens. All
results in Political Leaders
ing an increasingly inte-
ed direction and line, in short,
elds them together into an
ssoluble community.

The National Director of Organisation provides systematic
training to facilitate an efficient
personnel policy and the establishment of a suitable organisation. Moreover, he provides for
external alignment of Political
Officers, and for this purpose he
issues basic instructions regarding training facilities.

In the field of personnel policy
it is an essential task of the
National Director of Organisation continually to supervise the
training of potential leaders, particularly of those suitable for
higher, specifically political,
Party posts.

The National Director of Organisation also bears full responsibility for the organisation of
National Party Rallies.

The National Director of
Organisation is, at the same time,
Director of the German Labour
Front (D.A.F.).

The above outlines briefly the
National Director of Organisation's range of duties. In detail
this establishes the following
competences for the National
Director of Organisation:

The National Director of Organisation has to guard against
over-organisation and must, if
necessary, reduce the organisation to its fixed limit. Territorial
changes, and changes in office
structure must be authorised by
the National Director of Organisation. In addition, the National
Director of Organisation must
ensure that in organisations
where men are led, the community spirit should be fully expressed, and that the ideological
alignment of fellow citizens in
such organisation is safeguarded.
Organisations based on economic
status must be firmly dis-
couraged; only in exceptional
cases will association according
to occupational group be permitted.

## The task of Directors of Organisation in all areas:

It is necessary above all that
Directors of Organisation should
possess accurate knowledge of
their subject matter. Their work
will mostly be done behind the
scene of political events, and yet
it is among the most important
activities of the Party. Just as
the chief engineer in a factory, the
Director of Organisation must
supervise with great precision
the organisational apparatus in
his care, so that it may satisfy
any demands made by the Party.
Even small, insignificant mis-
takes must be stopped. **It must**

**never be tolerated that mis-
takes exist at all.**

Precisely because of the tremendous tasks, complicated by
an organisation comprising many
millions, an organisation without
its equal anywhere in the world,
perfunctory and careless work
does much harm.

The Director of Organisation is
the Party member who, in his
area, bears full responsibility for
implementing all orders and directives issued by superordinate offices, and for all organisational
tasks in general.

Orders or directives received
from a superordinate office must
not be put up for discussion, but
must be carried out at once.
In this context it must be pointed
out, however, that although work
must be conscientious and accurate, bureaucratic methods are
to be deprecated. The organisation should be lively, flexible,
and without rigid arrangements.

If no suitable Party members
are available locally, the Office
for Organisation must be taken
over by the Leading Functionary
himself.

It is one of the Director of
Organisation's special duties to
remain in constant personal contact with subordinate Directors
of Organisation. Thus the
Regional Director of Organisation should, from time to time,
meet the District Director of
Organisation, and the District
Director of Organisation the
Local Group or the Base Director
of Organisation, in order to dis-
cuss with them any outstanding
questions of organisation and
keep each other informed, so that
official communications between
Directors of Organisation may
not be confined to written orders
and reports. Without personal
contact between men in responsible positions, the striking power
of any organisation will be inef-
fectual.

This applies also to co-
operation with the Departmental
Directors of Organisation of individual sections and affiliated
bodies whose work will be supervised by their local Director of
Organisation.

It is advisable to call in these
Party members for personal discussions or for meetings, as indicated above, to ensure mutual
agreement with regard to organisational work. Above all, the Director of Organisation should in
every respect be an objective and
responsible adviser to his Leading
Functionary and relieve him of
all technical work relating to

Party organisation.

In cases of friction between
offices, or disputes about competences, etc., which may spring
up sometimes, he should act in a
conciliatory way and eliminate
tensions.

Any organisational or territorial change in the Regions may
only be made with the approval
of the Director of Organisation,
to whom a preliminary report
must also be sent prior to such
changes coming into force.

Directors of Organisation must
plan all measures well in advance.

The points below are directives
for the work of Directors of
Organisation:

(1) On behalf of his Leading
Functionary, the Director of Organisation must ensure that all
offices, organisations and affiliated bodies co-operate efficiently.

(2) He must ensure that the Party
machinery works entirely re-
liably in all organisations and
offices.

(3) It follows that the Director of
Organisation must, from time to
time, inspect every unit of the
Party (Block, Cell, Base, Local
Group, etc.).

(4) The Director of Organisation
is responsible for the planning
of Party Rallies. The internal
arrangements are in the hands of
the Director of Propaganda.

(5) The holding of membership
meetings in Local Groups and
Bases is incumbent on the Director of Organisation on behalf of
his Leading Functionary, unless
the latter wishes to take the
meeting himself. The actual arrangements for such meetings are
in the hands of the Director of
Propaganda.

(6) The Director of Organisation
must be exemplary in every respect when dealing with requests.
The setting of time limits for the
submission of reports is not some
bureaucratic request, but necessary for the implementation of
tasks for the Movement.

(7) The Director of Organisation
must see that the offices of the
Movement are not smothered by
a paper war or by bureaucratic
devices, but that everywhere the
life of the Movement should throb
vigorously. Thus reports on activities and on the atmosphere
among Party members are valuable and useful only if they can
be thoroughly dealt with and
utilised by the superordinate
office.

(8) It is one of a Director of
Organisation's special tasks to
organise the staff in his area
meticulously. As he is his Leading

Functionary's competent Administrator, the establishment of main offices, offices, Cells, Blocks, etc, requires his consent.

(9) The Director of Organisation must supervise the work of Political Officers and make sure

(a) that in their service for the people Political Officers are not overtaxed;

(b) that demands for service by different departments are sensibly distributed;

(c) that in conformity with Party directives the only assignments dealt with are ideological, or tasks which serve to imbue the people with National Socialist ideology;

(d) however, he must also make sure that Party members who do not participate actively are eliminated from the Political Leader Corps in the not too distant future.

(10) The Director of Organisation will keep records of Departments and offices, so that he may at all times be ready to give his Leading Functionary the opportunity of inspection.

(11) The Director of Organisation must take the greatest care to ensure that individual offices do not burden themselves with work outside their competence or outside the ideological tasks of the Party.

(12) On behalf of his Leading Functionary, the Director of Organisation must make sure that the essential activities of Political Leaders are undertaken among the people, by personal contact between man and man, and that the work of political leaders must on no account be restricted to more or less well-organised offices. Our strength will always be in our seeking out our fellow citizens and not in merely giving them the occasional opportunity of attending an appointment graciously accorded.

For this reason the responsible Director of Organisation must watch carefully that the development of Local Group or Base offices is limited to a minimum; at the same time he must ensure the perfect functioning of the Party's Block and Cell system and see that only the best Party members work as Block and Cell Leaders.

If the Party machinery is working efficiently, a wealth of Leader meetings will be necessary; these alone are suitable to align Political Officers and their helpers with each other and, at the same time, indoctrinate them

ideologically.

(13) The Director of Organisation is responsible for the internal and external alignment of the Political Leader Corps. For the implementation of the necessary physical and ideological training, a Training Officer will be at the disposal of the Director of Organisation.

(14) In the pursuit of his activities the Director of Organisation will work in close contact with the responsible N.S.D.A.P. Personnel Administrator and Indoctrination Officer.

(15) The Party rank order for Directors of Organisation is as follows:

Director of Organisation: Central Office for Organisation

Regional Director of Organisation

District Director of Organisation

Local Group Director of Organisation.

(16) The Director of Organisation is authorised to ensure territorial conformity in all fields of action of affiliated bodies, the N.S. Women's League, the N.S. Students' Association, etc. with Party sovereign areas. He is also responsible for all other problems of territorial organisation, such as the demarcation of Regional, District, Local Group, Base, Cell and Block boundaries.

(17) It is one of the duties of the Central Office for Organisation to agree upon and fix service designations for Political Officers, Administrators and Wardens, etc., as well as for affiliated bodies and their offices. The final decision rests with the Führer.

### The Training Supervisor and his Tasks

A Political Leader should excel through soldierly bearing and discipline, regardless of whether he is in civilian dress or in uniform. His demeanour, as an individual or in closed formation, at grand ceremonial parades and demonstrations of the Party (the Annual Party Rally, etc.), as well as the handling of his pistol, the weapon of honour bestowed upon him, all these demand appropriate training. His exhausting service as Political Leader demands counterbalancing through sport and physical training.

Thus the tasks of the Training Supervisor, working within the scope of the Director of Organisation, have been determined. They are:

(1) To carry out marching and

shooting training of Political Leaders. Duties will be determined in detail by the Leading Functionary in authority and may not take place more than twice monthly.

In the issuing and carrying out of commands, the Training Supervisor will follow the Regulations for the Training of Political Leaders of the N.S.D.A.P.; in small-arms training, he will follow the special regulation, entitled "The Pistol". An integral part of the training is the familiarisation of the Political Leader with individual commands so that during parades he will, if necessary, be in a position to give these himself.

(2) To carry out parades fixed by the Leading Functionary in authority.

(3) To supervise the observation of regulations when service dress is worn; to check the authority of individuals to wear badges of rank: for this purpose the Training Supervisor will be in charge of the Patrol Service, set up by the Leading Functionary.

(4) To take over (if possible) assignments of the Outdoor Service on behalf of the Director of Organisation.

(5) To supervise or possibly to carry out the sports activities, compulsory within the framework of the training scheme for Political Leaders.

Physical training will generally be carried out. Proper contests are forbidden, unless they are training exercises for the purpose of gaining the S.A. Sports Medal. The Training Supervisor will take part in sports activities. Physical training will be directed by sports instructors, seconded by the N.S. Association "Strength through Joy". The Training Supervisor will make the necessary arrangements. Insofar as arrangements with the "Strength through Joy" Association are not feasible for technical reasons, the Training Supervisor will himself take charge of the physical training of Political Leaders, as directed by the regulations laid down for this purpose. Marching, shooting, and physical training should take place not more often than twice monthly.

Since, for the Political Leader, this training is merely supplementary, in order to mould his exterior demeanour in a soldierly fashion, the Training Supervisor will have to be conscious of his great duty and the complexity of his tasks, namely thoroughly to train Political Leaders in the

comparatively short time available, without tiring them; rat[her] by means of additional sp[ecial] activities, to provide comp[en]satory relaxation from th[e] strenuous and responsible act[ivi]ties as Block Leaders, C[ell] Leaders, Administrators, L[ocal] Leaders, etc.

Under no circumstances m[ust] the Training Supervisor all[ow] himself to be carried away to [the] extent of using an insole[nt] peremptory tone, which mi[ght] incline Political Leaders to l[ose] that capacity for enthusiasm t[hat] has always distinguished th[em]. Only then will the Politi[cal] Leaders regard their training [and] sports duty as a welcome opp[or]tunity for relaxation and rec[re]ation from their strenuous wo[rk] and comradely association v[ill] make their duty pleasurable.

## 20. The Head Office for Organisation– Central Statistical Burea[u]

### (1) General remarks
The Central Statistical Bure[au] deals with the following matte[rs]

(1) Party member statistics
(2) Political Leader statisti[cs]
(3) Sectional statistics
(4) Affiliated Bodies statisti[cs]
(5) Statistical research on [the] subject of Party and Peo[ple]
(6) Population statistics in [the] Regions of the N.S.D.A.[P.]
(7) Special statistics.

These statistics are sub-divi[ded] into:

(a) National statistics
(b) Regional statistics
(c) District statistics
(d) Local Group and Base s[ta]tistics

and are composed of:

(i) Statistics relating to [mo]bility
(ii) Statistics relating [to] strength of establishme[nt]

to be compiled:

(A) regularly every two to th[ree] years
(B) separately, on request.

### (2) Tasks
It is the task of the Cent[ral] Statistical Bureau to determi[ne] by means of investigations m[ade] at certain intervals, any [de]ficiencies in the Party organi[s]ation; to create the conditions [for] furthering the tasks of the Par[ty] and to convey to the Führer [or] his representatives a true pictu[re] in accordance with the facts, [of] the Party in all its aspects, as [well]

this is possible through in-
...tigations.

...or that reason, statistical
...luation of incoming material
... be compiled not merely in
...ulated form, but will contain,
...addition to critical remarks,
...suggestions necessary at any
...n time.

...he main purpose of Establish-
...t statistics is to trace and
...ervise the following:

...Party members in relation to
...ulation, according to occu-
...ion and age
...Admissions and withdrawals
...Party members according to
...upation and age
...Exact intelligence of areas
...ses, Local Groups, Districts,
...ions) sparsely populated with
...ty members and thus falling
...ind in respect of the per-
...tage laid down of the number
...Party members per number of
...eral population
...Suggestions concerning de-
...nination of number of fellow
...zens to be admitted, according
...ccupation and age
...Increase or decrease of Local
...ups, as required, in a certain
...ition to households
...Activities of Party members
...Leadership analysed accord-
...to occupation and age
...Changes in rank (or promo-
...s) of Political Leaders
...Wear and tear on leadership
...irement, admission, and trans-
...of Political Leaders)
...Training and gatherings of
...itical Leaders
...Movement of Leaders and
...ty members in Party offices
...affiliated bodies. The Central
...tistical Bureau as well as all
...ional and District Statistical
...eaux are in continuous close
...tact with Government Statis-
...l Departments.

### Competence
...Central Statistical Bureau is
...sole authorised body to under-
...e any investigations essential
... the Party from an organis-
...nal and political standpoint.
...lot included in the above in-
...tigations are:
...Financial statistics and con-
...ious cash reports; these, as
...ninistrative matters, are
...lertaken by the National
...asury Department.
...Social and economic statis-
...; these are undertaken by the
...tistical sections of the relevant
...artments. There is, however,
...son with the Central Statisti-
...Bureau.
...n order to obtain the necessary
...terial, the Central Statistical

Bureau will, in the first place,
have at its disposal the Regional
head offices for statistics which,
moreover, are technically subordinate to it.

Apart from statistical assessments for the Regional Leader,
these offices will have to undertake research only as instructed
by the Central Statistical Bureau
of the N.S.D.A.P. and to create
the conditions necessary for such
research in Districts and Local
Groups.

The Central Statistical Bureau
will issue the forms necessary for
all statistical research and reports to Regions and Districts
and, if required, extend this to
Local Groups and Bases. Any
questions will be dealt with uniformly and when completed will
be reported through official
channels.

Existing sub-divisions of Party
offices, including organisations
and affiliated bodies, engaged in
statistical work, are technically
subordinate to the Central Statistical Bureau of the N.S.D.A.P.
Any investigations by these
offices will take place in agreement with the Central Statistical
Bureau and in closest co-operation with it.

Within the framework of their
competence, any material collected is at the disposal of Party
Offices for official purposes only.
In order to undertake statistical
research within the Party and
its affiliated organisations, permission of the Deputy Führer will
be required.

## 21. The National Director of Organisation

**Location:** Nuremberg.
**Tasks:** Arrangements and organ-
isation of all National Party
Rallies.

The Central Bureau for the
Organisation of National Party
Rallies works as an office within
the scope of the National Director
of Organisation. A permanent
office is maintained throughout
the year, staffed by a Manager,
an Assistant Manager, and an
Administrative Assistant. Some
time prior to the National Party
Rally, the following departments
will be staffed:
Management
Cashier and Administration
Transport and Parking
Accommodation
Congress and special meetings
Public entertainments and
"Fireworks"

Food and Camp construction
Telecommunications
Guests of Honour
Motor Transport
Sales
Press
Sanitation
Propaganda
Public address system
Road blocks and traffic control
Political Leader Corps Parade
  Staff
S.A. Parade Staff
S.S. Parade Staff
N.S.K.K. Parade Staff
H.J. Parade Staff
National Labour Service
Parade Staff
Armed Forces Parade Staff.

## 22. The National Socialist Motor Transport Corps

### Leadership
The National Socialist Motor
Transport Corps (N.S.K.K.), is an
independent section of the
N.S.D.A.P. and is led by the Corps
Leader of the National Socialist
Motor Transport Corps.

### Organisation and tasks
Next to the S.A. and S.S., the
National Socialist Motor Transport Corps stands as an independent section of the N.S.D.A.P.,
as its motorised unit. Growing
out of the Motor-S.A. and the
N.S.K.K. as it was in the years of
Struggle for Power, reared and
tested in the spirit of the S.A.,
drawing its strength from the
eager readiness for action and
ideological steadfastness of its
men, the Corps is the qualified
bearer of banner and will of the
idea of motorisation in our New
Germany. The higher the level of
motorisation, the stronger the
nation's defensive power!

It is in the intensification of
this realisation and in systematically preparing the way for
its practical consequences in a
National Socialist fellowship
spirit that the N.S.K.K. sees one
of its most important tasks. And
thus, not only Party members
but also young people, growing
up in the H.J. and in the Labour
Service, who are motoring en-
thusiasts, will find an eager welcome as new members of the
N.S.K.K. The Motoring Schools
of the N.S.K.K. all over the
country offer six-week courses in
which they provide systematic,
ideologically-orientated training
of prospective members in driving
technique and motoring as a
sport.

When the time comes for his
National Service, any young man
trained at one of these schools
will be well prepared, physically
and spiritually, to don with pride
the dress of one of the Nation's
arms-bearers – the German Armed
Forces – and when he has taken
it off once more, to return to the
ranks of the Corps, the right sort
of man now to be admitted into
the great comradeship of its broad
organisation which, sub-divided
into
  4 Senior Motor Corps
  3 Motor Divisions
  21 Brigades,
comprises German motorists
doing voluntary service.

Here, in steadfast concord, with
ideologically like-minded men
who, after a hard day's work,
meet in a National Socialist spirit
of fellowship for *Sturm* Evenings
and training rides every Sunday,
he will not only maintain his
flexibility but also retain and
enlarge the knowledge he has
acquired.

For this purpose, the sport of
cross-country driving, an activity
carried out by the N.S.K.K., is
eminently suitable. To take part
in it makes demands on the
whole man! Apart from mastery
of one's vehicle, courage, perse-
verance, the ability to make quick
decisions, the ability to find one's
way, and physical agility, are the
most important prerequisites for
this sport.

Thus the National Socialist
Motor Transport Corps is the
fountain of youth and the store-
house of strength of the motorised
nation: loyal, self-sacrificing and
ready for action!

### Notes
N.S.K.K. = *Nationalsozialistisches Kraftfahr-Korps*
Our New Germany: *Das Neue
Deutschland*, a Nazi concept, referring to Germany freed from
"liberalistic" ideas and wholly
immersed in National Socialist
thought.
*Sturm* Evenings: A *Sturm* or
Company is the collective word
for a group of Brown or Black
Shirts.

◁ An Oberscharführer (Colour
Sergeant) of the training
company of Motor Regiment
No. 86 of the N.S.K.K. in
motorcycling kit.
▷ An N.S.K.K. Mann in
service dress with crash helmet.

◀ *A* Scharführer *(Sergeant) of the N.S.K.K. Technical Leaders' School.*
▶ *A* Sturmführer *(Company Commander) on the staff of the 1st Squadron* (Staffel) *of Motorboat Regiment* (Kraftbootstandarte) *No. 1 in service dress.*

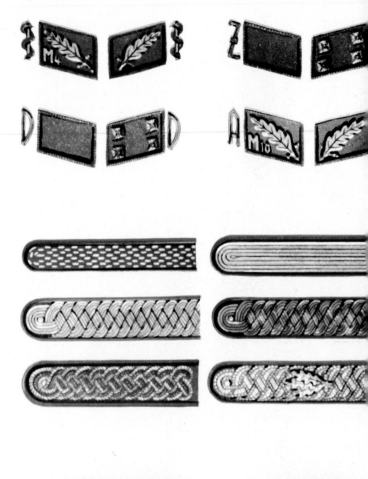

◄ *A* Scharführer *of Motor-boat Regiment No. 1 in service dre*
*with greatcoat.*

Δ *Insignia and headgear of the* Nationalsozialistische
Kraftfahrkorps:

Top two lines: *Specialist rank collar patches. These are for th*
*regimental doctor (*Standarten-Arzt*), squadron dental surgeo*
*(*Staffel-Zahnärzt*), squadron dentist (*Staffel-Dentist*), and*
*regimental chemist (*Standarten-Apotheker*).*

Centre three lines: *Epaulettes. These are, from left to right, to*
*to bottom:* Mann *to* Obertruppführer *in the "Saxony" Motor*
*Brigade,* Sturmführer *to* Sturmhauptführer, Staffelführer *to*
Standartenführer, Oberführer, Brigadeführer *to*
Obergruppenführer, *and* Korpsführer.

Bottom: *Service caps. These are, clockwise from top left:* Man
*to* Obertruppführer, *the field cap, and a* Sturmführer *on the*
N.S.K.K. *high command.*

*Opposite page:* N.S.K.K. *command flags.*

*Corps Leader (Korpsführer)*

*...s High Command (Korpsführung)*

*...ector of Technical Training ...Equipment (Inspekteur für ...chnische Ausbildung u. Geräte)*

*Reich Leader School (Reichsführerschule)*

*Senior Motor Corps "South"* (Motor-Obergruppe "Süd")

*Motor Division "East"* (Motor-Gruppe "Ostland")

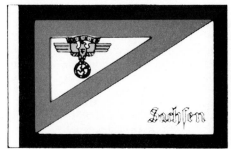

*Motor Brigade "Saxony"* (Motor-Brigade "Sachsen")

*Motor Regiment No. 84* (Motor-Standarte 84)

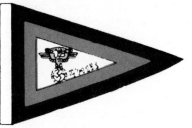

*Motor Squadron No. 2/ Regt. No. 133* (Motor-Staffel 2, Standarte 133)

## 23. The National Director of Organisation of the N.S.D.A.P.

### a. The Central Office for Political Indoctrination

Tasks and Responsibilities of N.S.D.A.P. Indoctrination Offices: A Survey of Activities in its Organisations and Affiliated Bodies:

The National Director of Organisation is at the same time National Director of Indoctrination.

The National Director of Organisation of the N.S.D.A.P. is responsible for ideological alignment and selection of Political Leaders working in the N.S.D.A.P., of Political Leaders seconded to organisations and affiliated bodies, as well as of administrators, wardens, and chairmen of organisations and affiliated bodies.

For the purpose of discharging this task he makes use of the Central Indoctrination Office which comes under his administrative scope. For ideological training purposes the following will be immediately included within the sphere of the Central Indoctrination Office or the Indoctrination offices of the N.S.D.A.P.:

(1) Political Leaders of the N.S.D.A.P. (including all Political Leaders of the N.S.D.A.P. seconded for service to affiliated bodies and organisations under the care of the N.S.D.A.P.);

(2) Members of the N.S.D.A.P. insofar as they take part voluntarily in Indoctrination activities;

(3) Women Leaders and Wardens of the N.S. Women's League and the German Women's Service (N.S.F.S. and D.F.W.);

(4) Chairmen, Administrators, and Wardens of the German Labour Front including those holding leading positions in the N.S. Association "Strength through Joy" and in the Labour Groups;

(5) Chairmen of, or all personnel in leading positions in the N.S. War Victims' Welfare Organisation (N.S.K.O.V.);

(6) Wardens of the N.S. League for Public Welfare (N.S.V.);

(7) Wardens of the Civil Servants' League (R.D.B.);

(8) Chairmen of the N.S. Physicians' League (N.S.A.B.);

(9) Wardens and members of the N.S. Teachers' League (N.S.L.B.);

(10) Leading personnel of the N.S. Lawyers' League (N.S.R.W.B.);

(11) Leading personnel and members of the N.S.D. Students' League (N.S.D.S.B.);

(12) Leading personnel and members of the N.S.D. University Lecturers' League (N.S.D.D.B.); and

(13) Wardens of the N.S.D. Technical League (N.S.B.D.T.).

The Central Office for Political Indoctrination is composed of the following five departments:

**(a) Department with Responsibility for Theoretical Indoctrination Tasks:** Preparation of teaching material, curriculum, teaching aids, and lists of guest speakers; collaboration with scientific institutions; alignment of instructors; publication of instructions concerning teaching materials for the purpose of indoctrination in the N.S.D.A.P.; and creation of a lecture library.
**Sections:** Curriculum Planning; Lecture Arrangements.

**(b) Department with Responsibility for Practical Training. Its tasks include:** Organisation and supervision of indoctrination activities at the Training Castles (*Ordensburgen*) of the N.S.D.A.P.; organisation and supervision of all other indoctrination arrangements; supervision of instruction at the *Ordensburgen*; supervision of adherence to curriculum; inspection of classes; supervision of technical training in affiliated associations; appointment, recall, and transfer of skeleton staff at the *Ordensburgen*; compilation and evaluation of reports; evaluation of assessment papers; and preparation of progress reports.
**Sections:** Indoctrination Activities; Reports.

**(c) Recruiting Office.**
**Tasks:** Collaboration with enlistment for the *Ordensburgen*; calling up of Political Officers for annual manoeuvres at District or Regional training establishments; close co-operation with Central Staff Office; and issue of cheap travel vouchers.
**Sections:** Special and Refresher Courses; Selection.

**(d) Administrative Office (Commissariat).**
**Tasks:** Control of establishment at Schools and *Ordensburgen*, and supervision of technical matters in connection with all indoctrination operations and activities.

**(e) Department with Responsibility for Indoctrination Circulars. Task:** Publication of N.S.D.A.P. Indoctrination Circulars and supervision of editorial training work in the Party. (The editor may be given the title of Head Office Director.)
**Sections:** Editor's Office; Management and Records; Inspection of Distribution.

## b. The Regional Office for Political Indoctrination

Regional Indoctrination Supervisors will be appointed by the Regional Leader in agreement with, and under the supervision of, the National Director of Organisation.

The structure of the N.S.D.A.O. Regional Office for Political Indoctrination corresponds with the structure of the Central Office for Political Indoctrination. In place of individual departments of the Central Office for Political Indoctrination, there are at the Regional Office for Political Indoctrination corresponding sections having the same tasks, of which the following may be specially mentioned:

(*a*) Management of Regional Schools; organisation and execution of political indoctrination at N.S.D.A.P. Regional Schools; and supervision of Technical Schools run by affiliated bodies and organisations;

(*b*) Selection of participants in Regional school indoctrination courses;

(*c*) Co-operation with training staffs of organisations and affiliated bodies within the framework of tasks and responsibilities laid down;

(*d*) Supervision of District Indoctrination Supervisors' work;

(*e*) Distribution of Indoctrination Circulars; and

(*f*) Formation and care of the necessary politico-ideological nucleus of Political Indoctrination Lecturers.

## c. The District Indoctrination Supervisor

District Indoctrination Supervisors will be appointed by the District Leader in agreement with the Regional Indoctrination Supervisor.

Generally, the tasks of the District Indoctrination Supervisor correspond to those of the Regional Indoctrination Supervisor. The following are the duties incumbent upon him and his regional office:

(a) To suggest participants for Indoctrination courses at the Regional school;

(b) organisation and execution of politico-ideological training in the District area;

(c) supervision of District school; arrangement of Indoctrination courses or week-end courses;

(d) distribution of Indoctrination Circulars;

(e) supervision of technical training of association; and

(f) formation and continuous alignment of all politico-ideological Indoctrination lecturers (Indoctrination Speakers).

The organisational structure of the Central Office for Political Indoctrination applies, by analogy, to all District Offices for Political Indoctrination.

With the District Office for Political Indoctrination there will be three Main Offices:

**(1) Main Office with responsibility for practical indoctrination**
**Tasks:** Creation and constant control of Indoctrination establishment;

**(2) Main Office with responsibility for theoretical indoctrination**
**Tasks:** Formation and constant control of staff of speakers; and

**(3) Main Recruiting Office**
**Tasks:** Inclusion of all Political Leaders, Administrators, and Wardens in Local Group Indoctrination; calling-up for Indoctrination course at District schools.

## d. The Local Group (or Base) Indoctrination Supervisor

The Local Group Political Indoctrination Supervisor will be appointed by the Local Group Leader in agreement with the District Indoctrination Supervisor.

The Local Group Indoctrination Supervisor has the following duties:

(a) organisational preparation of Indoctrination Evenings;

(b) placing of Indoctrination Speakers, particularly for the political indoctrination of Block and Cell Leaders and all leading members of the Party (including those of organisations and affiliated bodies) within the Local Group area, as well as Party members participating voluntarily;

(c) suggestions for participants at District schools from among participants in Local Group or Base indoctrination;

(d) distribution of Indoctrina[tion] Circulars; and

(e) supervision of technical t[rain]ing of associations within Local Group or Base area.

The Local Group Indoc[trin]ation Supervisor (or Base [In]doctrination Supervisor) mu[st] to the uniform executio[n] political indoctrination within the area of his Local G[roup] (or Base).

He has not been appointe[d] undertake indoctrination himself, but his task is the pr[epar]ation and organisation o[f in]doctrination functions, at w[hich] Regional or District Indoc[trin]ation Speakers will be mad[e] of as lecturers.

As far as all indoctrin[e] work is concerned, the princ[iple] in direct contrast with p[ro]ganda work, that it addr[esses] itself exclusively to a select c[ircle] of people must be borne in m[ind] and it is for that reason th[at] refrains from the usual for[m] propaganda at its functions.

The task of indoctrination be one of selection. This pr[ocess] of selection takes place, fir[st] all, by dint of the fact that fu[nda]mentally participation in i[ndoc]trination functions is on a vo[lun]tary basis for all Party mem[bers] and that Political Leaders will be called in compulsoril[y] indoctrination.

From among this circle, [selec]tion for attendance at Di[strict] and Regional schools wil[l] made at the suggestion o[f] Leading Functionary, acco[rding] to the candidate's particip[ation] and aptitude record during [Local] Group or Base Indoctrin[ation] functions.

Speakers will be put a[t the] disposal of Indoctrin[ation] Evenings from the staff [of In]doctrination Speakers of[ the] Regional Office for Politic[al In]doctrination or the District [Office] for Political Indoctrination[. The] Local Group (or Base) Indo[ctrin]ation Supervisor will be re[spon]sible for the fixing of date[s and] for notification of the Indo[ctrin]ation Speaker, just like the [Local] Group Propaganda Super[visor.] In addition, he has to take [care] that indoctrination [notes] arranged monthly by the Ce[ntral] Office for Political Indoctri[nation] are discussed exhaustively [and] in good time.

Thus, within his area, the [Local] Group (or Base) Indoctrin[ation] Supervisor bears the res[ponsi]bility for all indoctrinatio[n ac]tivities of the N.S.D.A.P.

…an Women's Service = …sches Frauenwerk (Organis-…n for the social and edu-…nal concerns of women)

…K.O.V. = N.S. Kriegsopfer-…rgung (care of war victims)

…V. = N.S. Volkswohlfahrt …gue for Public Welfare)

…B. = Reichsbund Deutscher …nter (Civil Service Organis-…n)

…B.D.T. = Nationalsozialis-…er Bund Deutscher Technik …man Technical League)

## …he Central Office …olitical Indoctrination

… Appointments of Political …ers, and the allocation of … will take place according to …ing staff regulations for all …w workers in Indoctrination …es.

… All politico-ideological In-…rination Speakers belong to …taff of their local N.S.D.A.P. …e for Political Indoctrina-… They will be made available … N.S.D.A.P. Indoctrination …ings at Local Groups, etc. …e Supervisor of the Indoctri-…n Office.

…Among others, the following …es are part of the whole …ect of politico-ideological …ment: the delineation of the …amental National Socialist …ude vis-à-vis internal politics, …gn affairs, racial and heredi-…science, economic and social …ics, history, geopolitics, cul-…l and educational politics,

## …ndoctrination of the S.A., …, H.J. and N.S.K.K.

…logical indoctrination of the …ers of the above formations … be undertaken in those for-…ons on the part of their local …es in mutual agreement with …National Director of Organi-…n, the Central Office for …ical Indoctrination or the …D.A.P. Offices for Political …ctrination.

…All Political Leaders, sec-…d to affiliated bodies on the … of the N.S.D.A.P., since, in … capacity as Political Direc-…they belong directly to the … of the Leading Functionary …heir area, will, notwith-…ding their activities as Ad-…strators, Wardens and Chair-…in the affiliated bodies, be …logically aligned solely and …ctly by their local Supervisor …doctrination.

…Indoctrination Depart-…ts in Affiliated Bodies are concerned with the technical training of their Administrators, Wardens, etc. on an ideological basis.

This technical training is independent; it will be supervised by the Indoctrination Offices of the N.S.D.A.P.

Insofar as purely ideological indoctrination is provided, (i.e. for teachers, students, and lecturers), this will be undertaken according to instructions by the competent Supervisor of Indoctrination.

Speakers on the subject of technical training in organisations and affiliated bodies will join the staff of the competent Administrator of Indoctrination of their affiliated body in Reich, Region, or District. They will have to be approved by their local N.S.D.A.P. Supervisor of Indoctrination.

Administrators of Indoctrination in affiliated bodies will have their seat of office at the offices of their affiliated body; they are attached to the staff of the leading Administrator of the affiliated body.

(6) Politico-ideological propaganda vis-à-vis members of organisations and affiliated bodies is incumbent upon the National Directorate for Propaganda, as well as upon N.S.D.A.P. Regional and District Directors of Propaganda and, on their behalf, upon Propaganda departments of affiliated bodies.

The Central Office for Political Indoctrination works in closest co-operation with the National Directorate for Propaganda.

## f. N.S.D.A.P. Indoctrination Castles and Technical Schools of Organisations and Affiliated Bodies

(1) The N.S.D.A.P. Indoctrination Castles serve for politico-ideological alignment of N.S.D.A.P. Political Leaders and Administrators of affiliated bodies. They are under the sole supervision of the Regional, or District, Supervisor for Indoctrination. Insofar as he does not reserve for himself the direction of the school, he may detail a fellow Party member to act as director of the school.

(2) All schools of affiliated bodies are technical schools. They work independently. Technically they are supervised by the Adminis-trator of Indoctrination of the body in question.

The number of schools will be determined in agreement with the National Director of Organisation in his capacity as Director of the Central Office for Political Indoctrination. Directors of technical schools must be Party members.

(3) **Staffing of N.S.D.A.P. Schools and Ordensburgen** The above will be staffed by the following:

A. **Administrative Staff** (Chief Financial Officer, Administrator, etc.); and

B. **Teaching Staff** (Castle Commandant or School Director, leading and teaching staff). Teaching staffs as a body will come under the auspices of the Central Office for Political Indoctrination. As far as skeleton staff in Ordensburgen is concerned, we must distinguish the following:

(a) The solely responsible leader in the Ordensburg is the Castle Commandant.

The Castle Commandant will remain at the same Ordensburg during his entire term of office. The Castle Commandant is supported by

(b) one adjutant, and

(c) the staff (drill sergeant, chief administrator, etc.). In this connection, the following subdivision should be noted:

(d) senior teachers for physical hardening and alignment of students (drill sergeant, sports coach, etc.);

(e) senior teachers for ideological and spiritual education of students.

(f) In addition, there will be a senior teacher, on whom it will be incumbent to impart knowledge of deportment.

Immediately subordinate to the Castle Commandant are

(g) three stand-to leaders (for 300–400 men).

Each stand-to leader also has an adjutant at his disposal. The most senior stand-to leader will lead the first stand-to squad. At the same time, he will act as deputy to the Castle Commandant, should the latter be prevented from being present.

The maximum age on appointment for stand-to leaders is 40. A stand-to leader will remain at the same Ordensburg during his entire term of office.

The following are subordinate to stand-to leaders:

(h) Leaders of Centuries:
All ten leaders of Centuries must have passed their sports coach's examinations.

Leaders of Centuries remain at Ordensburgen for six years' service. In future, they will be withdrawn successively from the Ordensburgen as and when their term of office expires. In due course, leaders of Centuries will be accepted for senior Party service. Maximum age on appointment for leaders of Centuries is 35.

The following are subordinate to leaders of Centuries:

(i) Squad (Kameradschaft) leaders (for 50 men).

The Squad represents simultaneously the seminar of spiritual and ideological education.

The Squad leader must be physically well trained, through and through. Squad leaders are changed every three years. In future, they will be withdrawn successively from the Ordensburgen, as and when their term of office expires.

If he is considered suitable, any Squad Leader, having completed his course of instruction, will be accepted into active Party service; only at a later point in time will he be ordered to return to do service as Squad leader. In due course, Squad leaders will be accepted for senior Party service. Maximum age will be 30.

The appointment of teaching staffs will take place on the strength of a muster, for which Regional Administrators, District Leaders, District Administrators, and Local Group Leaders will be considered.

For a muster of Skeleton Staff the regulations are similar to those for a muster of students at Ordensburgen.

C. **Guest Instructors**

(a) Full-time scientists, directly subordinate to the Central Office for Political Indoctrination and

(b) N.S.D.A.P. National, Regional and Central Administrators.

(c) There are, however, Instructors (called Indoctrination Specialists), who are attached to the teaching staff of an Ordensburg, and who may, at the same time, should this prove expedient, work as guest instructors at other Ordensburgen or Party schools.

D. **The following subjects will be taught:**

(1) Racial theory (to be taught by a biologist and a philosopher);

(2) History (to be taught by an instructor each for ancient, mediaeval, and modern history);

(3) Ideology and Philosophy;

(4) Art and Culture;

(5) Economics and Sociology; and

(6) Military science.

If instructors for the above-mentioned subjects are civilians, they will teach at any *Ordensburg* for three months in a year.

### E. Regulations concerning Recruitment for Prospective Participants in Ordensburg Courses

Recruitment will be carried out by a commission consisting of the National Director of Organisation, the Regional Leader, the District Leader, the competent Staff Administrator, and the confidential medical officer of the Department for Public Health. Application will be made voluntarily to the Local Group Leader.

### Conditions for admission to an Ordensburg:

(*a*) Applicant must have worked actively in the N.S.D.A.P.;

(*b*) Perfect health and freedom from defects;

(*c*) Aryan origin and freedom from hereditary disease;

(*d*) Favourable opinion of Leading Functionary after receipt of report from Staff Administrator;

(*e*) Age 23 to 30; in exceptional cases, applicants below and above the age limits may be considered.

After the age of 26, celibacy is undesirable.

## 24. The German Labour Front and N.S. Association "Strength through Joy"

Extracts from Regulations issued by the Führer on October 24, 1934, concerning the nature and aims of the German Labour Front.

"**Nature and aims:** The German Labour Front is the organisation for all Germans who labour with hands and brains.

"It includes particularly members of the former trade unions, the former Unions of Salaried Employees, and the former Employers' Association, as members enjoying equal rights.

"Membership of professional, socio-political, economic, or ideological organisations does *not* serve as substitute for membership of the German Labour Front.

"The Reich Chancellor may order legally recognised professional organisations to belong as a body to the German Labour Front. The aim of the German Labour Front is the creation of a genuine all-German fellowship of people and production.

"**Tasks:** The German Labour

Front must safeguard industrial peace by creating among management understanding for the justified claims of their employees, and, conversely, among employees, for the situation and potential of their place of employment.

"It is the task of the German Labour Front to establish between the justified interests of all parties a balance which corresponds with National Socialist principles, and which limits the number of cases which, according to the law of January 20, 1934, will have to be transferred to the competent State authorities for their decision.

"The representation of all parties involved, necessary for the achievement of that balance, is exclusively the concern of the German Labour Front. The formation of other organisations and activities of such organisations in this connection are prohibited. (signed) Adolf Hitler

Führer and Reich Chancellor"

### (1) Introduction

An end having been put by National Socialism to the many political parties and their seditious activities, it was necessary for group egotism and the class struggle caused by it, and manifesting itself in the shape of fighting units and trade unions, to disappear from among German workers.

A new organisation has been

ed according to the
onal Socialist principle of
lic Need Before Private
d", namely the National
list Co-operative Organis-
known as
e German Labour Front".

wship of the people has
the place of class struggle.
e German Labour Front, this
vship of the people is given
ble expression through the
poration of all Germans
ng their living by the labour
eir hands and brains.

e aim of the German Labour
t is the creation of a true all-
an fellowship of people and
iction. The German Labour
t must take care to see that
individual takes his place
e economic life of the Nation
spiritual and physical dispo-
a which will enable him to
eve the highest possible out-
nd thus ensure the greatest
it for the fellowship of the
e.

e N.S.D.A.P. retains the
ership of the German Labour
t. The National Director of
nisation is Director of the
an Labour Front. He is
inted by the Führer and is
nsible to him only. The
tor of the German Labour
t appoints and dismisses all
holders of the German
ur Front. Party members
should be appointed to such
t, in the first place.

e following are office holders
e German Labour Front:
.A.F. Foremen
.A.F. Stewards; and
.d.F. Wardens.

e geographical structure of
erman Labour Front corre-
ds to that of the N.S.D.A.P.
r the purpose of organisa-
of the German Labour
t, the target of organic order,
d down in the programme of
I.S.D.A.P., is decisive.

e geographical and technical
nisation of the German
ur Front will be determined
e National Director of Or-
sation of the N.S.D.A.P.

e financial administration
e German Labour Front will
inder the control of the
onal Treasurer of the
D.A.P., in accordance with
rst Regulation for the Imple-
ation of the Law for Safe-
ding the Unity of Party and
, of March 23, 1934.

th the incorporation into the
an Labour Front of the
nisations of commercial
omy, transport economy, and
rian economy, the foun-

△ *The uniform of a D.A.F. Werkschar-Mann, a D.A.F. Steward (Walter), and a "Strength through Joy" Warden (Wart). The* Werkschar *was a political organisation of factory employees.*
Opposite page: *Flags of the* Deutsche Arbeitsfront. *From top to bottom these are: the standard of the Aalen branch; the service pennant of a D.A.F. Gauwalter (Regional Steward), a Department Leader of the D.A.F. Central Bureau, and an Administrator in a Reich manufacturing industry; and a D.A.F. Leader's standard.*

dations have been laid for the creation of **social self-con-sciousness** which the Führer confirmed in his edict of March 21, 1935.

The German Labour Front is the holding organisation of the National Socialist association "Strength through Joy".

### (2) The Tasks of the German Labour Front

In fulfilment of the Regulations issued by the Führer and Reich Chancellor on October 24, 1934, and of the Law concerning the Regulation of National Labour, dated January 20, 1934, the tasks of the German Labour Front are as follows:

(*a*) the ideological education of all members of the D.A.F. so that they may become National Socialists;

(*b*) care of all members in safe-guarding their labour and social rights;

(*c*) their professional education and training;

(*d*) in its capacity as National Socialist Fellowship and accord-ing to the principle of "Public Need Before Private Greed", to maintain within the scope of their potential the livelihood of its members in case of need, or to offer able persons the possibility of advancement;

(*e*) care of members' staff-management relations by cre-ating a social balance in co-operation with the organisation of the economic sector as well as the Labour Trustee;

(*f*) organisation of leisure time through the N.S. Association "Strength through Joy" in the D.A.F.;

(*g*) social care of all German nationals abroad within the scope of the host country's laws; and

(*h*) any other tasks set the D.A.F. by Adolf Hitler, Führer and Reich Chancellor.

### Tasks of the N.S. Association "Strength through Joy"

It is the task of the N.S. Associ-ation "Strength through Joy" to gather together labouring German fellow citizens of all classes and occupations, in order to mould German working life in a uniformly National Socialist way.

Those contrasts which existed formerly in the assessment of workers, made possible by con-trasting and discriminatory as-sessment of their work, must be overcome through the experience of human values, which have their roots in that very work.

*D.A.F. uniforms:*
◁ *A member in field dress
with greatcoat.*
▷ *An Administrator or Warden
in field dress, with the D.A.F.
emblem on his left sleeve.*

3316

is therefore the special his-
task of the N.S. Association
ength through Joy" to do
y with the former exclusively
erialistic assessment of tech-
l-mechanical working life by
rtaining and putting forward
deal values of that work, and
ork as such.

or that reason, the leisure
ement organised by the N.S.
ociation "Strength through
" must always take care to
y out the organisation of
re time in the closest rela-
ship to working life.

ational Socialist leisure time
nising does not mean: Let's
way with work! but: Up and
!

is in work experienced men-
and spiritually that the N.S.
ociation "Strength through
" sees life's most lofty purpose
lled. For that reason, all
ural activities organised by
N.S. Association "Strength
ugh Joy" must always main-
their close relation to work-
life, artistically as well as
tually. Participation of the
man working class in artistic
nust always be aligned on the
s of working-class fellow citi-
natural relationship to art,
with special consideration
g given to possible under-
ding and increasing interest
he part of the workers.

he N.S. Association "Strength
ugh Joy" must strengthen
German worker's belief in
self and in his abilities, not
in the mechanical work
esses he carries out, not only
is manual work, but beyond
, in his mental and spiritual
ers and abilities.

this belief, the N.S. Associ-
n "Strength through Joy"
t be in a position to convince
German worker of his ability
day to give suitable artistic
ression to his mental and
itual experiences. However,
German worker will be able
ackle such tasks only when
belief in himself will be con-
ed by the experience of
eral ideals of beauty which
pel him towards creative ac-
ty. The path thither leads
ugh the experiencing of
re, of man, and of scenery. To
r this path for the German
ker is the aim of all organis-
nal endeavours and measures
e N.S. Association "Strength
ugh Joy". All cultural and
al activities must be chan-
ed in this direction.

o awaken and strengthen com-
al life, as demanded by

National Socialist ideology, the
N.S. Association "Strength
through Joy" will have to include the German worker in the
lofty world of ideals, treading
ever new paths and using ever
new means, so as to enable him to
believe with all his might in the
sense and in the greatness of that
German life which he helped to
fashion.

That is why the N.S. Association "Strength through Joy" is
not only the organisation for
spare time and leisure time arrangements, but wants to create
a totally

**new conception of life**
It is the most vigorous expression
of the life-affirming National
Socialist Idea.

**Notes**
former: The Nazis had, of course,
abolished all parties, trade
unions, and other organisations
which might have represented an
opposition.
does not serve as substitute: an
insidious way of pointing out that
membership of the German
Labour Front was compulsory.
employees: The German word
used here is *Gefolgschaft*. Only
in the Nazi period was this used
to describe employees. Its correct
meaning is "vassals", "followers", "partisans".

# 25. The N.S.
# Women's League

The N.S. Women's League, being
an organisation of the N.S.D.A.P.,
is found in every area, down to the
Block.

German girls or women, of
unblemished character, having
completed their twenty-first year
and belonging neither to any
Freemasons' Lodge nor to any
other Secret Society, may become
members of the N.S. Women's
League. If they are married, their
husbands must also be of Aryan
origin.
**Tasks:** It is the task of the N.S.
Women's League to educate
politically and ideologically
reliable women leaders for the
Führer, to lead German women
in the important spheres of work
of the N.S. Women's League; these
comprise all areas where the co-
operation of a nation's women-
folk is required.

This takes place
(1) through the exercise of total
ideological alignment within
women's work by the N.S.
Women's League;

(2) through the supervision of
ideological or political alignment
and attitude of all women's work
in places of education or on any
other occasions; and
(3) through the creation of establishments necessary for the execution of this work.

**Organisation:** Geographically
the structure of the N.S. Women's
League coincides without exception with the structure of the
areas of the N.S.D.A.P. Within
each Local Group area, there
exists a Local Group Women's
League. Cells and Blocks of the
N.S. Women's League correspond
in every way to Cells and Blocks
of the N.S.D.A.P.

**German Women's Service**
The N.S. Women's League looks
after its affiliated body, the
German Women's Service.

**Department with
responsibility for National
and Domestic Economy**
The task of the Department with
responsibility for Political and
Domestic Economy consists in
guiding the German woman, as
regards National Economy, in
her peculiar position as main
consumer of the national income.
Work carried out by women's
guilds up to now has been devoted to this work. The housewife as main consumer has to be
guided towards adapting her domestic tasks to the requirements
of German National Economy.
By thoughtful housekeeping, by
careful shopping, by wise
management of her store cup-
board, she must contribute to the
safeguarding of the German
people's nutrition and to a recovery of the National diet.

With the aid of lectures, courses
in domestic science, leaflets, exhibitions, films, practical cookery
demonstrations, as well as
through the Department's organ,
the periodical *German Domestic
Economy*, an attempt is made to
guide housekeeping in its entirety
from the point of view of political
economy. The younger generation, too, being the housewives
of the future, must be trained in
the same way as the housewives
of today.

There is a Regional Woman
Official responsible for this department in every Region, who is
subordinate to the Regional
Leader of the N.S. Women's
League. This applies also to Districts and Local Groups.

In co-operation with the
Central Employment Exchange

and Unemployment Insurance,
and the B.D.M., the Department
for Political and Domestic
Science organises the "Domestic
Year" during which a minimum
of domestic skill is imparted in a
family household to young girls
who have left school. The two-
year domestic apprenticeship is
the focal point for the training of
future housewives; it imparts
thorough training in domestic
science, together with a final
examination. With the institution
of two-year courses for the training of home economists, the
Department contributes towards
raising the status of housekeeping
in its entirety and, at the same
time, it creates a nucleus of
housewives, always ready for
action, to do instruction and
information work in connection
with the subjects of National and
Domestic Economy.

**The National Motherhood
Service**
Training courses arranged by the
National Motherhood Service,
the purpose of which is to help
create the preconditions for
healthy families, provide training
and drill for German women in
the following subjects:
(a) Housekeeping (cookery and
sewing);
(b) Health and hygiene (baby
care, domestic nursing, including
population policy as well as
genetic and race hygiene); and
(c) Education (with instruction
in handicrafts).

A Regional Woman Official will
be responsible for the organisation of this training work for
mothers within a Region. She
will be a specialist who must be
specially equipped with administrative skills.

The actual training courses
will be carried out by full-time
and part-time ideologically reliable specialists. Part-time
teaching staff will be drawn from
the ranks of District Women
Welfare Officers, women doctors,
women youth leaders, etc.

There are training courses for
mothers in town and country. In
town there are permanent Schools
for Mothers; in the country there
are mobile courses. Work has
been organised in such a way that
each political District in the
Reich is allocated a full-time
Supervisor of the School for
Mothers (District Woman
Specialist Officer), possessing the
necessary specialist qualifications, and who, working under
the District N.S. Women's League
Supervisor, will be responsible

for putting into practice all relevant work in the District with the help of part-time specialist instructresses. Courses will be run according to the skeleton syllabus worked out by the National Women's Executive. Work is most important in areas with a high infant mortality rate, or where there is still unemployment, or which require special attention because they are distressed or border areas.

The National Motherhood Service comprises German women from all walks of life, the housewife and the domestic help, the university woman and the working woman; but, above all, it is the woman worker who will be extensively enlisted in training courses for mothers, by dint of the happy co-operation which exists between the D.A.F. Women's Bureau and the N.S. Women's League.

The work of the National Motherhood Service is effectively promoted because of the close connection with Party and State Offices, especially the Ministry of the Interior and the N.S. Public Welfare, both of which give far-reaching and much valued support to the National Motherhood Service.

### Foreign Department
It is the task of the Foreign Department to give information in response to the many enquiries from abroad concerning the position and the work of women in our New Germany; to maintain connections with organisations abroad; to give to correspondents of important foreign newspapers insight into women's work; to report to journalists, professors, teachers, etc., about women's work in New Germany and to give them the opportunity of getting to know German women's work on the spot (by means of conducted tours of Women's Labour Service Camps, training courses for mothers, N.S.V. work). For the purpose of disseminating information about the position of women in the New Germany, the following should be used:
Short-wave radio (Woman's Hour);
the despatch abroad of publications of all kinds;
regular supply to news agencies representing foreign papers, and papers for German nationals abroad, of short articles about German women's work; as well as:
lectures to groups of foreigners temporarily in Germany as students.

### Notes
National economy: The German expression used here is *Volkswirtschaft*, the correct translation of which is "national economy". However, the text which follows clearly shows that what is meant is simply "management of domestic matters" or *Wirtschaft*. Tongue in cheek, the correct translation has been used throughout to illustrate the fact that the Nazi predilection for long words was not always backed by knowledge of their meaning.

# 26. The Reich Director of Propaganda of the N.S.D.A.P.

The responsibility for propaganda activities of the N.S.D.A.P., its organisations and affiliated bodies, is in the hands of the Reich Director of Propaganda.

### Tasks:
(1) He determines the entire propagandistic demeanour of the Movement, including its organisations and affiliated bodies.
(2) He issues guide lines to the Party including organisations and affiliated bodies, concerning the realisation of the Führer's cultural commands.
(3) He exercises control over the entire German radio network with regard to its internal organisational, cultural, and economic development.
(4) By using his initiative, he is concerned about the penetration of the entire German people with National Socialist ideology.
(5) He informs the people about the accomplishments of the leadership of Party and State.

For the purpose of propaganda, use will be made of press, radio and film.

The following are subordinate to the Reich Director of Propaganda: the Chief-of-Staff and the Adjutant.

The fields of duty of the Reich Propaganda Executive are divided into five parts, each of which is dealt with by a separate office administration:
(1) Active Propaganda
(2) Film
(3) Radio
(4) Culture
(5) Liaison.

### The Chief-of-Staff:
The following come under the immediate control of the Chief-of-Staff:

(1) The Reich Ring for National Socialist Propaganda and National Enlightenment;
(2) the "Reich Motor Column Germany" with the auxiliary "Motor Column Bavaria";
(3) the office of the Reich Propaganda Executive;
(4) the section for Press Propaganda; and
(5) the section for Exhibitions and Trade Fairs.
It is the task of **the Reich Ring for National Socialist Propaganda and National Enlightenment** to safeguard the unified leadership through the Party of propaganda activities in all organisations and associated bodies. The competent Leading Functionary will detail one representative from the Propaganda Offices of each of the organisations and affiliated bodies to serve with the Reich Ring. In addition, there will be further representatives of certain offices of the National Executive, etc.

**The Reich Motor Column Germany** is designated to supply the latest technical aids necessary to the Party, its organisations, and affiliated bodies at all important rallies. Moreover, the Reich Motor Column Germany will look after demonstrations which, outside the Party, are of political importance to the state.

**The Office:** The Office is responsible to the Chief-of-Staff of the Reich Propaganda Executive for all questions in connection with financial and administrative problems of the Reich Propaganda Executive.

**The Section for Press Propaganda:** It is the task of the Section for Press Propaganda to deal with all propagandistic measures arising from the general activities of all Offices of the Reich Propaganda Executive; to edit them for publication; and to direct them via the competent channels to the National Socialist Party as well as the remaining Press.

**The Section for Exhibitions and Trade Fairs:** It is the task of the Section for Exhibitions and Trade Fairs to supervise from a propaganda point of view all exhibitions in which the Party proposes taking part.

### (1) Office for Active Propaganda
It is the task of Active Propaganda to organise the execution of all propaganda campaigns devolving upon it, from large-scale functions of gigantic proportions with their architectural arrange-

ment to functions of Groups or Bases.

This necessitates the organisation of propaga[nda] speakers of Movement, org[anis]ations, and affiliated bodies concentrated in Active P[ro]paganda.

Parallel with the contin[uous] analysis of topical political [ques]tions goes the penetration [of the] entire speaking staff with [news] of information and the des[patch] to all propagandists in the [form] of the monthly journal *Ou[r Will and our Way*.

Furthermore, the us[e of] speakers requires the desig[nation] distribution of suitable p[amphlets] and leaflets, as well as ca[reful] examination of reports of [meet]ings on the part of speaker[s by] the immediately relevant p[ropa]ganda executives.

An overall picture of p[ropa]ganda activities will e[merge] through statistical analysis [of] reports from Districts [and] Regions (with reference to p[ropa]ganda).

**The Section for P[ublic] Speaking:** The Section [for] Public Speaking, in its [sub]ordinate office "Organis[ation] of Speakers", includes [all] N.S.D.A.P. Reich, Regional [and] District speakers and, in add[ition,] all specialist speakers of org[anis]ations and affiliated bodies. [The] speaking staff of the o[verall] Movement will be continu[ally] supplied with material b[y the] Speakers' Information Bu[reau] and this will be the only spe[aking] and information material o[f the] Party.

The supply of Reich spe[akers,] Mobile Squad speakers o[f the] Reich Propaganda Executive [and] trainees for the Mobile S[quad] will be in the hands o[f the] Speakers' Bureau.

The Speakers' Tra[ining] Bureau, subordinate to the [Sec]tion, will take care not o[nly of] prospective political and sp[ecial]ist speakers, but also o[f the] continuous extension of [the] knowledge of all active spe[akers.] For this purpose a special "[Reich] Speakers' School" has bee[n cre]ated.

### The Party Speaker
Speakers are registered und[er the] following titles:
(1) Reich speakers
(2) Mobile Squad speakers Trainee Mobile Squad speakers
(3) Regional speakers
(4) District speakers
(5) Specialist speakers.
When advertising mee[tings]

ers' titles, as listed above,
be strictly adhered to.
ployment of speakers will be
d
v performance
v a veteran Party fighter's
s.
principle, a distinction will
made between political
cers and specialist speakers.
is the task of the political
er, by means of the spoken
at public demonstrations
meetings, to make the
an people familiar with
nal Socialist ideology,. as
as with the measures of the
nal Socialist Government.
present, only those Party
ers will be confirmed as
cal speakers who were mem-
of the N.S.D.A.P. before the
mption of Power, and who,
t time, had worked actively
eakers, as Political Leaders,
the S.A., the S.S., or the

future, only those Party
bers will be used as Reich
cers or Mobile Squad
ers who have spent a pro-
nary period as Trainee Mo-
quad speakers.

**ilm Office**
he task of the Film Office to
ge regular film shows which
serve to enlighten and edu-
the public and which are
ble for spreading National
list ideology.

**Radio Office**
he duty of the Radio Organis-
of the N.S.D.A.P. to exercise
tant control over the entire
an broadcasting network,
der to weld the development
e broadcasting network, as
s internal organisation, cul-
technical know-how, and
omics are concerned, to
nal Socialist principles.

**Bureau for Culture**
the task of the Bureau for
ure to stimulate, further, and
rvise all artistic activities in
rdance with the formative
ession of National Socialist
ogy, and to make use of them
e propaganda work of the
y, its organisations, and af-
ed bodies.
e following departments will
e that purpose:

**artment for Architecture:**
office will issue directives
nstructions concerning ques-
s of architectural design of
uments and edifices which
e the official activities of the
onal Socialist Movement.

**Department for Artistic Design:** This office will issue directives and instructions concerning all remaining questions of artistic design for symbols, artefacts, etc., which are used in the official activities of the National Socialist Movement.

It will also issue directives and instructions for the artistic setting of demonstrations and for the design, through the use of cultural means, of the content of National Socialist ceremonies.

**Department for Selection:** Among the tasks of this office are the examination and selection of musical and poetic works from the point of view of their suitability for demonstrations and functions of the National Socialist Movement.

**Department for Programme Design:** It is the purpose of this office to prepare specimen programmes for functions of the National Socialist Movement and for designing the setting of National Socialist demonstrations on the basis of the design tradition which has grown up during the Time of Struggle.

Its tasks include: the exclusion of unsuitable designs which unauthorised elements may attempt to introduce; the struggle against *Kitsch*; the preservation of National Socialist lucidity in the design of functions; the prevention of mystical and pseudo-religious falsifications of ideology through the tortuous constructions of cranky cult-apostles; the commissioning of qualified artists according to the directives above-mentioned; suitable personalities will be called in by the Reich Propaganda Director to be regular contributors to the Bureau for Culture, for instance, in order to deal with special areas; and the organisation of practical courses for the encouragement of singing, in order to recruit suitable personnel for artistic planning work in all units of the Movement.

The monthly publication of the Bureau for Culture, *Suggestions for Planning of National Socialist Functions*, will furnish Directors of Propaganda and Directors of Bureaux for Culture with the material required for their work. In this publication will also be found instructions commensurate with our attitude of mind and excluding the danger of intellectual shallowness, for the organisation of lecture evenings, Party meetings, Social evenings of the H.J., Social gatherings of the S.A. and S.S., etc. The unity of Party

and official bodies within the realm of culture has been safeguarded by means of liaison between the decision-making departments.

## 27. The Reich Press Director

**Tasks:** Incumbent upon the Reich Press Director are tasks connected with editorial policies. He has been charged with creating for the German people a Press which is committed and responsible to him, and which reflects life and events in the German community. Moreover, the Reich Press Director's functions include the necessary arrangements for the realisation of the demands concerning editorial policies made in Article 23 of the Programme of the N.S.D.A.P., and to supervise their execution. The latter is particularly relevant to the decree of April 25, 1935 "for the protection of the independence of newspaper publishing" and concerning "the closure of newspaper concerns for the purpose of elimination of unhealthy competition". Finally, he has been charged with the publishing of all writings of significance to the National Socialist Movement.

**Competence**
The Reich Press Director has been authorised by the Führer to take all measures necessary for the execution of his task. In detail, his competence comprises the following:
(1) the acknowledgement of periodical printed publications as official Party organs;
(2) decisions concerning the establishment of periodical printed publications, published by Party members, even insofar as they do not aspire to acknowledgement as official Party organs;
(3) (*a*) the issuing of general regulations for the entire publishing business to the whole press owned by Party members (unless, in individual cases, special instructions are issued by the Reich Press Director, his regulations are orders);
(*b*) decisions concerning all publishing problems of fundamental importance beyond the individual publishing concerns, insofar as he wishes to make the decision himself (in this case, publishing houses are obliged to submit these problems to the Reich Press Director before a final decision is made); and

(*c*) insight, at all times, into all official Party publishing firms and their entire economic organisation and management, as well as the right of exercising whatever influence he wishes.

This does not in any way affect the responsibility of individual publishers for the management of their business.
(4) All publishers and responsible editors of official Party publications are subordinate to the Reich Press Director. The appointment of a responsible editor may only take place with his approval. Should the Reich Press Director demand the dismissal of a responsible editor, this will have to be granted, if necessary, by means of immediate leave of absence.

△ *The armband of the Party Press Office's Chief Editor* (Hauptschriftleiter).

## The N.S.D.A.P. Foreign Office

(1) The Office for Foreign Affairs of the N.S.D.A.P. (A.P.A.) comprises two spheres of activity: one is internal, the other external.
(2) Internally, it is the task of the A.P.A. to carry the aims and aspirations of the National Socialist State, as far as foreign policies are concerned, into all offices and organisations of the Party.
(3) Externally, it is the task of the A.P.A. to spread information about the aims and essence of National Socialism, both abroad and among foreigners visiting Germany or staying in Germany as representatives of foreign newspapers, and in this way to awaken the understanding of other peoples for the vital necessities of the German people and to convince those foreign peoples that National Socialism wants peace for constructive development in Germany, as well as peace with all nations without, however, relinquishing the defence of its vital rights.

**Notes**
*Kitsch*: "worthless pretentiousness"
A.P.A. = *Aussenpolitisches Amt*

## 28. The N.S. Parliamentary Group

### (1) Tasks

Just as the N.S.D.A.P. embodies and moulds the political will of the German people, the National Socialist Parliamentary Party Group must embody and mould the political will of the people's representatives (the *Reichstag*). By means of the Parliamentary Party Group it is intended to ensure that, at all times, the *Reichstag* is guided by the overall interests of the nation; that it does not become subservient to special interests; and that it renders responsible and disciplined allegiance to National Socialist government. It is also the task of the Party Group to pass on to competent Party or Government departments applications and suggestions received from members of the public.

### (2) Responsibilities

The Parliamentary Party Group is represented and led by the Group Leader. The Group Leader is responsible for Group discipline. He must see to it that in their entire conduct members of the Parliamentary Party Group show themselves worthy of the honour of being members of the *Reichstag* and of the Parliamentary Party Group, and, in case of misdemeanours, he must take the necessary measures. According to Paragraph 35 of the Reich Electoral Law of July 3, 1934, the Group Leader has authority to exclude members of the *Reichstag* from the Parliamentary Party Group with the effect that, at the same time, they lose their seat in the *Reichstag*. The same law authorises him, on the occasion of a member retiring (through death, resignation, or expulsion), to appoint a replacement from among applicants officially nominated at the last election but not yet called up for service in the *Reichstag*. By virtue of Party Group discipline, the Group Leader may prohibit a member exercising his parliamentary mandate until further notice (e.g. if there should be Party Court proceedings pending against the member). It is incumbent upon the Group Leader to evaluate applications for the withdrawal of a member's Parliamentary immunity. As far as is necessary, he makes his decision in agreement with other Party Departments (e.g. the Deputy Führer, the Supreme Party Court) and Government Departments

(e.g. when the member holds an official post at the same time). During sessions of the *Reichstag*, the Leader of the Parliamentary Party Group is responsible for the introduction of bills in the *Reichstag*.

## 29. The Office for Racial Policy of the N.S.D.A.P.

(1) The Office for Racial Policy has the task of unifying and supervising all indoctrination and propaganda work in the field of population and racial policies. By the Deputy Führer's decree of November 17, 1933, this task has been assigned to the head of the Office for Racial Politics, for the N.S.D.A.P. and its organisations.

(2) Only the Office for Racial Policy is authorised to make arrangements about indoctrination and propaganda in connection with problems of racial and population policies, and to issue press releases.

In consequence, all press releases in the field of racial or population policies require, without exception, the prior approval of the Office for Racial Policy of the N.S.D.A.P.

(3) On the part of the N.S.D.A.P., the Office for Racial Policy deals with all measures concerning the field of population and racial policies, in co-operation with the competent authorities. Consequently, the office for Racial Policy will continuously take part in Government legislative measures in this field.

## 30. The National Association of German Families with Four or more Children

The National Association of German Families with Four or more Children includes families with at least four (three in the case of widows) legitimate children; families must be German, free from hereditary disease, Aryan, and living in respectable circumstances. Admission will take place upon application by persons wishing to join if the above conditions are fulfilled.

The National Association of German Families with Four or

more Children is a militant association, population-politically orientated, whose aim it is to take National Socialist population-political thinking to the people.

Its purpose is the preservation and encouragement of the healthy German Aryan family. Its public-spirited activities do not extend to welfare work nor do they include the conducting of a business organisation.

## 31. The Bureau for Kinship Research

(Established on October 15, 1934, as directed by the Deputy Führer)

### (1) Tasks

The Bureau for Kinship Research is responsible for the following:

(*a*) during proceedings before a Party Court, it will have to decide whether or not a person is of German origin and free from the taint of Jewish blood, in accordance with conditions for admission to the N.S.D.A.P. (i.e. by delivering an expert opinion). On the basis of these findings the Party Courts will decide what conclusions are to be drawn.

(*b*) It will have to issue character references for Political Directors in connection with their proof of origin *vis-à-vis* Party offices.

(*c*) It will issue certificates about German origin, confirming an applicant's German origin and freedom from the taint of Jewish or Negro blood, in accordance with conditions for admission to the N.S.D.A.P.

### (2) Organisation and Classification

The head of the Bureau for Kinship Research is a member of the Deputy Führer's staff. He is at the same time Director of the Reich Office for Kinship Research at the Reich, as well as the Prussian, Ministry of the Interior, where all matters connected with origin are dealt with on behalf of the Party.

The organisation of the Reich Office for Kinship Research is as follows:

**Sub-divisions:**
(1) Research Department (preparation of expert opin concerning pure-blooded ori
(2) Research Department (auxiliary expert opinions cerning racial and genetic fac naturalisations, half-breeds)
(3) Protection of literary m ments
(4) Drafting of law for Kin Office
(5) Records of persons of a races
(6) Ancestral Register
(7) Library
(8) Photographic service
(9) Finance, cashier, person
(10) Record office, adm tration, etc.

The special tasks of the R Office have been determine the stipulations of several (such as the Reich Civil Ser Law, the Reich Civil Law, ditions for admission to N.S.D.A.P., and others), and consist in the establishmen purity of blood in the A sense, the safeguarding of t sources which are most vita proof of origin, by means photographic reproduction parochial registers in dan and in co-operation with the tection of literary monume In addition, by going thro personal records in existe (Register Office records, p chial registers, Reside Records, Citizens' Regist court records, etc.), it will be position to show genealog connections.

Moreover, it will be respons for awakening and encoura the appreciation of the popula for the significance of family kinship connections within re-organisation of the Ger people.

## 32. The Party Investigation Committ for the Protection of N.S. Literature

I. The Investigation Commi is no censorship office, but office for protection against resistance to pseudo-Natic Socialist literature; it gu against the adulteration National Socialist ideas by authorised persons, and t commercial exploitation i manner which may mislead general public.

**S. literature in the
est sense**
includes N.S. literature
was created under the im-
te influence of the Move-
In accordance with
nal Socialist ideology, this
ure is exclusively political;

**erature which is
tially related to
nal Socialism**
ologically this extends over
siderable period and in-
literature about political
ht and demands within the
h of National Socialism.

reliable staff of lecturers
s the Party Investigation
ittee as advisers.

tings against which no ob-
ns have been raised during
igation will be included in
J.S. bibliography (N.S.B.).
airman of the Party Investi-
Board will communicate
al decision to the publisher,
basis of evaluation by the
ers. This decision will in-
the following statements:
om the point of view of the
cal intentions represented
Party, this publication is
ectionable. In that case, the
ation in question will re-
an endorsement to that
, that is to say, the following
ce may be printed in it:
e are no objections on the
f the N.S.D.A.P. against the
ation of this book."

ere are no objections
st the contents of a publi-
. However, it cannot be
ed among National
ist literature in the
est sense.

his case, however, there is
ossibility of the publication
listed in the N.S.B. under
ture essentially related to
nal Socialism. Such a publi-
will contain no endorse-
in the text.

he publication in its state-
is not in accordance with
rinciples of the N.S.D.A.P.;
therefore rejected. In such
there are the following
bilities:
e sale of the publication is
itted, but not in connection
National Socialism; and
e publication may not be
buted. The formal ruling is
d by the President of the
Chamber of Literature.

# 33. The Central Archives of the N.S.D.A.P.

All documents, printed publications, reports etc., which may be
of interest to future historians,
will be collected, examined and
dealt with scientifically by the
Central Archives.

The Central Archives are divided into the following departments:

## A. Historical Archives
The Historical Archives deal with
the historical material of the
N.S.D.A.P., its organisations, and
affiliated bodies: Forerunners,
foundation, early years, different
phases in the Struggle, symbols;
compilation of the entire history
of the Party. Moreover, the questions of Judaism, of Freemasonry,
of Political Catholicism, and of
Racialism from the historical
point of view.

## B. Newspaper and Periodical Archives
A collection of newspapers and
periodicals of all former parties
and organisations and of the N.S.
press, particularly the press
during the Time of the Struggle.

Linked up with those archives
are the Archives of the Reich
Press Director as well as the
Foreign Press Director. Com-
bined with the archives is an
information service for all Party
offices.

## C. Library
The Library collects all N.S.
literature, the literature of
Marxism, the Trade Unions, and
other organisations of the old
régime. The Library is available
for the use of all Party offices.

## D. German People and Culture Abroad
A collection of all events concerning German people and culture abroad, as well as the
National Socialist Movement
abroad.

## E. Department for Cultural History and Cultural and Educational Policy
The preparation of historically
sound pictorial and textual
material for cultural purposes of
the Party and for propaganda
purposes; card-indexing of all
areas of working activities, with
particular reference to the Nor-
dic-Indo-European culture group.

## F. Collections
Collection of pictures, documents etc., of famous men of the
Party and of men of the Movement fallen in action; the preservation of mementoes of parties
and organisations of the old régime as well as of gramophone
records of political personalities.

## Notes
Parliamentary Party Group =
*Reichstagsfraktion*.
Residents' Records: Every resident in Germany had to register
with the *Einwohnermeldeamt*,
where he had to report any change
of address.
Indo-European: This used to be
"Indo-Germanic", and is actually
called *indogermanisch* in the
text. However, today, the linguis-
tically correct expression is
"Indo-European".
fallen in action: This does *not*
refer to war service, but to the
many street battles fought
against Socialists, Communists,
and the Police.

# 34. Party Jurisdiction

**Its nature and tasks:**
While during the Time of Struggle
the hatred of all others made
sure that no one joined the
N.S.D.A.P. who was not infused
with honest belief in the Führer's
aims; while in those days a declaration of loyalty to the Party had
as a result nothing but disad-
vantages of every kind; after the
Assumption of Power, individual
place hunters and climbers believed that membership of the
Party would be of advantage to
them, and for that reason they
allowed themselves to become
members of the Party. That
natural process of selection, as
we knew it particularly during
the Time of Struggle of the Party
before the Assumption of Power,
will now have to be complemented
by an artificial one.

**To be a Party member means
to have greater duties**

To watch over this field of
duty, extended beyond general
civic limits, in severe cases to
remove the guilty person from
the Party; in addition, to keep
obviously unsuitable fellow citizens away from the Party; that is
the task which has been entrusted to the Party Jurisdiction.

Thus the Party Jurisdiction is
essentially in part responsible
for the continued existence of
the pure idea of National
Socialism. It does not only see to
it that an obviously unsuitable
Party member is swiftly removed

from the Party, but it is equally
important that everybody who
endeavours to co-operate with an
honest will and a believing heart
should be preserved for the Party.
Every incorrect assessment does
not only wrong the individual
affected by it, but to a much
greater degree the Party which
could not survive the loss of
genuine old National Socialists
while place hunters were being
encouraged. Thus a sum total of
wrong decisions would create
an inverse selection in the Party,
on account of which it would be
bound to perish.

**Structure**
The Party Jurisdiction has been
entrusted to:
(1) District Courts
(2) Regional Courts
(3) the Supreme Party Court.
Organisationally, individual
Party Courts belong to the area
of their Leading Functionary. In
matters of proceedings only,
Party Courts are independent
and not tied to orders by the
Leading Functionary for their
decisions.

**Internal Organisation:**
According to its size, each Party
Court has one or more divisions.
Each division is manned by a
chairman and two or more assessors. One of the assessors must
belong to the S.A. or another
organisation, and if the accused
is a leader in the S.A., he must
hold a service rank not lower
than that of the accused. The
same goes for all other organisations. District Courts are almost exclusively manned by lay-
men. As far as Regional Courts
and the Supreme Party Court are
concerned, professional judges
predominate. They are there to
ensure that the facts of the case
in which judgement will have
to be given in collaboration with
Party members who are proven
National Socialists, are elicited
incontestably. For judgement
corresponding to justice can only
be based upon correctly established facts.

A Party Judge must therefore
spare no effort in order to fulfil
the first part of his task, namely
the ascertainment of the true
facts; only after he has done so,
he may venture upon the second
part, the critical examination
of the facts he has ascertained.

**Different types of
proceeding:**
The following five types of proceedings are provided for in the

The insignia of the Party's senior judiciary. On the left of each of the three groups is an example of the braid worn on the collar and cap. The insignia themselves are collar patches. The piping around each patch indicates the status of the wearer's department: yellow for the Party's Supreme Judiciary (Oberstes Parteigericht), red for the Regional Judiciary (Gaugericht), and black for the District Judiciary (Kreisgericht).

Left-hand column, top to bottom: Senior Judge and Reich Leader; Court President; two different patches for a Judge; Assistant Judge, Department Leader; and Department Assistant. [All in the Party Supreme Judiciary.]

Right-hand column, top to bottom: President; Court President; Judge; Department Leader; and Department Assistant [all in the Regional Judiciary]; and President; Court President; Judge; and Department Assistant [all in the District Judiciary]. The last two were both Department Leaders in the Kreisgericht.

ctives for Party Courts.
Disciplinary proceedings
Litigious proceedings
Protection of Honour pro-
ings
Rejection proceedings (in con-
on with applications for
ssion to the Party)
Proceedings in connection
race and Freemasonry
ers.

**iplinary proceedings:**
Leading Functionary should
ider necessary the punish-
of a Party member whom
iously he had attempted to
mand by means of kind or
re words, he will apply to his
etent Party Court for per-
ion to start proceedings
1st that Party member in
r to bring about his punish-
or, should the man have
ed altogether unsuitable, his
lsion from the Party. The
y Court will consider whether
ttitude of the Party Member
e particular case cited by the
ing Functionary calls for
shment. If, on the other hand,
ncident of that kind should
e to the ears of the Party
t or a Party member, then
Party Court or the Party
ber will ask the Leading
ctionary to make an appli-
n for sentence to be passed.
refuses, an appeal to his
rordinate Leading Function-
will be indicated. In all cases,
ultimate decision rests with
Supreme Party Court.

**gious proceedings:**
second kind of proceeding
e the purpose of which is to
g about an amicable settle-
t of personal disputes and
greements among Party mem-
With these proceedings it is
ible for both the accused and
plaintiff to be punished,
ld the Party Court consider
both to be guilty. Here, in
icular, it is the foremost task
e Party Judge to intervene
on as squabbles come to his
ce, and to nip these in the
Rather than by punishment,
s through successful arbi-
on that the close fellowship
he Party may be restored,
cially in its smallest groups.
ctly as in the Time of Struggle
re the Assumption of Power,
Party will have to rely even
y upon appearing to the
ide world as a close-knit unit.
that reason, there is no room
he N.S.D.A.P. for personal
ngling and squabbling be-
en members.

**Protection of Honour proceedings:**
The third kind of proceeding is one which any Party member may initiate against himself, in order to restore his own honour and thus the common honour of the Party, should it have been injured through an assertion against or an attack upon him. Here the co-operation of the Leading Functionary is not called for. In these proceedings, a Party member has the possi-bility of knocking the bottom out of rumours spread about him, without knowing their author. It is therefore the most effective protection of his honour imagin-able for every Party member to apply for proceedings to be taken against himself.

**Rejection proceedings:**
Even though Party Courts are competent for Party members only, and do not deal with out-siders other than in their capacity as witnesses, there exists an es-sential exception to this rule. Party courts participate in the rejection of applications for ad-mission to the Party. A Leading Functionary may not reject any application for admission without the approval of the Party Court. In every case, the rejection of new applicants will take place with-out explanation through the com-petent Local Group Leader in agreement with the competent Local or District Court. In this way, any unreasonable rejections of fellow citizens who are valu-able to the Party will have been obviated.

**Proceedings in connection with Race and Freemasonry matters:**
One of the Party Judiciary's special tasks is the removal of those Party members who, be-cause of their non-Aryan origin or kinship, or because of member-ship of Lodges, should never have been admitted in the first place. In these cases, the Party Court will act without an application by the Leading Functionary. These proceedings which almost always appear to be deceptively simple on the surface, frequently conceal great hardships for those affected, which, however, will have to be borne for the sake of the purity of the Party in its capacity as a fighting nucleus of National Socialism within the German people. Because the Party is a sworn racial fellowship, it cannot tolerate that its members maintain links with

international organisations, such as Masonic Lodges. Because the Party preaches purity of blood to the people, it cannot itself tolerate members within its ranks who do not comply with these standards.

**Proceedings before State courts of law:**
In every walk of life, a Party member must put the interests of the Party community before his own. Personal friction among Party members should not take place, and even when it cannot be avoided, it must be dealt with within the Party. That is why it is a part of maintaining Party discipline for a Party member not unnecessarily to drag internal Party matters before State law courts by instituting civil actions. The same is valid for all other legal proceedings.

Not every trifle is suitable to be inflated into legal proceedings. Often a warning or a simple hint suffices to draw the attention of a Party member to his duties *vis-à-vis* the Party. Besides, a com-radely hint of that nature will not leave the person affected with a bitter feeling of condemnation.

It is the task not only of Court, chairman, and assessors, but also of all parties concerned, of the accused as well as of the respon-sible S.A. or S.S. Leader, of the witnesses as well as of the Leading Functionary, to contribute their share towards establishing the true facts and, in so doing, to-wards arriving at true justice in the interest of the Movement.

**The course of proceedings:**
A summons for the main hearing will be made under safeguard of an eight-day time limit upon proof of delivery of writ. The chief difference between the main hearing and proceedings at State courts of law is that proceedings at Party Courts are not con-ducted in public. This is necessary so as not to draw the attention of wide circles inside or even outside the Party to the investi-gation by means of public pro-ceedings. The Party is itself deeply interested in the pureness of its own ranks. It is, however, not interested in carrying out the purification in public. A record will be kept of the main hearing. The guide lines determining the course of the proceedings, ap-proved by the Führer, have been issued not because of the Party's delight in legal subtleties, but in order to provide, by adhering to prescribed proceedings, a guaran-tee for the justice of a verdict

which is based on the proceedings and on the investigations made during the proceedings. A just verdict, the be-all and end-all of all proceedings, can only be ar-rived at if, first of all, the facts are established correctly and afterwards the verdict is given correctly. The course of pro-ceedings prescribed in the guide lines, during and after the main hearing, is devised solely to this end.

**The main hearing:**
After the calling of all concerned, they will be cautioned to be silent, the witnesses, in addition, being reminded of the need to be truthful, after which the latter will be given leave. There will follow the reading of the opening statement, and subsequently the examination of the accused. In contrast to proceedings at regular courts of law, the accused, too, is obliged to tell the truth. Thus, to lie before a Party Court repre-sents a punishable offence for the accused also. Not included, however, under this head is the obvious freedom for every ac-cused to present the established facts in a light most favourable for himself.

Following the examination of the accused, the hearing of evi-dence will begin. Witnesses and experts will be called indi-vidually, one after the other, and examined. Non-appearance and unwarranted refusal to give evi-dence before the Party Court will be punished as lack of discipline.

After the hearing of evidence, permission to speak will be given first to the Leading Functionary and subsequently to the Leader responsible for the organisation in question, for the purpose of putting their point of view. Finally, the accused will make his concluding remarks.

**The decision:**
The Party Court will take its decision in secret session. This decision requires delivery in writing, even if it is announced publicly.

Whereas a State court of law is obliged to apply a number of legally defined factors to the individual case, Party Courts are not bound in this way. For them, the essential law is represented by the relevant regulations con-tained in the Articles of the Party, as well as by general commands and orders of the Führer. The absence of concise rules as to what actions will be considered dishonourable, and damaging to the Party, although it gives greater freedom–in comparison with State judges–to the Party judge in his assessment of each individual case, places upon him, at the same time, much greater responsibility to examine whether the case before him might not be a private matter, not in the least affecting the good of the Party, or a matter which might be dealt with disciplinarily by the organisation concerned. Only an action which is culpable, whether committed negligently or deliberately, is punishable. Incapacity alone, therefore, can never furnish grounds for prosecution by a Party Court.

Party Courts, with the exception of the Supreme Party Court in cases of complaints, do not impose punishment themselves, but make application for punishment by the competent Leading Functionary. Once it has become valid, he will have to act on the decision, that is to say, if he has not made use of his right of appeal in time. In matters of complaints, the Supreme Party Court will itself enact whatever measures it has decided upon. The fact that, in general, Party Courts lack executive power is accounted for, just as in Courts Martial, by the military organisation of the Party. The Leading Functionary is the supreme judicial authority of his competent Party Court.

### Penalties:

The following penalties have been laid down:

(1) Expulsion from the Party, if the Party Court is convinced that the accused, by his behaviour, has forfeited the right to remain in the N.S.D.A.P.

(2) Caution, if the Party Court is convinced that the accused, because of the behaviour laid to his charge, has not become unworthy of remaining in the Party. Over and above the caution, the Party Court may inflict the following additional penalties:

(a) Loss of ability to hold Party Office for not more than three years.

(b) Loss of right to carry a weapon for not more than 12 months.

(c) Loss of right to appear as a public speaker.

(3) Reprimand, if the Party Court is convinced that the misdemeanour of the accused and the significance of the action laid to his charge, are trivial.

(4) Fines, or Imprisonment have been statutorily provided; however, up to now, the Party Jurisdiction has not made use of this means of punishment.

The Party membership book which, during the course of proceedings, must be filed in the dossier, will be impounded on expulsion. Any caution or additional penalties will be entered in the membership book.

When meting out punishment, the personality of the accused in relation to the Party must be taken into consideration in addition to the circumstances of the individual case. As a rule, services to the Party during the Time of Struggle justify the granting of extenuating circumstances and thus preclude expulsion which on consideration of nothing but the facts of the case in question, might have appeared necessary. On the other hand, services to the Party, however great, are not sufficient exoneration if the individual case to be dealt with should obviously be not a single lapse but the product of a character defect.

### Future development of Party Jurisdiction:

Party Jurisdiction has grown together with the Party. Its precursors, the Committees for Investigation and Arbitration date back to the time of the foundation of the Party. In the same way, the future development of Party Jurisdiction will take place consciously from within the Party. Never will it be possible for an impression to be created that something alien is to be implanted into the Party. In their capacity as conscience of the Movement, Party Courts, in preserving the increased spheres of duty of Party members, will take care to see that the old fighting spirit will never be lost and that the Party will increasingly become the Order of the Best of the German People.

### Notes

a number of legally defined factors: In Britain and the United States, the law is administered by precedent, whereas in Germany it is laid down in sets of rules.

## 35. The S.A.

Whereas the Political Organisation of the N.S.D.A.P. must carry out the practical political leadership, the S.A., on the other hand, is the Party's instrument of training and education.

According to the Führer's directions at the Reich Party Rally of

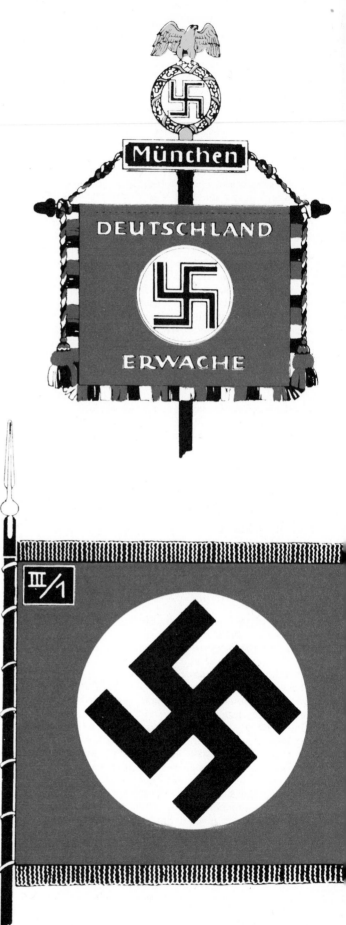

*Flags of the S.A. or* Sturmabteilung:
△ △ *The standard of the Munich Regiment.*
△ *The flag of the 1st* Sturm *(Company) of the* Leibstandarte, *Hitler's personal bodyguard.*

◄ *The* Standartenführer
*(Colonel) of* Standarte
*(Regiment) No. 5 "Horst
Wessel" service dress.*

prescribes its codes of action; it
is he who orders it into action.
On the Führer's behalf, a Chief-
of-Staff represents the S.A. as a
whole.

## Membership of the S.A.:

In principle, membership of the
S.A. is voluntary. However, it is
the Führer's will that every
German, from early childhood to
old age, should receive continuous education in a National
Socialist spirit.

In a National Socialist State
it is required, therefore, that once
a young German has joined the
S.A., he should devote himself,
body and soul, to it and to the
fulfilment of its tasks.

## Admission to the S.A.:

In principle, recruitment for the
S.A. will generally be made from
the H.J., and insofar as requirements cannot be supplied by the
H.J., by admission of other volunteers of German extraction who
fulfil the following conditions:
They must be:
(1) of irreproachable character
and willing, by dint of their
idealism and selflessness, to
identify themselves to the utmost
with the ideas of the Führer and
the tasks of the S.A.;
(2) able to prove Aryan descent
up to and including great-grand-
parents;
(3) worthy to be admitted to the
N.S.D.A.P.;
(4) physically suited to all demands by S.A. service (i.e. route
marches, physical training,
action in emergency service); and
(5) of unexceptionable reputation, with no previous conviction.
The procedure during ad-
mission is as follows:
To begin with, a volunteer will
report to the leader of the S.A.-
*Sturm* (Company) with headquarters in the volunteer's
quarter, his town, or his District.
Facing the *Sturm* Leader, he will
make the voluntary declaration
that he wishes to join the S.A. The
volunteer will then be registered
for examination by a selection
committee. This will establish the
applicant's physical fitness; it
will examine him from a genetic
point of view; it will examine his
*curriculum vitae* and his personal
documents, such as military and
work records, certificate of political conduct etc.; and evaluate his

▷ *An S.A. member of the* Gruppe "Hochland" *(Upper Bavaria and Schwabia) in sports kit with a javelin.*

appearance from a racial aspect.

On the decision of the Selection Committee depends the volunteer's admission as an S.A. trainee. After completion of a period of six months as a trainee (in exceptional cases a shorter period will be accepted) and after successful completion of a trainee examination, final admission as S.A. Man will take place. (In the case of men who are only conditionally suitable, the recruiting office will decide, in conjunction with the S.A. Doctor, whether there is a possibility of transfer to an S.A. Reserve Unit, or whether rejection will have to follow.

**Principles for promotion:**
S.A. Men who, according to their achievements and personality, have proved themselves as above average, may be promoted to Lance-Corporal after six months' service, and to Corporal after another six months. Further promotion to Troop Leader, Senior Troop Leader Section Leader, and Senior Section Leader will only be possible when, in the course of time, the S.A. Man has shown distinct qualities of leadership.

In particular, he must be able, according to the service rank in question, to weld together men of a Troop or a Section, to indoctrinate and train them to becoming excellent ideological (political) soldiers of the Führer, and to lead them, not only during peaceful parades and ceremonies, but also in action, in mortal combat. The demands made upon middle-ranking S.A. Leaders, *Sturm* Leaders, Senior *Sturm* Leaders, Chief *Sturm* Leaders, *Sturm* Unit Leaders, and Senior *Sturm* Unit Leaders, are based on the same principle as the demands which will have to be made on Troop Leaders and Section Leaders.

However, in all areas correspondingly higher and more demanding standards will, of course, have to be applied. Whoever would be appointed leader of a *Sturm*, or leader of a *Sturm* Unit, and accordingly promoted to a corresponding service rank, must, above all, have proved himself most convincingly at the front.

Training courses for leaders will take care of the appropriate extension of knowledge and of

practical ability. An examin⟨ation⟩ for *Sturm* Leaders or *Sturm* ⟨Unit⟩ Leaders will have to be ⟨one⟩ which will cover all areas o⟨f⟩ service. Last but not lea⟨st⟩ man's overall demeanour an⟨d⟩ general merits of his perso⟨n⟩ will carry considerable w⟨eight⟩ in his evaluation.

After prolonged activity ⟨as⟩ leader of units and on staf⟨f, as⟩ well as after completion o⟨f⟩ appropriate examinations, i⟨t will⟩ be possible for a middle ra⟨nking⟩ S.A. Leader to move up int⟨o the⟩ higher S.A. Leader Corps, w⟨hich⟩ comprises the service ran⟨ks of⟩ Standard Leader, Senior Le⟨ader,⟩ Brigade Leader, Group Le⟨ader⟩ and Senior Group Leader.

It is a matter of principle ⟨that,⟩ after the present state of ⟨tran⟩sition, every S.A. Leader ⟨will⟩ once again have to be a ⟨Party⟩ member, just as during the ⟨Time⟩ of Struggle.

The enhanced standing an⟨d the⟩ extended scope which are ⟨con⟩comitant with promotion or t⟨rans⟩fer to a higher service offic⟨e are⟩ meant to benefit not the pe⟨rson⟩ thus distinguished, but the ⟨S.A.⟩ and the Party.

**Notes**
S.A. *Sturm:* a *Sturm* is the c⟨ollec⟩tive term for a company of B⟨rown⟩ Shirts.
Lance-Corporal = *Rottenfüh⟨rer⟩*
Troop Leader = *Scharführe⟨r⟩*
Section Leader = *Truppfüh⟨rer⟩*
*Sturm* Unit Leaders = *St⟨urm⟩bannführer*. (A *Bann,* in ⟨the⟩ military sense, is a "unit"; ⟨it is⟩ likely that the Nazis derive⟨d the⟩ word from *Heerbann,* signif⟨ying⟩ "a body of vassals".)

**Resignation from the S.A.⟨:⟩**
Service in the S.A. is, and ⟨must⟩ always be, voluntary. Jus⟨t as⟩ when recruiting for the ⟨S.A.,⟩ there must be neither pro⟨mise⟩ of advantages nor pressure o⟨f any⟩ kind in order to persuade a ⟨man⟩ to join, the S.A. Man must ⟨have⟩ the opportunity of leaving ⟨the⟩ S.A. if he believes that he i⟨s no⟩ longer able to agree with the ⟨line⟩ taken by the S.A., or if he i⟨s no⟩ longer in a position to disch⟨arge⟩ fully the duties laid upon hi⟨m by⟩ dint of his being a member o⟨f the⟩ S.A. If there are honour⟨able⟩ grounds, the S.A. Man ma⟨y, at⟩ his own request, be "honour⟨ably⟩ discharged from the S.A.". Sh⟨ould⟩ he show lack of interest, or p⟨rove⟩ to be only a fellow trave⟨ller⟩ driven into the S.A. by capric⟨e⟩ or opportunist motives, ⟨"dis⟩charge from the S.A." will ⟨take⟩ place as an official meas⟨ure⟩

...uld he have become guilty of disciplinary, political, or pos-[...]y criminal, misdemeanours, competent disciplinary [...]rior may bring in a verdict of [...]manent and penal discharge [...] the S.A.". Should there be [...]us misdemeanours, the ver-[...]may be for "expulsion from [...]S.A.".

[...]sofar as the S.A. Man is, at [...] same time, a Party member, [...]manent and penal discharge [...] the S.A., as well as expulsion, [...] be reported forthwith to the [...]petent Party Court for a [...]sion as to whether a man thus [...]issed from the S.A. is still [...]thy to remain a member of the [...]y.

[...]ining of the S.A.:
[...]ional Socialism is governed [...]wo ideas, the idea of com-[...]ity and the idea of individu-[...]y. Particularly in the S.A., [...]relationship of individual and [...]munity to one another must [...] a form which is commensur-[...]with its task as instrument of [...]ic reinforcement within the [...]ulation. It is the aim of its [...]ning activities to enable S.A. [...]ders and S.A. Men to educate [...] widest circles possible in [...]ional Socialist ideology and [...]he physical hardening con-[...]ted with it.

[...] order to achieve uniform [...]ning, division into the follow-[...]three main groups has been [...]anged:
[...]ideological training
[...]general training
[...]operational service.
[...] the main, these groups com-[...]se the following individual [...]as:
[...](1) education and training [...]ed on the aims and teachings [...]he Führer, as formulated for [...]aspects of our life and National [...]ialist philosophy of life in [...]n Kampf and the Party Pro-[...]mme.
[...] the teaching of the history of [...] Germanic peoples and its [...]evance to the tasks of our [...]e.
[...] practice of the National [...]ialist doctrine of duty.
[...](1) Formation duty
[...]Physical culture
[...]Drill
[...]Field training
[...]Rifle practice
[...]Anti-gas and air raid defence [...]Service in special units (naval, [...]elligence, engineering, and [...]alry units).
[...](1) Parades and demon-[...]ations
[...]Contests and proficiency tests

◄ *A* Rottenführer *(Corporal) of the 100th Regiment of* Gruppe "Sachsen" *in service greatcoat.*

for the S.A. Sports Badge
(3) Security Service
(4) Home defence (emergency service, etc.).

**The S.A. Sports Badge:**
The new state demands a hard race with great powers of resistance. In addition to ideological indoctrination, we must demand combative training of the body by means of simple, useful and natural physical exercises.

In order to provide increased incentive and direction to youth's endeavours, I herewith renew the foundation for the entire S.A. and all its former formations of the
    S.A. SPORTS BADGE
which may be acquired, after completion of a training period conscientiously carried out, by taking a proficiency test.

In order to give conscious expression to the cultivation of a militant spirit in all parts of the German people, I furthermore decree that this S.A. Sports Badge may also be acquired and worn by those not belonging to the Movement, as long as racially and ideologically they conform to National Socialist requirements. The Chief-of-Staff will issue directives for the implementation of the above decree.
The Supreme S.A. Leader
(signed) Adolf Hitler

In the National Socialist State, the focus for every thought and every action is the Nation; within it, and in connection with it alone, the "I" and the "We" are decided. The National Socialist revolution comprises life in its entirety, giving us the lofty ethos of our idea of State, the brotherhood of the people, and the community of the people. And thus it consciously determines the Nation's new life. As for all areas of cultural life of the people, the motto of "Public Need Before Private Greed" holds good for sports too, and for physical culture in general. To do physical exercises is a serious obligation which the citizen has *vis-à-vis* the people.

It was reserved for our time, returning as it is to everything natural and, in so doing, to the purest sources of human life, to demand physical exercises for all fellow citizens. Today it is a matter of course that from his early days a child receives physical training and, in this way, is moulded to command greater vitality and efficiency. However, the Nation further demands a race which is hard, tough and strong. This vital demand has created a form of physical education which comprises not only the training of the body to fighting pitch, but also the ideological indoctrination of the mind. The tangible acknowledgement which may be gained in this connection is the

S.A. SPORTS BADGE.

It is called the S.A. Sports Badge–but that by no means signifies that only the S.A. may gain it; on the contrary, it is only because the thought of and the demand for physical and mental education of the body stems from the S.A.; because it was the S.A. which first carried out this kind of training, the spirit of which was created out of comradeship and the readiness to help each other, a spirit which must continue to live as such; that today the symbol of manly fighting-fitness still carries the honourable name of the S.A. And yet it is dedicated to the entire German youth, nay, over and above, to the entire German people.

The S.A. Sports Badge, in its clear and characteristic structure, embodies political education in a comradely spirit, and readiness for action in National Socialist Germany. It symbolises political indoctrination through the body, putting the Community before the Self. In addition to ideological training, all areas of sport and physical exercise have been utilised to help mould the National Socialist fighter. It is precisely here, in doing the exercises for the S.A. Sports Badge, in doing scouting exercises and nowhere else, that a German, whatever his age, may demonstrate to what degree he is capable of risking body and soul for any task set by the Führer; and what manly virtues, namely, discipline, courage, determination and a spirit of comradeship, he possesses. Any German, as long as he has completed his seventeenth year and complies with the general requirements laid down, may acquire the S.A. Sports Badge. The following are the general requirements: The would-be acquirer must be

**(1) eligible**, that is he must conform, racially and idelogically, to S.A. requirements;

**(2) able-bodied**, i.e. he must have been declared "capable of sports and marching activities" after a medical examination;

◀ *An* Obertruppführer *(Se Section Leader) of th Company of S.A. Regiment in ceremonial service d*

**(3) fully trained**, i.e. he be able to prove, accordin regulations, his training by r nised teachers of scouting cises (who must be holde teachers' certificates); and

**(4) fully examined**, i.e. training and proficiency tes quire authentication by r nised examiners. The acquis of the S.A. Sports Badge nec tates the passing of a profici test as termination of prepara training. This comprises t groups of exercises: physical cises, ground exercises, scouting exercises.

**Notes**

the history of the Germ peoples = *deutsch-völkische chichte*: a free rendering of untranslatable concept of the National Socialists and German National Party (*Deu Nationale Partei*).

scouting exercises = *Gelä sport*: Harrap's Standard Dict ary remarks that this ap "especially in the Nazi perio para-military training".

The physical exercises inclu the 100 metres, long jump, putting, and 3,000 metres. ground exercises included forced march, small bore shooting, and dummy gren throwing. Scouting exercises cluded map-reading, reconn sance, use of terrain, and sig ling, etc.

# 36. The S.A. Uniform

**I. General remarks**

(1) The service uniform is a d of honour. Whoever wears represents the Movement in lic. Therefore, his uniform m be neat and tidy, according regulations. If service unif is worn, it must always be service uniform. The wearin individual items of S.A. ser uniform together with civil dress, and conversely, wearing of individual items civilian dress (e.g. an overc together with S.A. service form, is prohibited. It is fitting for an S.A. Man, for stance, to appear in public w out head covering, without leather belt or in an open-nec shirt without a necktie.

(2) S.A. Leaders and S.A. Me S.A. service uniform must av acting in any way which may

△ A Marinesturmführer *(Naval Company Commander) of the 4th Company of S.A. Naval Regiment* (Marinestandarte) *No. 9 in service dress.*

△ A Marinescharführer *(Naval Sergeant) of the 3rd Company of S.A. Naval Regiment No. 52 in Naval S.A. greatcoat.*

Standartenführer *(Colonel) in charge of Regiment No. 16's medical services.*

Standartenführer *on the veterinary staff of the* Gruppe *"Hochland" group staff*

Standartenführer, *a chemist on the group staff of* Gruppe *"Franken" (in Bavaria)*

Sturmbannführer *(Major), a dentist of Regiment No. 222*

This page, left-hand columns: *S.A. specialist collar rank patches.*
This page, right-hand column: *S.A. epaulettes.*
Opposite page: *S.A. service collar rank patches.*

S.A. Mann *(Private) of the 2nd Company of Cavalry Regiment No. 25 of* Gruppe *"Berlin-Brandenburg"*

S.A. Mann *of the Signals Company of Regiment No. 32 of* Gruppe *"Thüringen"*

S.A. Mann *of the 15th (Pioneer) Company of Regiment No. 69 of* Gruppe *"Westmark" (on the Rhine)*

S.A. Mann *of the 5th Company of Naval Regiment No. 27*

Sturmführer *(Company Commander) on the staff of the* Reichsführerschule

Musikzugführer *(Bandmaster) of Regiment No. 100 of* Gruppe *"Sachsen" (Saxony)*

detrimental to the standing of the S.A. in public, such as eating and smoking in public places, lounging about with hands in trousers pockets, idly hanging about at street corners, especially at main thoroughfares, sitting about on park benches, walking in the street arm in arm with one's female companion, carrying a cane or an umbrella, pushing a perambulator, carrying a child on one's arm, etc.

(3) Every member of the S.A. *must* wear his service uniform on duty, and he *may* wear it off duty. Men applying for admission into the S.A. must be in possession of an S.A. service uniform by the time they are admitted, at the latest. Whoever wears his service uniform off duty is subject to S.A. regulations and to S.A. senior personnel, even though they may be in civilian dress themselves, as long as they are known to the S.A. Leader or S.A. Man in question, or prove their identity as senior personnel.

It is forbidden to wear S.A. service uniform in exercising one's civilian occupation as commercial traveller, street trader, newspaper vendor, etc., if in so doing the impression may be created that the S.A. service uniform was being worn for the purpose of obtaining personal gain.

Similarly, S.A. service uniform must not be worn in the exercise of occupations where the work process may result in soiling the service uniform, thus possibly affecting unfavourably the wearer's standing; or in the exercise of occupations which require the rendering of personal services to customers. The entire service uniform may be worn at all times in the exercise of one's occupation in public offices, schools, banks, etc.

(4) It is forbidden to appear in court wearing S.A. service uniform, or the S.A. Civilian Badge, whether as plaintiff, accused, witness, juryman, expert, assessor, etc.

(5) S.A. Leaders and S.A. Men in service uniform are, in principle, forbidden to frequent public restaurants after midnight. In the event of functions at public restaurants, at which members of the S.A. in S.A. service uniform take part, and which are planned to extend beyond midnight, exceptions are permissible. However, it is forbidden for members of the S.A. in S.A. service uniform to visit other restaurants after the function. The S.A. service

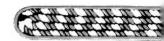

S.A. Mann *to* Obertruppführ... *(Senior Section Leader)*

Sturmführer *(Company Commander) to* Sturmhauptführer *(Captain*

Sturmbannführer *(Major) t* Standartenführer *(Colonel*

Oberführer *(Brigadier-Gener... to* Obergruppenführer *(Gener...*

Stabschef *(Chief-of-Staff)*

uniform demands the keeping... the midnight curfew.

(6) It is forbidden to col... money, or sell post-cards... badges while wearing S.A. serv... uniform, either in the street o... public restaurants. The Chief... Staff is the sole person authori... to grant exceptions to this ru...

(7) Unless exceptions are spec... cally granted, clothing for... members of the S.A. must... uniform in cut as well as... colour.

(8) The following are forbidd... visibly displayed watch chai... fobs, handkerchiefs in bre... pockets, etc.

(9) Only persons possessing va... S.A. passes, i.e. bearing auther... cation for the current month, ... permitted to wear S.A. serv... uniform, or the S.A. Civil... Badge with their civilian su... Applicants waiting to join... S.A. will wear the S.A. Civil... Badge with their civilian su...

Any S.A. Man unable to id... tify himself must be prepared... have his service uniform or... S.A. Civilian Badge taken aw... from him. In case of doubt, S... Leaders holding the rank ... *Sturm* Leader and above ... authorised to ask men weari...

### Description of different
iforms

ere are four kinds of service
iform:
Full Dress uniform
Battle dress
Sports dress
Evening dress.

### Full Dress Uniform con-
ts of:
Service cap with coloured
nd
Brown shirt
Epaulettes
Collar flash
Service rank badge
Service station badge
Necktie
Party badge (for Party mem-
rs only)
Armband
) Breeches
.) Footwear
) Leather belt with shoulder
ap
) Dagger with adjustable
ap.

### neral remarks concerning
ll dress uniform:
full dress uniform will be
rn on solemn occasions, such
parades in the presence of the
hrer, inspections by the Chief-
Staff, swearing-in ceremonies,
nsecration of colours, funeral
remonies, tattoos, etc.
Decoration clasp with decor-
ons as well as any other
corations, worn at the neck or
the chest, are part of regu-
tion full dress uniform.
In principle, the leather belt
th shoulder strap must always
worn with full dress uniform.
the office or in closed society
e dagger may be taken off.

### Battle Dress consists of:
Uniform cap with coloured
nd
Uniform jacket
Epaulettes
Collar flash

Mann *of the 32nd Company of
the* Leibstandarte *of* Gruppe
"Hochland"

Obertruppführer *(Warrant
Officer) of the 2nd Company
of Regiment No. 4 of* Gruppe
"Kurpfalz"

Standartenführer *(Colonel) of
Regiment No. 7 of* Gruppe
"Schlesien" *(Silesia)*

Sturmmann *(Lance-Corporal)
of the 33rd Company of
Regiment No. 1 of* Gruppe
"Nordsee" *(Oldenburg)*

Sturmführer *(2nd Lieutenant)
of the 3rd Company of* Jäger
*Regiment No. 3 (*"Ostmark"*)*

Oberführer *(Bdr.-Gen.) on the
staff of the S.A. high command*

Rottenführer *(Corporal) of the
13th Company of Regiment No. 2
of* Gruppe "Pommern"
*(Pomerania)*

Obersturmführer *(1st Lieutenant)
of the 4th Company of Regiment
No. 25 of* Gruppe "Niederrhein"

Brigadeführer *(Major-General)
in command of the 56th Brigade
of* Gruppe "Südwest"

Scharführer *(Sergeant) of the
1st Company of* Jäger *Regiment
No. 15 of* Gruppe "Ostmark"

Sturmhauptführer *(Captain) of
the 5th Company of Regiment
No. 5 of* Gruppe "Ostland"

Gruppenführer *(Lt.-Gen.) in
command of* Gruppe "Sachsen"

Oberscharführer *(Colour-
Sergeant) of the 21st Company
of Reserve Regiment No. 76 of*
Gruppe "Hansa"

Sturmbannführer *(Major) of
the 4th Battalion of Regiment
No. 8 of* Gruppe "Westfalen"

Obergruppenführer *(General) in
command of* Gruppe "Berlin-
Brandenburg"

Truppführer *(Sergeant-Major)
of the 24th Company of Regiment
No. 21 of* Gruppe "Franken"

Obersturmbannführer *(Lt.-Col.)
of the 3rd Battalion of Regiment
No. 9 (*"Berlin-Brandenburg"*)*

Stabschef *(Chief-of-Staff)*

(5) Service rank badge

(6) Service station badge

(7) Armband

(8) Brown shirt with turn-down collar and tie

(9) Party badge (for Party members only)

(10) Breeches

(11) Footwear

(12) Leather belt with shoulder strap

(13) Dagger with strap.

**General remarks concerning Battle Dress:**

(1) Battle dress will be worn on

(c) **Sports Dress consists of:**

(1) White sleeveless sports vest with badge

(2) Brown twill sports trousers

(3) Light-weight heelless sports shoes.

**General remarks concerning Sports Dress:**

Care must be taken to ensure uniform sports dress for any unit lined up for sports activities.

(d) **Evening Dress consists of:**

(1) Uniform cap with coloured band

all official and non-official occasions which do not require the wearing of full-dress uniform.

(2) Unless otherwise instructed, a small decoration clasp will be worn with battle dress.

(3) On as well as off duty, the leather belt with shoulder strap must always be worn in public with battle dress. In public places, theatres, and restaurants, the leather belt will be taken off. The dagger is retained by the wearer and will be fastened on the ring of the left-hand jacket pocket. In closed society and at the office the dagger may be taken off.

(4) The wearing of white shorts with battle dress is not permitted.

(2) Uniform jacket

(3) Epaulettes

(4) Collar flash

(5) Service rank badge

(6) Service station badge

(7) Armband

(8) Light-coloured shirt with brown tie

(9) Party badge (for Party members only)

(10) Long black trousers

(11) Black boots

(12) Dagger.

**General remarks concerning evening dress:**

(1) Unless special orders are issued in exceptional cases, evening dress is worn off-duty only.

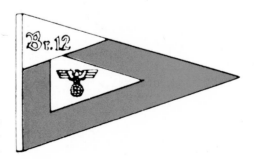

*S.A. flags:*
◁ ◁ *The standard of Motor Regiment No. 8*
△ ◁ *The Chief-of-Staff (Stabschef).*
◁ *The High Command (Oberste S.A.-Führung*
▽ ◁ Gruppe ''Hochland
▽ ▽ ◁ *The 12th Brigade*
△ △ ▷ *Regiment (Standarte) No. 231 and the 3rd Battalion (Sturmbann) of Regiment No. 134.*
△ ▷ *The 1st Naval Brigade (Marine-Brigade).*
▷ *Naval Regiment (Marine-Standarte) No. 130 and the 1st Naval Battalion (Marine-Sturmbann) of Naval Regiment No. 112.*
▽ ▷ *Cavalry Regiment (Reiter Standarte) No. 133.*
▽ ▽ ▷ *The pennant of 4th Cavalry Company (Reitersturm) of Cavalry Regiment No. 41.*

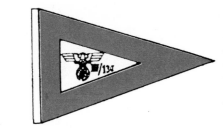

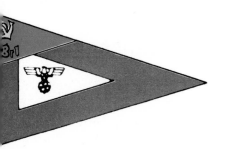

(2) Unless otherwise ordered, a small decoration clasp will be worn with evening dress.

(3) With evening dress, the dagger will be worn on the ring of the left-hand jacket pocket. In closed society and for dancing the dagger may be taken off.

(4) If an overcoat is worn with evening dress, the leather belt will be omitted. The dagger will be fastened on the ring of the left-hand overcoat pocket.

(*e*) Members of the *Hochland* Group may wear leather shorts, white stockings, and black or brown lace-up shoes with their brown shirts. In closed units, dress must be uniform.

(*f*) For the rifle Regiments One and Three of the *Hochland* Group, battle dress consists of mountain and ski cap, mountain and ski jacket, climbing and ski trousers, climbing boots. For full-dress uniform, brown shirt will replace mountain and ski jacket, and S.A. uniform cap the mountain and ski cap.

In summer, the above standards may wear shorts, white knee stockings, or *Wadenstutzen*, and black or brown shoes.

In closed formations, dress must be uniform.

In future, the phrase "S.A. brown" will describe the brown-green colour introduced in Ordinance I No. 1648, of November 3, 1933. The word "brown" will describe the colour prescribed before the above Ordinance came into force.

### Notes

fobs: the German word *Bierzipfel* describes "a ribbon worn on watch chain displaying the colours of a student club".

*Wadenstutzen*: These are the traditional knee stockings without feet, worn by Bavarians with their national dress.

## 37. The Hitler Youth

The leader of the entire H.J. is the Reich Youth Leader of the N.S.D.A.P. who is also Youth Leader of the German Reich.

Created during the Years of Struggle of the National Socialist Movement, and enlarged during the years of rebuilding of a new Reich, the Hitler Youth symbolises the expression of purpose and development of the new rising generation.

While that small handful of former Hitler Youths had fought for the realisation of the aims of National Socialism shoulder to shoulder with the fighters of the Movement, not conscious of any task other than that of holding their own in that struggle, the Hitler Youth, since the Assumption of Power, has accepted the great responsibility and the important task given to it by the Führer of introducing Germany's youth to National Socialist ideology. Once they are in the Hitler Youth, these young people, through constant political indoctrination, will be trained to become true and keen National Socialists. In addition to the work of political education which the Hitler Youth must carry out, there is also the task of the physical training of Germany's youth. On the one hand, they must be taught obedience and discipline; on the other hand, through the educational work of the H.J., the foundations of true leadership must be laid. Later on, when arrangements will be made for German boys and girls to join the Party, they must already be staunch National Socialists. The Hitler Youth must solve its tasks in close co-operation with home and school. Lofty and sacred is the trust left behind by those who fell in the struggle for this Reich, and likewise the obligation which the Hitler Youth bears because it bears the Führer's name.

The Hitler Youth is aware of its obligation; it realises its task, and it is going to carry it out because of its belief in the Führer and for the sake of the future of his Reich.

The Hitler Youth is responsible for all matters concerning youth. In co-operation with the respective Party Offices, it deals with all questions concerning youths aged between ten and eighteen, and girls between ten and twenty-one. However, it is not allowed to develop its own education policy.

Any German boy and any German girl who is Aryan and free from hereditary disease may join the H.J., the D.J., the B.D.M., or the J.M.

In general, new members will be enrolled only on the Führer's birthday, April 20 of each year. Similarly, the transfer of German *Jungvolk* (or of *Jungmädel*) to the Hitler Youth (or to the League of German Girls) will take place annually on April 20 for those who have reached the age of 14.

A solemn symbolical transfer of members of the H.J. or the B.D.M. to the Party and its organisations will take place an-

## Bannfahne

## Gefolgſchaftsfahne

nually on November 9.

Members of the Hitler Youth who have completed their 18th year will be admitted into the Party, as will members of the League of German Girls who have completed their 21st year, on the following conditions:

Boys must have been members of the Hitler Youth for four consecutive years before admission into the N.S.D.A.P.

Girls must have been members of the B.D.M. for four consecutive years before admission into the N.S.D.A.P.

It is a further condition for admission of boys and girls into the N.S.D.A.P. that they should have proved themselves reliable National Socialists by enthusiastically carrying out their service duties and by impeccable conduct on as well as off duty, so that there will be no doubt of their becoming valuable members of the N.S.D.A.P. after admission.

Enrolment of individual boys and girls will have to take place by means of the usual correctly completed enrolment forms. Applications for admission will have to be sent to the Central Executive through official channels–that is to say via Local Groups, Bases, or Regions.

Together with the application for admission, a certificate issued by the competent Hitler Youth Unit Leader or the Junior Woman Regional Leader, confirming membership of the relevant organisations as well as satisfactory conduct to date, must be submitted. No admission fees will have to be paid by members of either the Hitler Youth or the League of German Girls.

It is the duty of all offices to submit only application forms of boys and girls who have al-

ready completed their 18th or 21st year.

Applications for admission may be submitted to the Central Executive throughout the year, as long as the member of the Hitler Youth or the League of German Girls has completed his or her 18th or 21st year, and as long as the conditions outlined above apply.

According to regulations, the day of admission will be determined exclusively by the Central Executive. The day of admission will be the first day of the month in which the application has been received by the Central Executive. Thus the day of application is not the day of admission. Similarly, November 9 is not the day of admission. What happens on November 9 is simply a solemn symbolic act in which all those members of the Hitler Youth and of the German Girls' Organisation who have, up to that time, reached the age of 18 or 21, take part.

Lawful admission into the N.S.D.A.P. will be implemented according to an administrative decree of the Central Executive and will have taken legal effect only after the handing over of the membership card issued by the Central Executive.

From the point of view of organisation and discipline the Hitler Youth is independent. However, it is a matter of course that Leading Functionaries may exercise the right of supervision.

### Personnel Office:

The activities of the Personnel Office comprise two major tasks:
(1) selection of the most able comrades, and
(2) elimination of harmful elements.

### (1) Selection of the most able comrades:

The selection of the best members of the Hitler Youth for the purpose of forming the leadership of the future is of vital importance for the development both of Hitler Youth and Party. The principles of selection are guided by the following criteria:

A member of the Hitler Youth must display qualities of leadership which will enable him to lead not only during his limited time of activity in the Hitler Youth, but which, over and above this, destine him in years to come for greater responsibilities in Party and State. Hence follows the necessity of carrying out the selection of leaders with the greatest possible care. With the increased responsibility of the Hitler Youth towards the future of our people, the standard applied to the young leader with regard to his ideological reliability, his character as well as his physical and mental alertness, has become steadily more demanding. Appointments of *Sturm* Unit Leaders and Junior *Sturm* Unit Leaders will take place only after careful examination by the Reich Youth Executive. In addition, lower-ranking leaders are subject to strict control through the Personnel Department of the Reich Youth Executive. Only he whose bearing reflects an impeccable character, who has proved himself as a National Socialist, who, on duty, during hiking expeditions, and in camp, has shown himself the best among his comrades, and who fulfills certain mental and physical demands, only he may be confirmed as a leader.

These severe conditions for selection are effective for lower-

ranking leaders up to Tⁱ Leaders who are confirmed by Area Personnel Department.

Unit Leaders, the following ditions have been laid down:
(1) Successful activity as le of smaller units for a numbe years
(2) Completion of compul labour and national service
(3) Successful attendance Reich School for Youth Lea or the Leaders' Academy of Hitler Youth
(4) Fulfilment of conditions the H.J. Proficiency Badge
(5) Successfully completed sc or vocational education
(6) Proof of Aryan origin
(7) Proof of freedom from her tary disease.

By analogy, these conditi are valid for all other male female leaders. The aim of selection is the formation leader corps composed of most outstanding young Germ from all walks of life, and wh one day, will take over smoo the leadership of Party and St

### (2) Elimination of harmful elements:

Any member harmful to the c munity will be expelled from Hitler Youth through reg expulsion proceedings. At same time, care will be take see that this fellow citizen be kept away from all Yc leader and Youth education wo and, in severe cases, from greater responsibilities in P and State.

In addition to this most se punishment there exist sev punishments intended to the young comrade an op tunity of showing his ear endeavour to fulfil the conditi expected from a member of

## Jungbannfahne

## Fähnleinfahne

er Youth.

opposite page: *Flags of the* tlerjugend *or Hitler Youth.* the left is that of the 33rd riment or Bann, *a unit some* 00 strong, and on the right t of the 2nd Company of the 86th Gefolgschaft. s page: *Flags of the* Deutsches ngvolk *or German Youth. On* the left is that of the 1st pany of the 1st Regiment or ngbann, *and on the right that of the 1st Squad or* nlein *of the 150th Regiment.* he Fähnlein *was 150-boys strong.*

itler Youth jurisdiction is d upon the terms of reference he Supreme Party Court. ever, taking into account character of a youth organis- n, it must, in its assessment nisdemeanours, look upon ishment as a corrective sure to a far greater degree would be possible in an t organisation.

es

= *Hitler-Jugend* (Hitler th)

M. = *Bund Deutscher Mädel* gue of German Girls)

= *Deutsches Jungvolk*

= *Jungmädel*

### ce for Ideological octrination:

greement with, and according nstructions from the repre- ative of the Führer for the rvision of all spiritual and logical education in the D.A.P., this office directs and rvises the entire work of ctrination in the Hitler th and its junior section, the ung Folk" (*Jungvolk*), of the gue of German Girls and its junior section, the "Young Girls" (*Jungmädel*). The work of this office is sub-divided, as fol- lows:

(1) Indoctrination of leaders
(2) Indoctrination of units
(3) Schools for leaders
(4) Department responsible for literature
(5) Ideological supervision
(6) Direction of seminar for H.J. Leaders at the College for Political Studies.

Special Indoctrination Depart- ments working according to in- structions from the Reich Youth Executive have been assigned to the staffs of all areas. Indoctrin- ation work in the smallest units will be carried out by Formation Leaders.

All indoctrination material will be distributed free to all units in the Reich.

### Office for Physical Training:

It is the aim of Hitler Youth Physical Training that every German boy should acquire a basic knowledge of physical exer- cises, air rifle and small-bore shooting, and of scouting exer- cises. These activities go side by side with systematic training of every German girl by means of physical culture. To include every boy and every girl in this scheme of physical training, and to lead German youth in its entirety towards a systematic and steady increase in their physical pro- ficiency, is a vital task of the Hitler Youth's physical training. Another important task consists in creating for all young people in town and country oppor- tunities for and forms of exercise which will ensure the systematic physical training of all young Germans. Moreover, the Hitler Youth must create healthy and efficient future soldiers for the army. For that reason, one of its tasks is the training of prospective personnel for the special weapons unit of the armed forces. This training takes place in the special units of the Hitler Youth.

The entire implementation of this work is in the hands of the Office for Physical Training of the Reich Youth Executive. This office is sub-divided into three main columns:

(1) General training
(2) Special training
(3) B.D.M. physical training.

### Office for Cultural Activities:

Early attempts by the Hitler Youth to organise cultural ac- tivities have developed into the steadily increasing readiness of German youth to come face to face with all cultural values. What is most essential for the Hitler Youth is

### Vitality.

And thus it is not surprising to learn that it is song, as well as musical activities altogether, that is most popular and most as- siduously practised among mem- bers of the Hitler Youth. In the foreground of our cultural work can be found activities such as the organising of ceremonial oc- casions, morning assemblies, parents' evenings, producing plays, handicrafts, the making of posters, book jackets, pictures for the hostels, and building and furnishing hostels.

We realise that only by daily uninterrupted detailed work in all cultural matters will we be in a position one day to produce an achievement which will seize the imagination of German youth and imprint upon it the stamp of a coherent cultural purpose. Out of the radio work of the Hitler Youth numerous works and, at the same time, ideas have emerged which have become trend-setting for the continuation of our cul- tural work. Out of that work was created the "workshop of young Hitler Youth artists", which is not a new and self-sufficient or- ganisation, but which, on the contrary, joins together and com- mits all creative forces in order to bring to German youth new works and values as their heritage.

The Hitler Youth knows that it will be able to solve these cultural problems only if, on the one hand it includes German youth as a whole, and, on the other hand, it works together with all organisations of the Movement. For that reason, it strives particularly hard to keep in constant touch and work hand in hand with the S.A., the S.S., the N.S.K.K., the Labour Service, the N.S. Association "Strength through Joy", the Reich Propa- ganda Executive, the Reich Agri- cultural Board, and others.

### The Legal Office:

It is the task of the Legal Office of the Reich Youth Executive to deal uniformly with all legal interests of the Hitler Youth (including the B.D.M., D.J., and J.M.).

Thus it is incumbent upon the Legal Office to conduct a legal advisory service for the leader- ship and also to deal with the legal aspects of a large variety of matters concerning all offices of the Reich Youth Executive. Par- ticular mention should be made of legal actions which take place in close consultation with the Reich Legal Department of the N.S.D.A.P.

Further tasks arise out of the great demands made upon the

H.J. If the H.J. is to include youth as a whole and, at the same time, take charge of each individual member and of all his actions, then, in special cases, the young person must be afforded legal protection. In more important cases, this will be arranged directly through the Legal Office, whereas in cases of minor importance the legal expert of the unit in question will be called in.

Out of the character of the H.J. as an élite organisation arises its duty to pay close attention to the strictest purity among its ranks. In this connection, the Legal Office will help by putting at the disposal of the Personnel Office its legal experts for the purpose of interrogations, and for supervision in the case of court proceedings.

To this extent, the sphere of activities of the Legal Office does not differ materially from that of similar offices of other organisations. But as the significance and the tasks of the H.J. as such are unique and cannot be compared to those of any other organisation, the activities of the Legal Office must not be limited to such laborious details. In the Third Reich, youth has been given an area of tasks and responsibilities of its own. The Legal Office must co-operate in the development of a whole series of new laws concerning different aspects of youth care.

### The Broadcasting Department:

The Broadcasting Department of the Reich Youth Executive has been established as the centre for all German youth broadcasting activities.

In May 1933 the H.J. began its work in various German broadcasting centres and was in a position, during that year, to install specialists in charge of Hitler Youth broadcasting at all stations. Within the Reich Broadcasting Executive the post of a representative of the Reich Youth Leader was created, and the direction of all H.J. broadcasting activities is incumbent upon him. Today, at every broadcasting station, there are radio drama groups whose task is not only the creation of broadcasts, but also the organisation of active borderland work which receives the greatest possible radio support.

H.J. broadcasting is, in addition, responsible for spreading among the German people the treasury of folk songs accumulated by the H.J. Moreover,

Kameradschafts-
führer *(250th* Bann,
Gefolgschaft *1)*

Bannführer *of the
22nd* Bann

Gebietsführer

Obergebietsführer
*(Department Leader
in the Reich Youth
Leadership)*

Stabsführer *(highest
rank in the H.J.)*

Scharführer *(on the
staff of* Gebiet *4)*

Unterbannführer
*(on the staff of the
Reich Youth
Leadership)*

Oberbannführer
*(on the staff of
a Gebiet)*

Oberbannführer
*(on the staff of
the Reich Youth
Leadership)*

broadcasting has become a[n] ...tive cultural source.

In closest co-operation ... the Office for Ideological In... trination within the R.J.F., ... Broadcasting Department ... ates the weekly "Hour of ... Young Nation", which is ... centrepiece of Social Even... arranged by the Hitler Yout... particular, the Broadcasting ... fice takes part in all major ... paigns organised by the H.J. ... for instance, the Reich Vocati... Competition, the Drive for ... Hostels, or the H.J. Su... Camp.

With regard to listeners, ... Broadcasting Department of ... R.J.F. carries out prelimi... work for the safeguarding ... communal reception, by m... of an organisation specially ... ated for this particular pur... namely the H.J. Broadca... Wardens Organisation. Radi... ceivers obtained through ... Radio Set Supply Campaign ... be installed and serviced by ... Radio Wardens. They rec... their training and educatio... the Reich Radio School ... Göttingen, where there are w... shops and laboratories suppl... every device necessary for ... class technical training. Y... amateur radio operators who ... also members of the H.J. Br... casting Organisation are tra... in special courses. After ta... an examination set by ... D.A.S.D. and the German P... Authority, they will receive ... operator's licence which per... the operation of a short-w... transmitter. There are radio ... gineering groups attached ... many area headquarters w... are employed in tackling a l... variety of radio enginee... tasks.

### The Youth Hostelling Offic...

The Youth Hostelling O... which is connected with ... Executive of the Reich Ass... ation of German Youth Ho... by sharing some of its staff, ... the task of acting in an ... cational capacity by propaga... the idea of hiking as well as y... hostelling among young ... mans.

The Office organises h... which bring together boys ... girls from all parts of the R... and contribute towards level... regional differences by brin... together people from diffe... regions. The activities of ... Office support the work of ... German Youth Hostels As... ation which has established

ther 2,000 youth hostels all
· Germany. These youth hos-
·serve as quarters for the H.J.
·in addition are used by wider
·es of the Party for the purpose
·holding training courses.
·ugh international agree-
·ts with 20 Youth Hostels
·ociations all over the world,
· youth hostels are open to
·igners and may be used by
·n, just as youth hostels abroad
· at the disposal of young
·nans. By this means a be-
·ing has been made towards
·lowship of young people and
· towards the understanding
·outh beyond the frontiers of
·r own countries.

**·ce for Youth
·anisations:**
·J.V. includes two major fields
·tivity.

·rst: in collaboration with the
·ial departments in existence
· this purpose, all manifes-
·ns of opposition in the field
·outh work will be observed
· suitably interpreted. Simi-
·y, any incidents between the
· and other youth groups will
·ealt with.

·cond: the Office acts as Police
·son Office. With the help of
·ial Police organs, all mis-
·eanours of a criminal charac-
·which, after all, are unavoid-
·in an organisation as large
·he H.J., will be dealt with.
·vidual units of the Hitler
·th will be watched to as-
·ain whether they are, in fact,
·oving all criminal elements
·their ranks, and whether
·· are taking the measures
·essary for reducing to a mini-
·n misdemeanours of a crim-
·nature.

·the Police Liaison Office,
·ral records will be kept about
·ain misdemeanours, and these
· not only provide a survey,
· also render impossible the
·rgence of certain criminal
·ients in different districts.
·causes of crimes which young
·ile are most likely to commit
· be especially investigated,
·general guide-lines for their
··ention will be sought.

·addition, the Office for Youth
·anisations is responsible for
· supervision of the Hitler
·th Patrol Service which is
·g built up throughout the
··h and which is to supervise
· behaviour in public of the
·er Youth.

·l tasks of the Office for Youth
·anisations will be carried out
··o-operation with Party and
·e offices, such as the Secret

*For* Landjahr
*service (The*
Landjahr *was a*
*year's compulsory*
*service on the land)*

Gefolgschaftsführer
*of a Flying* Gefolg-
schaft *in the 250th*
Bann

Bannführer *(as*
*Financial*
*Administrator in*
*a Gebiet)*

Hauptarzt *(Senior*
*Doctor)*

Hilfsapotheker
*(Assistant Chemist)*

*Epaulettes of the* Hitlerjugend. *This was run on military lines, and*
*before the war its organisation was as follows: the smallest unit*
*was the* Kameradschaft *of 15 boys, under a* Kameradschaftsführer;
*two to four of these made up a* Schar, *under a* Scharführer; *two*
*to four* Scharen *made up a* Gefolgschaft, *under a* Gefolgschaftsführer; *three to five* Gefolgschaften *made up an* Unterbann, *under*
*an* Unterbannführer; *four to eight* Unterbanne *made up a* Bann,
*under a* Bannführer; *and 10 to 30* Banne *made up a* Gebiet, *under*
*a* Gebietsführer. *This was the highest level at which H.J.*
*activities took place, but on the administrative level there was*
*the* Obergebiet, *led by an* Obergebietsführer, *to co-ordinate*
*the activities of four to six* Gebiete.

State Police, the S.D., the Reich
Leader of the S.S., the Reich
Minister for Church Affairs, and
other relevant bodies.

**The Frontier and Foreign
Office:**
The tasks of the Frontier and
Foreign Office are as follows:
(1) to deal with all immediate
youth problems in the area of
frontier and foreign work, in
co-operation with the Party and
State political offices working in
this field;
(2) to indoctrinate all young
people in the spirit of National
Socialist work for and knowledge
of our national heritage and the
foreign policies of the Third
Reich. It is the aim of this indoctrination one day to bring
about the awakening of our people
to the sensitivity and instinct
required for these matters;
(3) to look after the borderlands
and to take care of frontier and
foreign travel.

Out of these tasks and within
this wide framework arises the
organisation of work in the Reich
Youth Executive's Frontier and
Foreign Office.

It consists of four main political
sections:
(1) Ethnical German Section;
(2) Foreign Section;
(3) Area 26: Abroad of the Hitler
Youth;
(4) Colonial work.

The activities of these main
political sections are supported
by two further sections:
(5) Hiking Office;
(6) Foreign Press Office; in addition, from the point of view of
indoctrination, they are carried
down to the most subordinate
units of the Hitler Youth, the
Young Folk and the League of
German Girls through Section 7:
G.A. Indoctrination.

The following aspects of the
G.A.'s practical work should be
mentioned: The holding of
ethnical-German indoctrination
conferences; work in the borderlands through cultural and social
development of borderland youth;
camps of German and French or
English young people; German/
Polish exchange radio programmes; socio-political discussions with foreign youth
leaders; and, above all, constant
care of foreign visitors in
Germany.

**The Langemarck Section:**
On November 11, 1934, the day
on which, 20 years earlier,
Germany's youth from all sectors
of the people had charged and

A Stammführer *of the D.J. or*
Deutsches Jungvolk *in winter
service dress.*

A Jungzugführer *(Youth Troop
Leader) in summer service dress
with drum.*

A Jungbannführer *(Youth*
Deutsches Jungvolk *in winter
service dress.*

n Untergauführerin *(Deputy Gau Leader) of the B.D.M. in winter costume.*

A Jungmädel *(Young Girl) of the B.D.M. in standard summer costume.*

*An* Untergauführerin *of the B.D.M. in standard summer costume.*

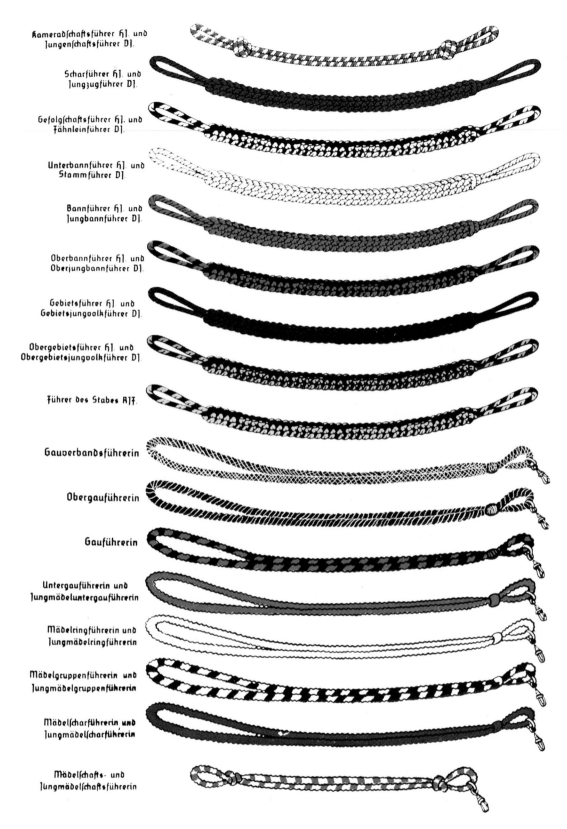

Kameradschaftsführer HJ. und
Jungenschaftsführer DJ.

Scharführer HJ. und
Jungzugführer DJ.

Gefolgschaftsführer HJ. und
Fähnleinführer DJ.

Unterbannführer HJ. und
Stammführer DJ.

Bannführer HJ. und
Jungbannführer DJ.

Oberbannführer HJ. und
Oberjungbannführer DJ.

Gebietsführer HJ. und
Gebietsjungvolkführer DJ.

Obergebietsführer HJ. und
Obergebietsjungvolkführer DJ.

Führer des Stabes RJF.

Gauverbandsführerin

Obergauführerin

Gauführerin

Untergauführerin und
Jungmädeluntergauführerin

Mädelringführerin und
Jungmädelringführerin

Mädelgruppenführerin und
Jungmädelgruppenführerin

Mädelscharführerin und
Jungmädelscharführerin

Mädelschafts- und
Jungmädelschaftsführerin

Kraftwagenstander
für Stabsführer RJ

Kraftwagenstander
für Amtsleiter der R

Kraftwagenstander
für Führer der Gebi

Kraftwagenstander
für Führer eines Bann

△ △ Top nine rows: *Leader lanyards of the* Hitlerjugend *and* Deutsches Jungvolk, *ranging from that of a* Kameradschaftsführer *of the H.J. and a* Jungenschaftsführer *of the D.J. to that of the* Stabsführer *of the* Reichsjugendführung.

△ Bottom eight rows: *Leader lanyards of the* Bund Deutscher Mädel *and* Jungmädel, *ranging from that of the* Gauverbandsführerin *to that of a* Mädelschaftsführerin *of the B.D.M. and a* Jungmädelschaftsführerin *of the J.M.*

▷ *Car pennants of the H.J. From top to bottom these are the pennants of the* Stabsführer *of the* Reichsjugendführung *(R.J.F.), an* Amtsleiter *(Department Leader) of the R.J.F., the* Gebietsführer *of Gebiet No. 20 "Württemberg", and the* Bannführer *of the 193rd Bann "Neustettin".*
Opposite page, top to bottom: *the obverse* (Vorderseite) *and reverse* (Rückseite) *of the D.J. Leader of Gebiet No. 20, the B.D.M. Leader of Obergau No. 25 "Pfalz-Saar", the obverse and reverse of a J.M. Leader in the same Obergau, and the* Reichsjugendführung *and* Gebiet *staff car pennant.*

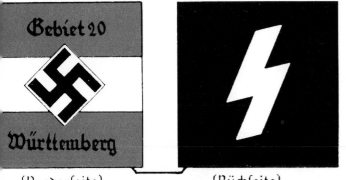

(Vorderseite)    (Rückseite)

aftwagenstander für Führer des DJ. im Gebiet

Kraftwagenstander
für die Führerin
eines Obergaues

(Vorderseite)    (Rückseite)

aftwagenstander für die Führerin der Jungmädel
im Obergau

Wimpel für den Stab
der RJF. und die Gebietsstäbe

died at Langemarck, the Reich Youth Leader took charge of Langemarck work for German youth in its entirety and established the "Langemarck Section".

Its work comprises the following tasks:

(1) to honour our heroes by showing respect and reverence for their sacrifices;

(2) for the heritage of our front line soldiers to be received and faithfully administered by Germany's youth who, standing shoulder to shoulder with living front-line soldiers, inspired as were those who died before them, must in turn be inspired to perform similar deeds and achievements for Germany.

(3) In serving the community, the will to emulate the spirit of our Langemarck comrades must be placed first and foremost as the loftiest fulfilment of genuine and true National Socialism.

**Notes**

R.J.F.: *Reichsjugendführung* = Reich Youth Executive

D.A.S.D.: I have been unable to ascertain the exact meaning of this abbreviation, but it probably stands for: *Deutscher Amateur-Sender Dienst* = German Amateur Radio Operators' Service.

J.V.: *Jugendverbände* = Youth Organisations

Secret State Police = *Geheime Staatspolizei* or Gestapo

S.D.: *Sicherheitsdienst* = Security Service

Area 26: Abroad: It must be assumed that areas 1–25 represent the German Reich.

G.A.: *Grenz- und Auslandsamt* = Frontier and Foreign Office

Langemarck: On the Ypres front in 1914 a unit of German students advanced against the British with arms linked and singing, and was cut to pieces by British rifle and machine gun fire.

# 38. The S.S.

**Leadership:**

The *Schutzstaffel*, an independent unit of the Party, is led by the *Reichsführer*-S.S.

**Tasks:**

The first and foremost task of the S.S. is to take care of the protection of the Führer.

By order of the Führer, the scope of the S.S. has been enlarged to include the country's internal security.

**Selection of Members:**

In order to carry out these tasks,

a fighting force, uniform, closely-knit, and ideologically dedicated to one another, has been created whose fighters are selected from among the best of Aryan stock.

The realisation of the importance of *Blut und Boden* is a directive in the selection for the *Schutzstaffel*. Every member of the S.S. has got to be permeated with sense and essence of the National Socialist Movement. Ideologically and physically he will receive exemplary training so that individually or with his unit he may be sent into action successfully in the determined fight for National Socialist ideology. Only racially outstanding Germans are suitable for this combat. Therefore it is necessary for a continuous process of selection to be carried out among members of the *Schutzstaffel*, first roughly and then with ever increasing care.

However, this selection is not only confined to the men, for its purpose is the preservation of a pure-bred race. Therefore every S.S. Man is required to marry only a racially compatible woman. From year to year, demands for keeping the S.S. untainted are becoming more exacting.

Loyalty and honour, obedience and valour determine the S.S. Man's actions. His weapon bears the inscription awarded by the Führer: "Loyalty is my Honour!" Both those virtues are inextricably joined together. Whoever transgresses against them is no longer worthy of being a member of the S.S.

Unconditional obedience is demanded. It arises out of the conviction that National Socialist ideology has got to rule. Whoever possesses it and supports it passionately will, of his own free will, submit to compulsory obedience. For that reason, an S.S. Man is ready to execute blindly every order coming from the Führer or given by one of his own superiors, even if it demands of him the greatest sacrifice.

To an S.S. Man, valour is the highest manly virtue in the struggle for his ideology.

Openly and mercilessly he fights the Reich's most dangerous enemies: Jews, Freemasons, Jesuits, and Political Clergy.

At the same time, by his example he will woo and convince those who are weak and wavering and who have not yet been able to fight their way through to a National Socialist philosophy of life.

Whoever is fighting, like the

S.S. Man, for lofty ideals will have to be able to accomplish extraordinary feats, physically and mentally. The S.S. engages in every sport. Wherever the S.S. Man enters into competition publicly, he is conscious that he has to give his best, his utmost, for the honour of his S.S. Squad.

One of his most outstanding publicity aids is the magazine *The Black Corps*. It is published on Wednesdays. Every S.S. Man is obliged to read this fighting and propaganda paper of the S.S. and to do his utmost to see that it is distributed among the entire German people.

**Organisation and Scope:**
The organisation of the S.S. arises from the variety of its tasks.

The following are directly responsible to the Reichsführer S.S.: The chiefs of: the three main Offices, the Adjutant's Office, the Staff Chancellery, the S.S. Tribunal, the Administration, the Board of Health, and the Office for Population Policy.

**The Central Office of the S.S.,** being the highest command post of the *Reichsführer*-S.S., has been assigned the job of forming, training for their allotted tasks and sending into action the three sections into which the S.S. has been sub-divided: the General S.S.; the S.S. Stand-by Troops; and the S.S. Guard Troops.

Hence follows the necessity for establishing the offices mentioned. These have the following tasks:

**Central Chancellery:**
The Chief of the Central Chancellery, together with his staff of Assistants, directs the command post of the Chief of S.S. Head Office. He is in charge of registering and sorting the entire incoming mail. He reports immediately to the Chief of the S.S. Head Office concerning any important occurrences. He carries out decisions and receives instructions and orders from the Chief of S.S. Head Office. He looks after liaison with all offices under the authority of the Chief of S.S. Head Office. He supervises and checks the entire business administration within S.S. Head Office.

**(1) Operations Section:**
The Operations Section deals with all matters in connection with training and organisation of the three sections of the *Schutzstaffel*.

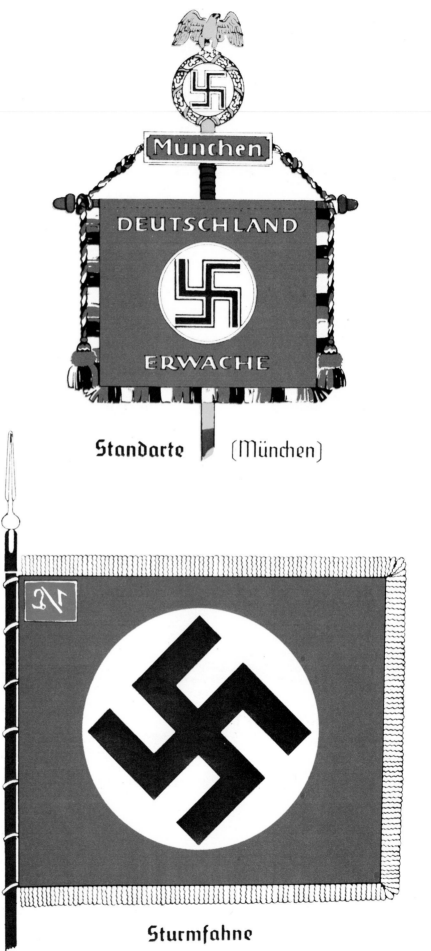

**Standarte** (München)

**Sturmfahne**
(Sturm 1 d. Leibstandarte)

Chief of the Staff Chancellery, Chief of the Staff Office is a member of the Personal Staff of *Reichsführer*-S.S. The three Offices of the S.S. Head Office, the Race and Settlement Office and the S.D. Head Office work under the authority of the Staff Chancellery. The Staff Chancellery is responsible for dealing with all staff matters of S.S. Leaders and of Junior Leaders of the entire Squadron who have been commissioned to Leaders' posts.

Within the scope of the Staff Chancellery falls the drafting of trainees for training courses for prospective leaders, as well as the care of standard bearers, discharged from S.S. Leader training schools.

### Administrative Office:

The Chief of the Administrative Office is simultaneously Chief of S.S. Administration (on the personal staff of the *Reichsführer-S.S.*). He is responsible for all administrative and domestic affairs of the three Head Offices.

As sole representative of the *Reichsführer* S.S. he is also in charge of negotiations concerning these matters with all offices outside the S.S.

He is sole authorised representative of the National Treasurer for the entire S.S.

For the purpose of strengthening the means for expansion and routine work of the S.S., an establishment has been created, the Administrative Office, where the names of Aryans not belonging to the S.S. are kept as Supporting Members, as long as they undertake to pay a monthly contribution, the amount to be stipulated by themselves.

### ) Medical Office

The Chief of the S.S. Medical Office deals with all areas concerning the medical service of the S.S. In his capacity as "National Medical Officer of the S.S." he is, at the same time, responsible to the *Reichsführer*-S.S. for the entire medical service of the S.S.

### 5) Recruitment Office:

The Recruitment Office deals with all admissions of Junior Leaders and Men, as well as with re-admissions, appointments, transfers and removals, secondments and dismissals. Among its tasks are also the inclusion in a card-index with intelligence about their particulars of all members of the S.S., as well as computation and statis-

Opposite page: *S.S. standards. Above is that of the Munich Regiment, and below that of the 3/1st S.S. Regiment.*
△ *An S.S.* Unterscharführer *(Senior Corporal) of the cordoning detail at Nuremberg in service dress.*

tics regarding the total force of the S.S.

### (6) Office for Security Matters:

Its scope corresponds with the title of the office.

Of the three sections of the S.S., S.S. Stand-by Troops and S.S. Guard Troops are equipped with light and heavy infantry weapons, the General S.S. only with daggers.

The two **S.S. Leader (Training) Schools** are meant to train prospective leaders.

At the Riding School, S.S. riders and drivers are perfected in their riding and driving training.

The School of Motoring trains members of the S.S. Motor Unit and the Motorised Convoys to become exemplary drivers and teachers.

**The Race and Settlement Office (R.u.S.)** provides the equipment for the S.S., being a kinship community selected according to Nordic-racial principles, to enable it to realise among itself, by living in a way characteristic for the species, the idea of *Blut und Boden*, to serve as an example to the entire people. The R.u.S. is divided into the following six offices:

### (1) Office for Organisation and Administration:

It creates the organisation, personnel, and material basis for the remaining offices in order to facilitate their work.

### (2) Race Office:

It is the task of this Office to prove and exploit the fact that blood alone determines history, morality, law, and industry.

### (3) Office for Indoctrination:

The purpose of the Office for Indoctrination is the ideological education of the S.S. Its aim is to bring every S.S. Man to accept, in its totality, the National Socialist ideological point of view and thus to create a self-contained ideological block within the population.

### (4) Kinship Office:

Incumbent upon the Kinship Office is the examination, from the point of view of race, parentage, and freedom from hereditary disease, of S.S. Men, Junior Leaders, and leaders already in the S.S., as well as those about to be admitted.

**Dienstanzug der SS.-Verfüg.-Truppe**
Sturmmann

3344

**Feldmütze**

**Sportanzug**

*Uniforms of the* Schutzstaffel:
*An* Unterscharführer *of the* Allgemeine S.S. *(General S.S.)
in parade dress.*
Sturmmann *(Lance-Corporal) of the S.S.* Verfügungstruppen
*(the S.S. military arm) in* Dienstanzug *or service dress.*
△ △ *The S.S. field cap (*Feldmütze*).*
△ *S.S. sports kit (*Sportanzug*).*
Scharführer *of the S.S.* Verfügungstruppen *in* Paradeanzug
*(parade dress).*

3345

The examination and selection takes place according to the directions of the *Reichsführer*-S.S., according to his principle that the S.S. is to be the élite of the best German Nordically-determined blood; through the extension of the S.S. to become a kinship community and by recording the best pedigrees in the Kinship Book it is intended that this valuable heritage of blood should be preserved for the German people and increased for future generations.

### (5) Settlement Office:
It puts into practice the thought of *Blut und Boden* by settling racially valuable S.S. families in connection with the re-creation of German peasantry and "homestead" settlement.

### (6) Records and Newspaper Office:
This Office has been given the task of putting at the disposal of all offices items of literature, the daily press and pictorial material for the purpose of adaptation and utilisation. In addition, this Office is to propagate the attitude of the S.S. in questions affecting the Head Office for Race and Settlement beyond the limits of the S.S. and, if necessary, to influence the General Press, Radio, Film, and Exhibitions in our favour.

### (7) Office for Population Policy:
This Office deals with all questions of population policy within the S.S. It has been appointed by the *Reichsführer*-S.S. as Chief Assessment Office for Freedom from Hereditary Disease.

In collaboration with offices run by the State (Advice Bureau for Heredity and Race Affairs attached to State Health Offices) it exploits scientifically the genetic stock-taking of the S.S. In short-term training courses it instructs all S.S. medical officers in the subjects of genetics, hereditary health hygiene, and marriage counselling.

### S.D. Head Office
The Security Service of the *Reichsführer*-S.S. is the source of political intelligence of the Movement and Reich.

This Head Office supervises and assesses all political events. As quickly as possible it transmits to the leadership of Movement and Reich its evaluation of the political situation at any

*◄ An S.S. Gruppenf[ührer] (Lieutenant-General) in se[rvice] dress with greatcoat (Ma[...]*

given time, to serve as basi[s of] their decisions.

The organisation of [the] Security Service correspon[ds to] these tasks. Its directorate m[akes] use of three offices. The [...] subordinate offices of [the] Security Service are bran[ches] working either for a divisio[n of a] subordinate Government B[...] or for a District Office of [the] N.S.D.A.P.

### S.S. Tribunal
On behalf of the *Reichsfü[hrer]* S.S., the S.S. Tribunal carrie[s out] investigations into matter[s of] discipline, complaints, [and] affairs of honour. Taking [into] consideration the instruct[ions,] orders, and directions issue[d by] the *Reichsführer*-S.S., it ju[dges] all cases exclusively accor[ding] to National Socialist ideolo[gy and] soldierly principles.

### The Relationship of the S.[S.] within the Party, and with[...] Government Offices
Within the framework of [the] tasks set by the Führer to [the] *Reichsführer*-S.S., all S.S. Le[aders] are urged by the *Reichsführer*[-S.S.] to create harmony in co-oper[ation] with Leading Functionarie[s of] the Party, and to see to it [that] National Socialist authori[ty is] preserved.

### Supporting Members of th[e] S.S.
Service with the S.S., makin[g as] it does exceptional demand[s es-] pecially at meetings of Lea[ders,] is economically a great [deal] harder because individual u[nits] of the S.S. are geographi[cally] more widely distributed [than] units of the S.A. As a re[sult] the S.S. has considerably hi[gher] transport costs in the execu[tion] of their duties.

For that reason, the Fü[hrer] has consented to the estab[lish-] ment by the S.S. of the [F.M.] Organisation. Supporting M[em-] bers, who need not be p[arty] Members, pay fixed amo[unts] monthly. Only those S.S. O[ffices] which have been specifically [ap-] pointed for this purpose by [the] R.F.S. (Administrative Office[s)] are authorised to collect t[he] contributions. The F.M. Org[anis-] ation is of the greatest import[ance] for the existence of the S.S., [and] it must not be impeded in its w[ork] by any other office.

tes

*utzstaffel* = "Defence Squad-
" (S.S.)
*chsführer*: Reich Leader
*t und Boden* = "Blood and
l"
. = *Sicherheitsdienst* (Security
vice).
tional Treasurer: of the Party,
of the Reich.
pporting Members: *Fördernde
tglieder*.

## Tasks
## d Organisation of the
## ich Labour Service

a sub-division of the
.D.A.P., the N.S. Labour Ser-
e has provided the basis for
law relating to compulsory
our service (issued on June
1935).

he N.S. Labour Service has
ome the Reich Labour Service.
he Reich Labour Service is
ordinate to the Reich Minister
the Interior.

he Reich Labour Service
resents an honorary obli-
tion *vis-à-vis* the German
ople: all young Germans of
th sexes are liable to Labour
rvice (Reich Labour Service
w).

Young men will be called up
compulsory labour service for
eriod determined by the Leader
the Reich Labour Service. The
me goes for young women with-
the framework of possibilities
ven at present. (The eventual
pansion of the Women's Labour
rvice is a matter of course).

**asks:**

its name conveys, the Labour
rvice is a service which, in
ntrast to military service, is
rried out, not with the help of
ms, but through labour.

he R.A.D. has an educational
well as an economic task.

The education takes place in
soldierly manner in closed
mps outside towns. Its chief
m is to provide an education
wards a National-Socialist out-
ok on labour and towards the
llowship of the People.

Because he labours for
ermany in a community and
ithout pay, the worker will be
ought to realise that the in-
insic meaning of labour lies
ot in wages earned, but in the
irit in which it is performed.
he elevation of labour to a
rvice will teach him that labour
not a curse but an honour. And

*◀ The standard of the "Andreas
Bauriedl" Detachment
(Abteilung) of the R.A.D. or
Reichsarbeitsdienst (Reich
Labour Service).
▽ The flag of an R.A.D. Camp
or House (Lager or Haus).*

### Abteilungsfahne

### Lager- u. Hausfahne

3348

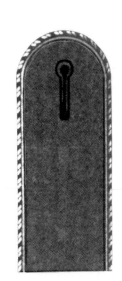

**Arbeitsmann**

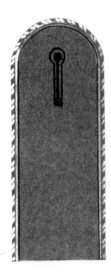

**Vormann**

**Obervormann**

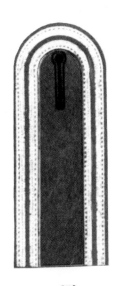

**Truppführer**

**Obertruppführer**

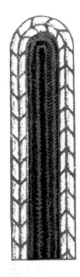

**Unterfeldmeister**

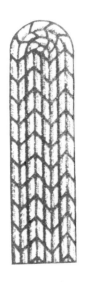

**Feldmeister**

**Ober-
feldmeister**

**Oberst-
feldmeister**

*niforms and insignia of the*
Reichsarbeitsdienst:
*An* Arbeitsführer *(Leader).*
*An* Arbeitsmann *(Worker).*
*Collar rank patches, from*
*of an* Arbeitsmann *(top),*
*Vormann,* Obervormann,
Truppführer *and*
Obertruppführer, *and*
Unterfeldmeister *to*
*berstfeldmeister (bottom).*
▷ *R.A.D. epaulettes.*

3349

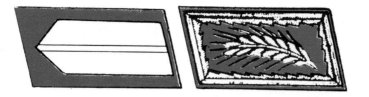

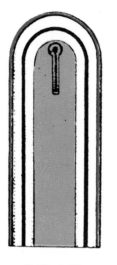

**ħeilgehilfe**
im Range eines Truppführers

**Arzte**
hier Arbeitsarzt

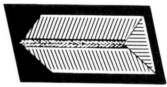

**Mufikzugführer**

**Ober-
mufikzugführer**

*R.A.D. specialist collar patches and epaulettes:*
△ △ ◁ *Medical Assistant* (Heilgehilfe) *with the rank of*
Truppführer.
△ △ ▷ *Doctor* (Arzt).
△ ◁ *Bandmaster* (Musikzugführer).
△ ▷ *Senior Bandmaster* (Obermusikzugführer).

thus he will realise that th
no difference between m
and white-collar workers
rather that the value of
labour will be determined t
attitude of mind with whic
carried out. Therefore, the
characteristics of Labour Se
education are soldierly bea
closeness to the soil, a Nat
Socialist outlook on labour
a community spirit.

(2) The Reich Labour Se
labours for the reclamatior
amelioration of German
Germany is obliged to utilis
land to the uttermost, an
that reason she must trans
fallow plains, waste land and
into fertile soil. The product
of German agriculture ma
significantly increased by
cesses of amelioration. The R
serves this important tas
safeguarding the people's
supplies from their own soil

**Regulations concerning
careers as leaders:**
There exists in the Labour Se
a junior career as leader,
prising the ranks of Troop Lea
Senior Troop Leader, Se
Lieutenant; as well as an i
mediate and a higher caree
leader, which includes lea
from Lieutenant upwards. T
is no rigid and final separa
between these careers.

Conditions for the accept
of applications for places
trainee leaders are:
(1) the applicant must have
pleted his seventeenth year
produce evidence of permis
of parents or guardian;
(2) the applicant must pro
proof of Aryan origin;
(3) the applicant must pro
proof of unblemished chara
by means of a certificate of
duct issued by the Police, an
extracts from the penal recor

Applications for enrolmen
trainee leader must be mad
the Regional Labour Leade
means of a written requ
General suitability having
proved, final acceptance as
nee leader will take place
after a period of six months
Private. There follows a
bationary period, including
years' National Service, for
trainee leaders. During this tr
ing period, no difference ex
between trainees for the lo
the intermediate, or the hi
career levels.

At the end of the probatior
period those trainees who
most suitable will be selected
the intermediate career, while

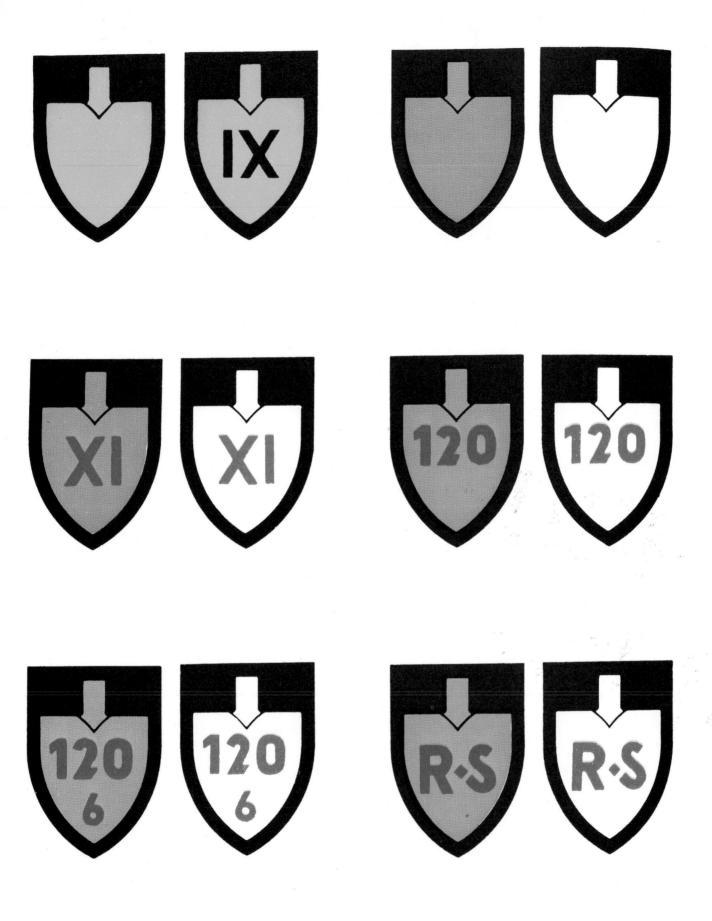

*Shoulder patches of the* Reichsarbeitsdienst:
op row, left to right: Reichsarbeitsführer *(Reich Labour Leader),*
bergeneralarbeitsführer, *and* Generalarbeitsführer *of the Reich*
*Labour Executive;* Generalarbeitsführer *as* Gauarbeitsführer
(Gau *Labour Leader) of* Gau *No. 9; and two patches for the*
Reichsleitung *(Central Executive) up to the rank of*
Oberstarbeitsführer.

Centre row, left to right: *Two patches for the* Arbeitsgauleitung
(Gau *Labour Executive) of* Gau *No. 11, up to the rank of*
Oberstarbeitsführer; *and two patches for the* Gruppenstab *(Group*
*Staff) of* Gruppe *No. 120.*
Bottom row, left to right: *Two patches for* Abteilung *(Detachment)*
*No. 6 of* Gruppe *(Group) No. 120; and two patches for the*
Reichsschule *(Reich School).*

3351

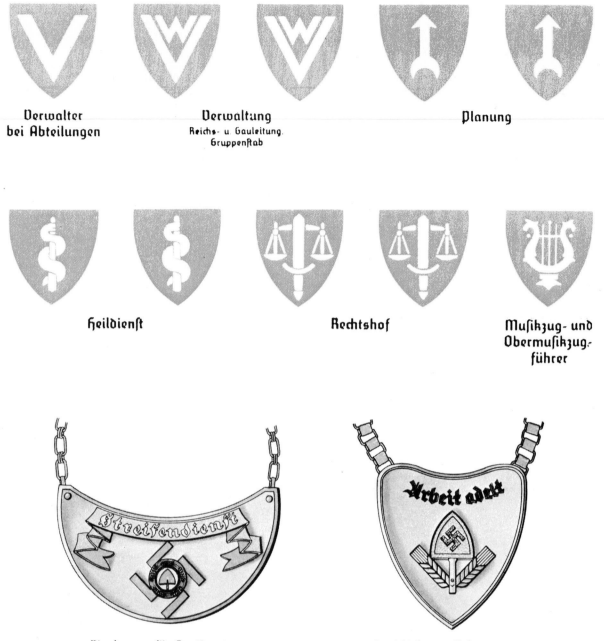

**Verwalter bei Abteilungen**

**Verwaltung**
Reichs- u. Gauleitung.
Gruppenstab

**Planung**

**Heildienst**

**Rechtshof**

**Musikzug- und Obermusikzug-führer**

**Ringkragen für Streifendienst**

**Brustschild des Fahnenträgers**

remaining men will, if suitable and having signed a ten-year agreement, continue with the lower career, and as vacancies occur, they will be finally accepted into the Reich Labour Service as regular Troop Leaders.

At a later stage, able leaders will have an opportunity to gain promotion to the intermediate career after taking an examination.

Commensurate with the great demands made upon intermediate career leaders, severe standards will have to be applied during the process of selecting applicants for the intermediate career, after completion of their probationary period. In addition to personality, what must be expected from trainee leaders for the intermediate-

and thus possibly for the higher-leader career is an appropriate mental aptitude as well as a level of education corresponding to the average level of a person having completed their grammar school education. Proof may be provided not only by means of a leaving certificate from a Grammar School, but also by passing a special examination.

Gifted trainee leaders who do not possess a leaving certificate from a Grammar School, but who, according to their personality, are suitable for the intermediate leader career, will be given an opportunity of preparing for this examination.

Trainees for the intermediate career will have to undergo a further year of training, on com-

pletion of which, that is to say, after successful attendance of the *Feldmeister* School as well as having proved their mettle in field work, they will receive their appointment as lieutenant.

Further training of Labour Service leaders will be carried out at District Schools and at the Reich Labour Service School, as well as, under certain circumstances, in special technical courses.

Retiring leaders and their surviving dependents are entitled to maintenance, according to Article 24 of the Reich Labour Service Law.

In addition to the above-mentioned leader careers, there exists the possibility of entry as "Long Service Volunteer". There

Top row, left to right: *R.A.D. specialist shoulder patches. From left to right these are for an* Abteilung Verwalter *(Detachment Administrator), Administrative Branch in the Reich or Regional Executive* (Reichs- *or* Gauleitung)*; the Reich or Regional Planning Department (*Planung). Centre row, left to right: *the Reich or Regional Health Ser* (Heildienst)*; the Reich or Regional Judicial Branch* (Rechtshof)*; and a Bandmaster and Senior Bandmaster.* Bottom row, left: *The gorget (*Ringkragen*) for R.A.D. patro* Bottom row, right: *The breast plate (*Brustschild*) for R.A.D. standard bearers.*

special regulations for their
ice promotion.

### flag of the Reich Labour
### vice:
symbol of the Reich Labour
ice is the union of spade and
of corn. The spade indicates
closeness to the soil of the
h Labour Service which, with
help of that implement, is
ting new land for the German
le; the ear of corn signifies
fruits of labour, the crop
h grows in the newly created

tween two crossed and
sed ears of corn stands the
e of the spade: black, on a
d, white field, on red cloth.
s the symbol of the Reich
our Service is repeated on all
ags, banners and standards.
o further ornament and no
bol other than this appears
he house flag, while on the
sional flag the symbol rests
swastika, angled at 45 deg-
In addition, the standard
he Reich Labour Leader dis-
s the embellishment of a
ath of golden ears of corn.
k surrounds or black
onal bars designate indi-
al offices which obtain further
tification by means of a sys-
of different combinations of
res.

es
.D. = *Reichsarbeitsdienst*
ch Labour Service)
nd Lieutenant = *Unterfeld-
ster:* the rank of *Feld-
ster* was created specifically
he Labour Service.
rate = *Arbeitsmann:* another
k created for the Nazi Labour
vice.

## The Party
## d the State

### The State
State has been created out of
necessity to regulate the
munity of a people according
ertain laws. Its distinguishing
k is its power *vis-à-vis* every
nber of the community. The
te has the right to demand
t every fellow citizen should
y the law. Whoever acts con-
ry to the laws of the State will
punished. To supervise its
s and regulations the State
its civil servants. The con-
ution of the State is the basis
ts legislation. The State is the
odiment of power! In a State,
ple holding differing con-

victions and different views may
live side by side. The State
may not demand that all men
should hold the same convictions.
However, it may demand that all
men should respect its laws.

### (2) The Party
In contrast to the State, the Party
is a community of like-minded
men. It was born out of the
struggle for ideology. In order to
come out of this struggle vic-
toriously, the Party rallied all
those who were ready to fight for
this ideology. And it is this
ideology that is the foundation
of the order according to which
men live within the Party. While
in the State many citizens consider its laws to be oppressive,
hindering and difficult, the laws
of the Party are no burden, but
represent the will of the community. The characteristic of the
State is the "I must", that of the
Party is the "I will".

### (3) The tasks of Party and
### State
(*a*) It is conceivable that Party
and State might be one and the
same thing. That will be the case
if all fellow citizens are convinced of the Party's ideology
and if, at the same time, the laws
of the State are the clear expression of that ideology. Then
it is the State that will be the
great community of like-minded
people. This ideal State will but
rarely be achieved in history.
Altogether, it is conceivable only
if that ideology is the sole basis
of an attitude of mind which has
completely penetrated all men.
(*b*) If the ruling Party possesses
no ideology at all, but is merely
an artificial organisation for the
purpose of achieving temporal
aims, then Party and State will
decline into a technical institution, where no spiritual values
are given to the people, and
which, acting merely as watch-
man and police state, maintains
peace and quiet. This is the state
of affairs which prevailed in the
past few decades.
(*c*) If the people are not totally
penetrated by the Party and its
ideology, then Party and State
must remain separate. In that
case, the Party will represent an
Order where a selection of leaders
and fighters takes place. It is by
these fighters that the ideology
will be taken to the people. The
Party must prepare the state of
receptiveness and the will of the
people for legislation, so that
the spiritual disposition of the
people will correspond to the

actual legislation of the State.
It is therefore not enough that
the Party is uniformly held together as an élite, as a minority.
Rather, it is the task of the Party
to carry out the political education and the political union of
German people. That is why it
has a right to the leadership of
what are known as affiliated
bodies. Through them the Party
is accomplishing its most vital
task: the ideological conquest
of the German people and the
creation of "the people's organisation". The State then becomes a
technical aid for this community
of the people: it is the instrument
for implementing the ideology.
The Party, thus, is the in-
trinsically vital body which,
again and again, gives life and
the will to live to defunct matter.
The State apparatus functioned
before the war, and it also functioned after the war. Nevertheless, the whole German people
experienced Black November 9,
1918; nevertheless it experienced
the terrible collapse of the post-
war years in all spheres of political, cultural, and economic life.
Only the spirit, the will and the
readiness for action of the German
Freedom Movement were able to
save Germany from drowning in
a Communist chaos. Only the
German Freedom Movement's
volitional and spiritual strength
have made possible the country's
reconstruction. It is the right
and the task of the Party again
and again to pump the stream of
its spiritual and volitional
strength into the State
machinery.
The Party must reserve this
function to itself, and it must also
take care that it does not become
too closely connected with the
administrative machinery of the
State; for, unless it takes care, it
runs the risk of being devoured
by the bureaucracy of the State
and of becoming itself petrified
as a Party bureaucracy.
All over the world we observe
this struggle for new forms of
government. Gone are those soul-
less days when parties represented merely a pragmatic programme, and when the State was
a dead machine. We call it the
age of materialism. In the 20th
Century, nations struggle for
their souls and for a new life style
which must necessarily find expression in forms of government.
We have seen these struggles in
Italy, in Hungary, in Germany,
and in other countries, such as
Spain.
After each revolution, bureau-

cracy fights for its position, and in
most cases it is victorious. In the
National Socialist revolution it
may already be clearly observed
that the struggle between
bureaucracy and Party has been
decided in favour of the Party.
Not even a few rearguard actions
can alter that fact.
According to the Führer's will,
the connection between Party and
State in Germany will take the
following form:
The link at the summit between
Party and State has been forged
by the appointment of the Deputy
Führer as Party-Minister and, of
course, through the Führer as
Leader of the Party and Reich
Chancellor. It is not necessary for
the remaining National Executive of the Party to be merged
with the State.
A further connection at the
summit of Party and State will
be the Great Senate, the creation
of which has been planned for a
later date. The Great Senate is
purely a Party institution, while,
at the same time, it will also be
the highest national State
authority.
The third link between Party
and State in National Socialist
Germany may be found in the
person of the Regional Leader
who is, at the same time, Reich
Governor.
This intention of the Führer
will be taken into account in the
reforms of the Reich.
There is a further connection
of Party and State in the establishment, through the German
Communities Regulation, of a
Party Representative within
every community, who has been
given certain rights of participation in the shaping of community life.
In any form, the State is bound
to be somewhat rigid; the Party,
however, must at all times stay
alive and flexible. If it wishes to
be the conscience of the people, it
must take its impulse from its
ideology alone.

## 41. The Law to Safeguard
## the Unity of Party and
## State (December 1, 1933)
The Government of the Reich has
decreed the following law which
is promulgated herewith:

### Article 1
(1) After the victory of the
National Socialist revolution, the
National Socialist German

Workers' Party has become the carrier of the principles of the German State and is indissolubly linked to the State.

(2) It is a body incorporated under public law. Its statutes will be determined by the Führer.

**Article 2**

For the purpose of safeguarding closest co-operation between Party offices, the S.A., and official authorities, the Deputy Führer and the Chief-of-Staff of the S.A. will become members of the Government of the Reich.

**Article 3**

(1) As the leading and motive power in the National Socialist State, increased duties *vis-à-vis* Führer, people, and State are incumbent upon members of the National Socialist German Workers' Party and the S.A. (including its subordinate formations).

(2) In case of failing in these duties they are subject to a special Party and S.A. judiciary.

(3) The Führer may extend these regulations to include members of other organisations.

**Article 4**

Any action or omission will be regarded as violation of duty which attacks or jeopardises the existence, organisation, activities, or standing of the National Socialist German Workers' Party, and, in the case of the S.A. (including its subordinate formations) especially any contravention against discipline.

**Article 5**

In addition to the usual penalties, arrest and detention may be imposed.

**Article 6**

Within the framework of their competence, authorities will have to render legal and administrative assistance to Party and S.A. offices, entrusted with Party and S.A. jurisdiction.

**Article 7**

The law concerning official penal power over members of the S.A. and the S.S. of April 28, 1933, is repealed herewith.

**Article 8**

The Reich Chancellor as Führer of the National Socialist German Workers' Party and as Supreme Leader of the S.A. will decree the regulations required to execute and complement this law, in particular concerning development

and proceedings of Party and S.A. jurisdiction. He will determine the date of coming into force of the regulations concerning the said jurisdiction.
Berlin, December 1, 1933.

(signed) Adolf Hitler
Reich Chancellor
Frick
Reich Minister of the Interior

**Notes**

Black November 9, 1918: the day of Germany's internal collapse in World War I. That, and the "shameful treaty" (*Schandvertrag*) of Versailles were among the stock phrases in Nazi demagogics.

## 42. The Law for the Protection of German Blood and German Honour (September 15, 1935)

Imbued with the realisation that the purity of German blood is presuppositional for the continued existence of the German people, and inspired by the unswerving will to safeguard the German Nation for all times, the Reichstag has unanimously decreed the following law, which is promulgated herewith:

**Article 1**

(1) Marriages between Jews and German nationals of German or kindred blood are forbidden.

(2) Only the Public Prosecutor is authorised to institute nullity proceedings.

**Article 2**

Extra-marital intercourse between Jews and German nationals of German or kindred blood is forbidden.

**Article 3**

Jews are not permitted to employ female German nationals of German or kindred blood.

**Article 4**

(1) Jews are forbidden to hoist the Reich national flag or to display the national colours.

(2) However, they are permitted to display Jewish colours. The exercise of this right is protected by law.

**Article 5**

(1) The contravention of the prohibition of Article 1 carries a punishment of penal servitude.

(2) Contravention of the regu-

lations of Articles 3 and 4 carries a penalty of up to 12 months' imprisonment and an additional fine, or either.

**Article 6**

In agreement with the Deputy Führer and the Reich Minister of Justice, the Reich Minister of the Interior will issue the legal and administrative regulations for executing and complementing this law.

This law will come into force one day after promulgation; Article 3, however, will come into force on January 1, 1936.
Nuremberg, September 15, 1935, at the Reich Party Rally of Freedom

(signed) Adolf Hitler
Führer and Reich Chancellor
Frick
Minister of the Interior
Dr. Gürtner
Reich Minister of Justice
R. Hess
Deputy Führer
Reich Minister without Portfolio

## 43. The Reich Citizenship Law (September 15, 1935)

The Reichstag has unanimously decreed the following law which is promulgated herewith:

**Article 1**

(1) A person is a German national if he lives under the protection of the German Reich and so is indebted to it.

(2) Nationality may be acquired according to the regulations of the Reich Citizenship and Nationality Law.

**Article 2**

(1) Only a German national of German or kindred blood who by his demeanour proves his willingness and suitability faithfully to serve the German people and the German Reich may become a Citizen of the Reich.

(2) Citizenship of the Reich will be acquired by means of granting of the Patent of Citizenship.

(3) A Citizen of the Reich is the sole possessor of full political rights, according to the law.

**Article 3**

In agreement with the Deputy Führer, the Reich Minister of the Interior will issue the legal and administrative regulations required for the execution and implementation of this law. Nur-

emberg, September 15, 1935 the Reich Party Rally of Free

(signed) Adolf Hitler
Führer and Reich Chancellor
Frick
Reich Minister of the Interio

## 44. The First Directive the Implementation of Reich Citizenship Law (November 14, 1935)

On the basis of Article 3 of Reich Citizenship Law of S tember 15, 1935, the followin decreed herewith:

**Article 1**

(1) For the time being, and u further regulations concern the Patent of Citizenship issued, Citizens of the Reich be all persons who are Gern Nationals of German or kind blood and who, at the time of coming into force of the Re Citizenship Law, were entit to vote in Reichstag electic or to whom the Reich Ministe the Interior, in agreement w the Deputy Führer, has gran temporary Reich Citizenship.

(2) The Reich Minister of Interior may, in agreement w the Deputy Führer, withdr temporary Reich Citizenship.

**Article 2**

(1) The regulations of Articl apply also to Jewish mix parentage German nationals.

(2) A Jew of mixed parentage a person who is descended fr one or two racially wholly Jew grandparents, unless he is a J according to the definition Article 5/2. A grandparent immediately considered to wholly Jewish if he was a me ber of the Jewish religic community.

**Article 3**

As possessor of full politi rights a Citizen of the Reich the sole person entitled to ex cise his voting rights in politi affairs and only he is entitled hold public office. During t period of transition, the Minis of the Interior, or the off authorised by him, may all exceptions for the admission public offices. The affairs of ligious societies are not affect

**Article 4**

(1) A Jew may not be a Citizen the Reich. He is not entitled

e in political affairs: he may hold public office.

After December 31, 1935, all ⁓ish civil servants will retire. ⁓ Jewish civil servant who, in ⁓ Great War, fought at the ⁓t for Germany or her Allies, ⁓l, up to retirement age, con⁓e to receive the full emolu⁓ts he received upon retire⁓t; however these emoluments ⁓ no longer increase according ⁓cale of seniority. On reaching ⁓rement age, the pension will ⁓ewly calculated according to ⁓ last full pension-related ⁓luments received.

The affairs of religious ⁓ieties are not affected by this ⁓ulation.

Until fresh arrangements for ⁓ management of Jewish ⁓ools have been made, the ⁓tract of employment of ⁓chers at Jewish state schools ⁓l remain unaffected.

## ⁓ticle 5

A person is a Jew if he is de⁓nded from at least three ⁓ially wholly Jewish grand⁓ents. Article 2/2, Sentence 2, ⁓lies.

A Jewish mixed-parentage ⁓rman national who is de⁓nded from two wholly Jewish ⁓ndparents will also be held to ⁓ Jew,

if at the time of issue of this ⁓ he was a member of a Jewish ⁓gious community, or is subse⁓ntly admitted as a member,

if at the time of issue of this ⁓ he was married to a Jew, or ⁓sequently marries a Jew,

if he is the child of a marriage ⁓h a person who is a Jew ⁓ording to the definition of ⁓agraph (1), which has been ⁓tracted after the Law for the ⁓tection of German Blood and ⁓rman Honour of September 15, ⁓5, came into force,

if he is the child of extra⁓rital intercourse with a person ⁓o is a Jew according to the ⁓inition of Paragraph (1), and is ⁓n after July 31, 1936.

## ⁓ticle 6

Insofar as requirements con⁓ning the purity of blood are ⁓nanded in laws of the Reich or ⁓ regulations of the National ⁓cialist German Workers' Party ⁓d its organisations, which ex⁓d Article 5, they are deemed to ⁓ unaffected.

Other requirements concern⁓ the purity of blood exceeding ⁓ticle 5 may only be stipulated ⁓ agreement with the Reich ⁓nister of the Interior and the

Deputy Führer. Insofar as requirements of this kind already exist, they will become void on January 1, 1936, unless they are approved by the Reich Minister of the Interior in agreement with the Deputy Führer. Application for approval must be made to the Reich Minister of the Interior.

### Article 7

The Führer and Reich Chancellor may grant exemption from the regulations of this directive.
Berlin, November 14, 1934

(signed) Adolf Hitler
Führer and Reich Chancellor
Frick
Reich Minister of the Interior
R. Hess
Deputy Führer
Reich Minister without Portfolio

## 45. The First Directive for the Implementation of the Law for the Protection of German Blood and German Honour (November 14, 1935)

On the basis of Article 6 of the Law for the Protection of German Blood and German Honour of September 15, 1935, the following is decreed herewith:

### Article 1

(1) German nationals according to the definition of the Reich Citizenship Law will be deemed to possess German nationality.
(2) Article 2/2 of the First Directive of November 14, 1935, to the Reich Citizenship Law defines a Jewish mixed-parentage person.
(3) Article 5 of the same Directive defines a Jew.

### Article 2

Included in marriages prohibited according to Article 1 of the law are marriages between Jews and Jewish mixed-parentage German nationals with only one wholly Jewish grandparent.

### Article 3

(1) Jewish mixed-parentage German nationals with two wholly Jewish grandparents, wishing to marry either German nationals of German or kindred blood, or Jewish mixed-parentage German nationals with only one wholly Jewish grandparent, require the permission of the Reich Minister of the Interior and the Deputy

Führer, or of the office appointed by them for that purpose.
(2) In making the decision, allowance must be made for the physical and mental qualities as well as the personality of the applicant; for length of residence in Germany of his family; or for his father's participation in World War I, as well as for the rest of his family history.
(3) Applications for permission to marry must be made to the higher administrative authority of the district where the applicant is domiciled or where he normally resides.
(4) The Reich Minister of the Interior in agreement with the Deputy Führer will regularise the procedure.

### Article 4

Marriages between Jewish mixed-parentage German nationals with only one wholly Jewish grandparent must not take place.

### Article 5

The impediments to marriage due to the infusion of Jewish blood have been exhaustively regulated through Article 1 of the law, and through Articles 2–4 of this Directive.

### Article 6

In addition, a marriage should not be contracted if it is to be anticipated that the offspring of such a marriage may jeopardise the continued purity of German blood.

### Article 7

Before contracting a marriage, each partner must prove, by means of a certificate of qualification (as per Article 2 of the Law for the Preservation and Safeguard of Racially Healthy Stock of October 18, 1935) that there is no impediment to the marriage according to Article 6 of this Directive.

The following are points from the Law for the Preservation and Safeguard of a Racially Healthy Stock which may apply:

### Article 1

(1) A marriage must not be contracted
(a) if one of the partners suffers from a contagious disease which it is to be feared may result in considerable damage to the health of the other partner or their descendants;
(b) if one of the partners has either been declared incapable of managing his, or her, affairs, or has been temporarily placed

under the care of a guardian;
(c) if one of the partners, although not declared incapable of managing his, or her, affairs, suffers from a mental disorder which appears to render the marriage undesirable for the community;
(d) if one of the partners suffers from a hereditary disease, in accordance with the Law for the Prevention of Hereditarily Diseased Offspring.
(2) The regulations of paragraph (1)(d) do not stand in the way of a marriage if the other partner is sterile.

### Article 2

Before contracting a marriage, the partners must prove by means of a certificate from the Public Health Department (certificate of qualification) that there is no impediment according to Article 1.

### Article 8

(1) The nullity of a marriage contracted in contravention of Article 1 of the law or Article 2 of this Directive may only be enforced by way of plea of nullity.
(2) For marriages contracted in contravention of Articles 3, 4, and 6, the consequences of Article 1 and Article 5/1 of the law do not apply.

### Article 9

If one of the partners holds foreign nationality, the decision of the Reich Minister for the Interior must be obtained prior to refusal to publish the banns because of an impediment according to Article 1 of the law or Articles 2–4 of this Directive, as well as prior to refusal of a certificate of qualification in cases relating to Article 6.

### Article 10

A marriage contracted before a German Consular authority is held to have been contracted in Germany.

### Article 11

Extra-marital intercourse in accordance with Article 2 of the law is understood to refer to sexual intercourse only. In addition punishable according to Article 5/2 of the law is extra-marital intercourse between Jews and Jewish mixed-parentage German nationals with only one wholly Jewish grandparent.

### Article 12

(1) A household is Jewish (Article 3 of the law) if a Jewish male is

head of the household or a member of it.

(2) Any person who has been accepted into the household within the framework of a contractual relationship or alternatively who performs diurnal household tasks or other diurnal tasks in connection with the household, is deemed to be working in the household.

(3) Female German nationals of German or kindred blood who were working in a Jewish household when the law came into force, may remain in that household in their former contractual employment, if they have completed their thirty-fifth year by December 31, 1935.

(4) Foreign nationals who are neither domiciled nor normally resident in the country are not affected by these regulations.

### Article 13

Any person contravening the prohibition of Article 3 of the law in conjunction with Article 12 of this Directive will be punishable according to Article 5/3 of the law, even if he is not a Jew.

### Article 14

For offences against Article 5/1–2 of the law, the Central Criminal Court is the competent Court of primary jurisdiction.

### Article 15

Insofar as the regulations of the law and its ordinance refer to German nationals, they must be applied to stateless persons who are domiciled or normally resident in this country. Stateless persons who are domiciled or normally resident abroad will only be affected by these regulations if previously they held German nationality.

(1) The Führer and Reich Chancellor may grant exemption from the regulations of the law and its directives.

(2) Prosecution of a foreign national requires the approval of the Reich Ministers of Justice and of the Interior.

### Article 17

This directive comes into force on the day following its promulgation. The Minister of the Interior will determine the date of the coming into force of the law; up to that date, certificates of qualification need to be submitted in cases of doubt.
Berlin, November 14, 1935

(signed) Adolf Hitler
Führer and Reich Chancellor

Frick
Reich Minister of the Interior
R. Hess
Deputy Führer
Reich Minister without Portfolio
Dr. Gürtner
Reich Minister of Justice

# 46. The Reich Citizenship Law and the Law for the Protection of German Blood and German Honour (by Reich Minister Dr. Frick)

As with so many other vital problems, it has been left to the National-Socialist Movement to realise the importance of finding a solution to the race problem for the German people.

According to what history and the theory of population have taught us, the continued existence of a nation depends essentially on keeping its blood pure and healthy. Even though external circumstances may influence the life of a people, whether that people can sustain its belief in the concept of the purity of blood must always be of vital importance. For it is on this peculiar quality of a people that its existence, its culture, its achievements etc., are based. If, on the other hand, a nation does not keep its blood pure, but absorbs elements of blood of a different kind, then a rift in its unity and completeness will necessarily appear in consequence, and its intrinsic nature will be lost.

In its programme, the National-Socialist Movement has already outlined directions which take this line of thought into consideration. Starting out from the fact that, in Germany, the race problem is the Jewish problem, it follows that members of the Jewish people must be excluded from exerting any influence whatsoever on the organic life of the German people. Points four to six of our Programme read as follows:

(4) Only a member of the fellowship of the people may be a citizen. And only if, regardless of creed, he has German blood in his veins, may he be a member of the fellowship of the people. Consequently, no Jew may be a member of the fellowship of the people.

(5) A person who is not a citizen should be able to live in Germany.

(6) Only a citizen has the right to determine leadership and laws of the State. We demand therefore that public offices of any kind whatsoever, whether in the Reich, the provinces or the community, may only be held by citizens of the Reich . . .

On the basis of these sentences from our Programme, the Reich Citizenship Law which, like the Reich Law of the Flag and the Law for the Protection of German Blood and German Honour, was unanimously accepted by the Reichstag at its gathering at the Party Rally of Freedom on September 15, 1935, regulates the future shape of political life in Germany: The German Reich belongs to the German people.

The Reich Citizenship Law distinguishes between the "national" and the "citizen of the Reich". By separating these two concepts, one of the main principles of the liberalistic era has been discarded. According to that principle, all nationals, regardless of race, religion etc., had equal rights and equal duties. Today formal membership of the German polity is no longer decisive in entitling one to the civic rights and for being called upon to do one's duty. Instead the concept of nationality serves primarily to distinguish Germans from aliens and stateless persons. The status of "national", therefore, is independent of the race to which the individual may belong. Rather, any one who, according to the regulations of the Reich Citizenship and Nationality Law, has acquired German nationality, and accordingly belongs to the protective commonwealth of the German Reich, is a German national.

Conversely, only a national who is entitled to full possession of political rights and duties is a citizen of the Reich. To achieve citizenship of the Reich is dependent, in particular, on two conditions. In principle, no one who is not of German or kindred blood (of German extraction) may become a citizen of the Reich; in addition, he must, by his demeanour, have manifested his will and suitability to serve the German people.

Since to be of German blood forms a condition for the acquisition of Reich citizenship, it follows that no Jew may become a citizen of the Reich. However, the same holds valid for members of other races whose blood is not akin to German blood, for example for gypsies and negroes.

German blood does not in itself constitute a race. Rather, [the] German people is compose[d of] members of several races. Bu[t] those races have one peculia[rity] and that is: their blood is [com]patible, and its interming[ling] does not – unlike blood that is [not] kindred – produce inhibition[s or] tensions.

Unhesitatingly, therefore[, one] may put on the same footing [as] German blood the blood of t[hose] peoples whose racial constitu[tion] is related to the German. Th[is is] the case consistently with [all] self-contained peoples of Eu[rope]. In every respect, kindred b[lood] will be treated in the same wa[y as] German blood. For that rea[son] members of minority gr[oups] living in Germany, such as P[oles,] Danes etc., may become citi[zens] of the Reich.

Citizenship of the Reic[h is] acquired by the granting [of a] Patent of Reich Citizenship. [De]tailed conditions· for the ac[qui]sition of this document wil[l be] determined in due course. In [this] context, we shall also out[line] ways in which evidence of [the] will and suitability to serve [the] German people will have t[o be] adduced. As a rule, comple[tion] of compulsory Labour Ser[vice] and of National Service will h[ave] to be demanded. Applicants m[ust] also have reached a specific [age.] It must be emphasised, howe[ver,] that it is not by any means [in]tended to restrict the grantin[g of] Reich citizenship to member[s of] the N.S.D.A.P., that is to say, [a] fraction of those who are Ger[man] nationals. Rather, it is plan[ned] that the great mass of the Ger[man] population should become R[eich] citizens. Exceptions will be m[ade] only in the case of persons [who] have committed offences aga[inst] country or people; who have b[een] sentenced to penal servitude [or] in similar cases. This inten[tion] has already found expressio[n in] the First Directive to the R[eich] Citizenship Law of Novembe[r 14,] 1935. It is likely to be some [con]siderable time before the f[inal] granting of Reich Citizens[hip,] since this requires extensive [ad]ministrative preparations. Th[ere]fore, and until further regulati[ons] concerning the Reich Citizen[ship] Patent are published, all Ger[man] nationals of German or kind[red] blood who held electoral rig[hts] when the Reich Citizenship [Law] came into force, that is to say [on] September 30, 1935, or on wh[om] provisional Reich Citizenship [was] conferred by the Reich Mini[ster] of the Interior in agreement w[ith] the Deputy Führer, will

ned to be Reich Citizens.
vision for special conferment
Reich Citizenship had to be
e in order to afford possession
eich citizenship particularly
young people reaching ma-
ty as well as to those who have
ly acquired German national-

ust as regulations have been
vided regarding the loss of
l Reich citizenship, it has
n necessary to create the
sibility of withdrawing pro-
onal Reich citizenship in case
holder should prove himself
vorthy of it. This decision may
pronounced by the Reich
ister of the Interior in agree-
nt with the Deputy Führer.
he Reich Citizen is the sole
sessor of political rights, as
cted by law. For that reason,
he alone who is entitled to
e in political elections.
ther, it is he alone who is
tled to hold public office.
ever, during the time of tran-
on, the Reich Minister of the
rior may grant exceptions,
vidually or generally, for ad-
sion to public office, particu-
y for the purpose of enabling
sons who, because of their age,
not yet in a position to acquire
ch Citizenship, to enter the
il Service, particularly the
ning service.
ince a Jew cannot be a citizen
he Reich, a regulation was
uired to clarify once and for
who is to be deemed to be a
. This has been done in Article
f the First Directive to the
ch Citizenship Law.
follows from the fact that a
cannot be a Reich citizen
t he is excluded in every
ect from participating in any
irs involving civic rights.
ish civil servants at present
ffice will, therefore, have to
gn; after December 31, 1935,
y will officially retire; for
se among them who fought
he front, special arrangements
e been made to the effect that
il they reach retirement age,
y will continue to receive
ir last salary by way of pension.
he separation of the German
ple from the Jewish people,
vever, could not be confined
the province of civic rights.
aration in the personal field
f equal importance. We must
phatically prevent new Jewish
od being introduced into the
man people. Consequently,
h marital and extra-marital
ances between Jews and per-
s of German stock are for-
den and represent a punish-

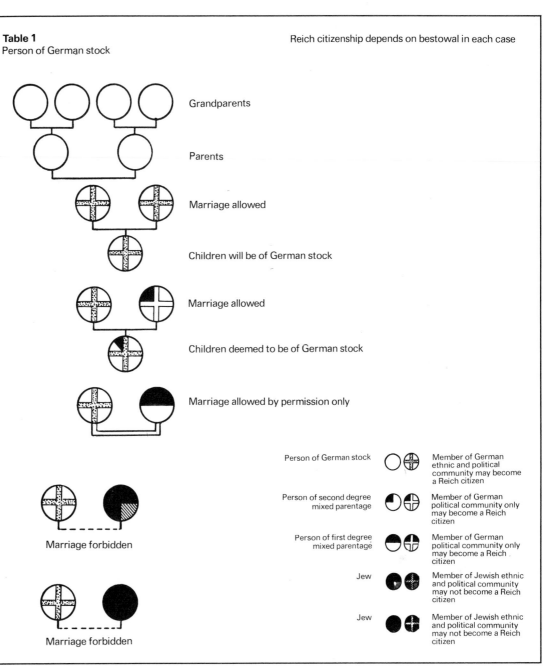

**Table 1**
Person of German stock

Reich citizenship depends on bestowal in each case

Grandparents

Parents

Marriage allowed

Children will be of German stock

Marriage allowed

Children deemed to be of German stock

Marriage allowed by permission only

Marriage forbidden

Marriage forbidden

| | | |
|---|---|---|
| Person of German stock | | Member of German ethnic and political community may become a Reich citizen |
| Person of second degree mixed parentage | | Member of German political community only may become a Reich citizen |
| Person of first degree mixed parentage | | Member of German political community only may become a Reich citizen |
| Jew | | Member of Jewish ethnic and political community may not become a Reich citizen |
| Jew | | Member of Jewish ethnic and political community may not become a Reich citizen |

able offence. Marriages contracted in contravention are null
and void. In all other respects,
however, the position of Jews
regarding civic rights is unaffected. In particular, in economic
life, they are subject only to
legally fixed restrictions. In principle, those of mixed parentage
must receive special treatment.
As they are not Jews, they cannot
be put on an equal footing with
Jews; as they are not Germans,
they cannot be put on an equal
footing with Germans. And although, in principle, they have
the possibility of acquiring Reich
citizenship–as illustrated by the
extension of provisional Reich
citizenship to include persons
of mixed parentage–they remain
subject to the restrictions pronounced in legislation up to the

present time, as well as in regulations of the N.S.D.A.P. and its
organisations. Thus in future
entry to the Civil Service will no
longer be open to them, nor will
they be able to become members
of the N.S.D.A.P. or its organisations. Economically, however,
they are entirely on equal footing
with persons of German stock.
Further, insofar as persons of
mixed parentage have been excluded from membership of organisations of all kinds, including
the N.S.D.A.P., by dint of orders
to that effect, such orders will
become void as from January 1,
1936, unless they have received
the consent of the Reich Minister
of Justice in agreement with the
Deputy Führer.

For the rest, care must be taken
to bring about the disappearance

of persons of mixed origin as
swiftly as possible. On the one
hand, this has already been
achieved by lumping together
with the Jews persons of mixed
parentage who tend over-
whelmingly towards Judaism; on
the other hand, it has been
achieved by making marriage of
persons of mixed parentage with
two wholly Jewish grandparents
and persons of German stock
subject to permission. And although they are allowed to marry
among themselves, according to
medical science only a small
number of offspring may be expected from such unions, if both
partners each show half of the
same composition of blood.
Persons of mixed parentage with
only one Jewish grandparent will
be helped to become absorbed into

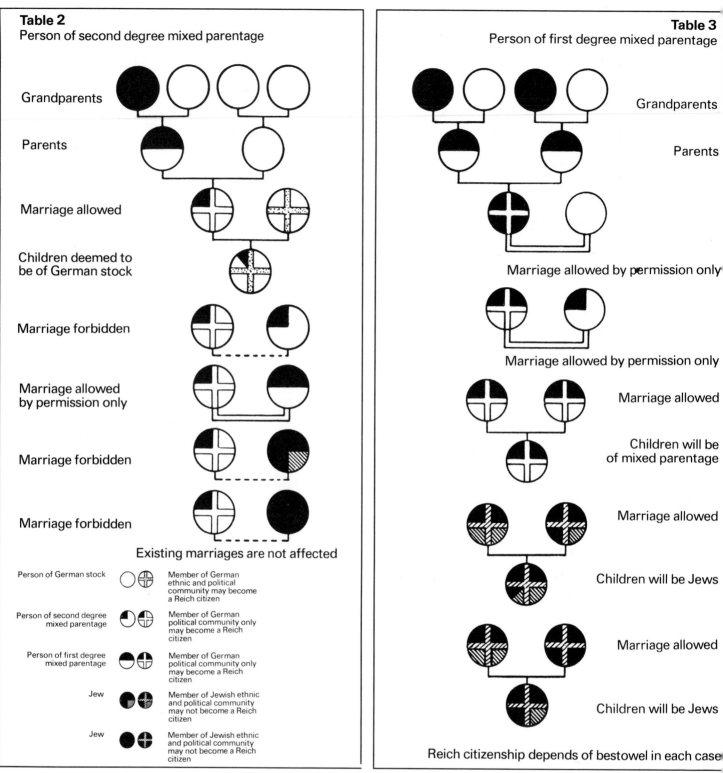

**Table 2**
Person of second degree mixed parentage

- Grandparents
- Parents
- Marriage allowed
- Children deemed to be of German stock
- Marriage forbidden
- Marriage allowed by permission only
- Marriage forbidden
- Marriage forbidden

Existing marriages are not affected

| | | |
|---|---|---|
| Person of German stock | ○ ⊕ | Member of German ethnic and political community may become a Reich citizen |
| Person of second degree mixed parentage | ◑ ⊕ | Member of German political community only may become a Reich citizen |
| Person of first degree mixed parentage | ◑ ⊕ | Member of German political community only may become a Reich citizen |
| Jew | ● ● | Member of Jewish ethnic and political community may not become a Reich citizen |
| Jew | ● ● | Member of Jewish ethnic and political community may not become a Reich citizen |

**Table 3**
Person of first degree mixed parentage

- Grandparents
- Parents
- Marriage allowed by permission only
- Marriage allowed by permission only
- Marriage allowed
- Children will be of mixed parentage
- Marriage allowed
- Children will be Jews
- Marriage allowed
- Children will be Jews

Reich citizenship depends of bestowel in each case

---

Germanity by marriage with persons of German stock, which is absolutely permissible. In order not to delay this process, marriage among themselves is forbidden.

The Reich Citizenship Law and the Law for the Protection of German Blood have not been framed for the purpose of placing members of the Jewish people in a worse position only because of their membership of that people. The elimination of Judaism from public German life and the prevention of further intermingling of races are, on the contrary, imperative necessities if the continued existence of the German people is to be safeguarded. The Jews in Germany are not to be deprived of the possibility of existing in Germany. German destiny, however, will in future be shaped solely by the German people.

**Note**
This article was published in the *Deutsche Juristen-Zeitung* on December 1, 1935.

## 47. Diagrammatic Survey of the Reich Citizenship Law and of the Law for the Protection of German Blood and German Honour

The law distinguishes between Jews, persons of mixed parentage, and persons of German stock. The distinguishing characteristic is the ethnic group to which grandparents belong.

Those who have three or f[our] wholly Jewish grandparents [will] be regarded as Jews.

Those who have one or [two] wholly Jewish grandparents [will] be regarded as of mixed parent[age]. In this context, a person with [three] Jewish grandparents is of f[irst] degree mixed parentage; a per[son] with one Jewish grandparen[t is] of only second-degree mi[xed] parentage.

Thus only a person who ha[s]

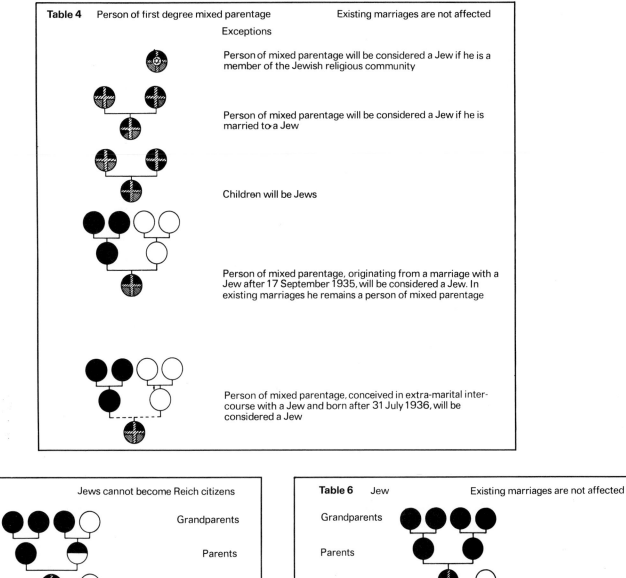

**Table 4**   Person of first degree mixed parentage          Existing marriages are not affected

Exceptions

Person of mixed parentage will be considered a Jew if he is a member of the Jewish religious community

Person of mixed parentage will be considered a Jew if he is married to a Jew

Children will be Jews

Person of mixed parentage, originating from a marriage with a Jew after 17 September 1935, will be considered a Jew. In existing marriages he remains a person of mixed parentage

Person of mixed parentage, conceived in extra-marital inter-course with a Jew and born after 31 July 1936, will be considered a Jew

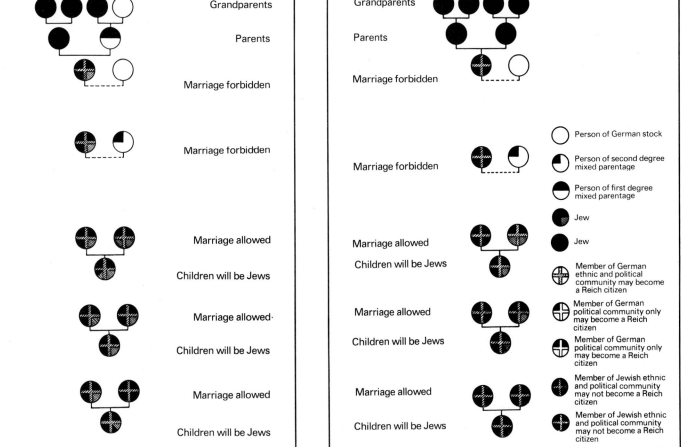

**Table 5**   Jew          Jews cannot become Reich citizens

Grandparents

Parents

Marriage forbidden

Marriage forbidden

Marriage allowed

Children will be Jews

Marriage allowed·

Children will be Jews

Marriage allowed

Children will be Jews

**Table 6**   Jew          Existing marriages are not affected

Grandparents

Parents

Marriage forbidden

Marriage forbidden

Marriage allowed

Children will be Jews

Marriage allowed

Children will be Jews

Marriage allowed

Children will be Jews

○ Person of German stock

◔ Person of second degree mixed parentage

◑ Person of first degree mixed parentage

Jew

Jew

Member of German ethnic and political community may become a Reich citizen

Member of German political community only may become a Reich citizen

Member of German political community only may become a Reich citizen

Member of Jewish ethnic and political community may not become a Reich citizen

Member of Jewish ethnic and political community may not become a Reich citizen

3359

Jews among his four grandparents can be considered to be of German stock.

Decisive for membership of Jewry is, naturally, not the religious but the ethnic factor. Thus a grandparent may be a Jew even though he belonged to a Christian religious community, or to no religious community at all. Needless to say, if a grandparent did belong to the Jewish religious community, he will immediately be regarded as wholly Jewish. The justification for this lies in the fact that, although at the time of the grandparents of the present generation there were Jews who left the Jewish religious community, there were conversely never any instances of persons not belonging to the ethnic community of the Jewish people entering the Jewish religious community. Thus the Jewish religious community was composed, at all times, only of those belonging both to the ethnic and religious Jewish community.

From the remarks by the Reich Minister of Justice it is clear who may be regarded as being of German stock. They are all those who originally formed the European peoples, or members of those peoples of mixed parentage.

A detailed account will be given below of different possibilities of marriage. In this connection, it must be emphasised, however, that only those conditions will be discussed which apply according to the Blood Law. The Law for the Preservation of Racially Healthy Marriage has not been included. Therefore, wherever marriage is contemplated, it will be necessary for the partners to find out whether, according to the law, there may not be health reasons which throw doubt on the advisability of their intended marriage.

## Table 1:

Persons of German stock and kindred persons may marry each other unhesitatingly (Case 1). Children of such a marriage will unhesitatingly belong to the German ethnic and political community.

Similarly, persons of German stock may unhesitatingly marry a person of second-degree mixed parentage (Case 2). Children of such a union similarly belong to the German ethnic and political community. The proportion of Jewish blood in a child of such a marriage is so comparatively insignificant that in practical terms

it is of no importance, and there are thus no serious objections to the child's absorption into the German ethnic and political community.

However, things are different in the case of a person of German stock and a person of first-degree mixed parentage (Case 3). Here the proportion of Jewish blood is considerably higher than in Case 2. For that reason, whether pure German blood may be allowed to mingle with that of a person of mixed parentage has, in this instance, been made conditional upon special permission. The granting of such permission will depend on how long the family of mixed parentage has been living in Germany and on the attitude of its members towards the German people, that is to say, whether they have served in the German armed forces or whether they have supported the cause of the German community. Whether the children of a marriage which is conditional upon permission will have to be regarded as persons of mixed parentage, or whether they belong to the German or Jewish ethnic community, will have to be determined in each individual case.

Marriage between a German and a Jew is, of course, forbidden (Cases 4 and 5). If such a marriage takes place in contravention of

the law, it will be null and void.

## Table 2:

A person of second-degree mixed parentage is unhesitatingly free to marry a person of German stock (Case 1). That fact had already been elaborated in Table 1 (Case 2). However, persons of second-degree mixed parentage are forbidden to marry each other (Case 2). The percentage of Jewish blood which is comparatively small in the parents, would be much higher in the children, and thus new persons of mixed parentage might be created. The absorption of persons of second-degree mixed parentage into the German ethnic community would be delayed.

Marriage between persons of second-degree mixed parentage and those of first-degree mixed parentage is allowed (Case 3). It is, however, subject to permission being granted. For this permission the same grounds apply as for permission of marriages between persons of German stock and persons of first-degree mixed parentage (cf. Table 1, Case 3).

Marriage between persons of second-degree mixed parentage and Jews is forbidden (Cases 4 and 5).

## Table 3:

With persons of first-degree mixed

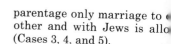

parentage only marriage to ⟨ other and with Jews is allo⟨ (Cases 3, 4, and 5).

Marriage between person⟨ first-degree mixed parentage persons of German stock is ⟨ ject to permission (Case 1).

The same applies for marr⟨ between persons of first-de⟨ and those of second-degree m⟨ parentage (Case 2).

It has been possible to al⟨ marriage between persons of f⟨ degree mixed parentage with⟨ hesitation, because from exp⟨ ence these marriages result ⟨ rarely in offspring, thus minir⟨ ing the danger of creating ⟨ persons of mixed parentage. ⟨ marrying a Jew (Cases 4 and ⟨ the person of first-degree mi⟨ parentage, whose percentage ⟨ Jewish blood is, after all, s⟨ comparatively large, decla⟨ himself a member of the Jew⟨ ethnic community. The child⟨ of such marriages will unhe⟨ tatingly be Jews. In contrast ⟨ the person of second-degree mix⟨ parentage, such a person shou⟨ not be prevented from maki⟨ this declaration of belonging ⟨ the Jewish ethnic communi⟨ exactly because his percentage ⟨ Jewish blood is comparative⟨ high.

## Table 4:

A number of special cases ha⟨ been provided for in connecti⟨ with persons of first-degree mix⟨ parentage, all of which have the⟨ inner justification in that ve⟨ declaration of belonging to t⟨ Jewish ethnic community. F⟨ such a person of mixed parenta⟨ will unhesitatingly be considere⟨ a Jew if he belongs to the Jewi⟨ religious community or if he ⟨ married to a Jew. Therefore, ⟨ person of mixed parentage hel⟨ to be a Jew is permitted to marr⟨ only Jews or persons of firs⟨ degree mixed parentage. The chi⟨ dren of such a union will be Jew⟨ In addition, persons of mixe⟨ parentage, born from a marriag⟨ with a Jew after September 17⟨ 1935, will be regarded as Jews. I⟨ existing marriages the child wil⟨ remain a person of mixed paren⟨ tage. Correspondingly, a perso⟨ of mixed parentage originatin⟨ from extra-marital intercours⟨ with a Jew and born after July 31⟨ 1936, will be regarded as a Jew.

## Tables 5 and 6:

Finally, Jews have only the possibility of marrying other Jews or persons of first-degree mixed parentage. Their children will in any case be Jews.